The American Presidency

THE COMPLETE IDIOT'S GUIDE® TO

The American Presidency

by Alan Axelrod, Ph.D.

ALPHA

A member of Penguin Group (USA) Inc.

For Anita, First Lady

ALPHA BOOKS

Published by the Penguin Group

Penguin Group (USA) Inc., 375 Hudson Street, New York, New York 10014, USA

Penguin Group (Canada), 90 Eglinton Avenue East, Suite 700, Toronto, Ontario M4P 2Y3, Canada (a division of Pearson Penguin Canada Inc.)

Penguin Books Ltd., 80 Strand, London WC2R 0RL, England

Penguin Ireland, 25 St. Stephen's Green, Dublin 2, Ireland (a division of Penguin Books Ltd.)

Penguin Group (Australia), 250 Camberwell Road, Camberwell, Victoria 3124, Australia (a division of Pearson Australia Group Pty. Ltd.)

Penguin Books India Pvt. Ltd., 11 Community Centre, Panchsheel Park, New Delhi—110 017, India

Penguin Group (NZ), 67 Apollo Drive, Rosedale, North Shore, Auckland 1311, New Zealand (a division of Pearson New Zealand Ltd.)

Penguin Books (South Africa) (Pty.) Ltd., 24 Sturdee Avenue, Rosebank, Johannesburg 2196, South Africa

Penguin Books Ltd., Registered Offices: 80 Strand, London WC2R 0RL, England

International Standard Book Number: 978-1-59257-912-9
Library of Congress Catalog Card Number: 2009920704

11   8 7 6 5 4 3

Interpretation of the printing code: The rightmost number of the first series of numbers is the year of the book's printing; the rightmost number of the second series of numbers is the number of the book's printing. For example, a printing code of 09-1 shows that the first printing occurred in 2009.

Printed in the United States of America

Note: This publication contains the opinions and ideas of its author. It is intended to provide helpful and informative material on the subject matter covered. It is sold with the understanding that the author and publisher are not engaged in rendering professional services in the book. If the reader requires personal assistance or advice, a competent professional should be consulted.

The author and publisher specifically disclaim any responsibility for any liability, loss, or risk, personal or otherwise, which is incurred as a consequence, directly or indirectly, of the use and application of any of the contents of this book.

Most Alpha books are available at special quantity discounts for bulk purchases for sales promotions, premiums, fund-raising, or educational use. Special books, or book excerpts, can also be created to fit specific needs.

For details, write: Special Markets, Alpha Books, 375 Hudson Street, New York, NY 10014.

Publisher: *Marie Butler-Knight*
Editorial Director: *Mike Sanders*
Senior Managing Editor: *Billy Fields*
Executive Editor: *Randy Ladenheim-Gil*
Development Editor: *Lynn Northrup*
Senior Production Editor: *Janette Lynn*
Copy Editor: *Amy Borrelli*

Cartoonist: *Steve Barr*
Cover Designer: *Rebecca Harmon*
Book Designer: *Trina Wurst*
Indexer: *Heather McNeill*
Layout: *Brian Massey*
Proofreader: *Mary Hunt*

Contents at a Glance

Contents

Introduction

It's usually a bad idea to begin a book by saying what it is not. But in this case, it really needs to be said. This book is not about the American presidents—who was the best, who was the worst, who was the fattest, who had the most children, who was the only bachelor. You will get none of that here. (Okay, the fattest was William Howard Taft, at 332 pounds. But that's it.)

This is a book not about the American presidents, but about the American presidency. It is a history of the creation and the development of the office, the institution.

The American presidency comes with only the thinnest of instruction manuals, Article II of the U.S. Constitution, which consists of just 1,046 words as originally written. The framers of the Constitution supplied a loose outline and left the rest to those who would actually occupy the office. As a result, the American presidency remains a work in progress. That's what makes the subject so fascinating. It has a past, a present, and a future—which we can only imagine.

Now a word about sex. (Or, at any rate, gender.)

The 2008 election season brought to American history three historic firsts. For the first time in our nation's political journey, a woman, Hillary Rodham Clinton, had a serious prospect of becoming president. She came in second in the Democratic primaries to Barack Obama, the first African American nominated by a major party as its presidential candidate and, as it turned out, after 220 years of white presidents, the first African American elected to the office. Obama and his vice presidential running mate, Sen. Joe Biden, were opposed by Republican Sen. John McCain and his running mate, Alaska governor Sarah Palin—only the second woman (Democrat Geraldine Ferraro was the first, in 1984) in U.S. history to receive a major-party nomination for the vice presidency.

It is inevitable that women will serve as American presidents. But since it has not happened yet—since every American president so far has been a man—I have used the masculine pronoun exclusively throughout this book in all generic references to "the president." When will history compel a change in this grammatical convention? Stick around for subsequent editions.

How to Use This Book

This book is divided into seven parts:

Part 1, "Presidential Precedents and Prototypes," explores American government before there were presidents, why the founding fathers decided that there should be presidents, and how they drew up the outlines for the presidency. We will look at the constitutional specifications for the office and how the first six presidents modeled the presidency. This part also offers a chapter on the vice presidency and its progress from a largely ceremonial office to a powerful, even controversial, feature of the executive branch.

Part 2, "Uncommon Common Men," begins with Andrew Jackson, who radically redefined the relationship between the chief executive and the people, building the first "people's presidency." This part traces the mixed legacy of Jackson, especially how his presidency affected the next eight as the nation marched toward civil war. We end with the uncommonest common man of all, Abraham Lincoln, who restructured the presidency in a heroic effort to restore the Union and the American democracy he believed was the "last best hope of earth."

Part 3, "Retreat and Advance," shows how the Congress, recoiling from the extraordinary power President Lincoln had amassed for his office, acted to reclaim government for the legislative branch. The struggle began dramatically with impeachment of Lincoln's crude, obstinate, and unpopular successor, Andrew Johnson, and continued variously through the last three decades of the nineteenth century, leaving the presidency a much-diminished office.

Part 4, "The Progressive Presidency," presents the reemergence of presidential power at the start of the twentieth century, beginning with the spectacular presidency of Theodore Roosevelt, whose progressivism was diminished, along with the presidency itself, by his handpicked successor, William Howard Taft, only to be raised to an even loftier height by Woodrow Wilson, the first president to make the Oval Office a center of world leadership.

Part 5, "From 'Normalcy' to the Personal Presidency," narrates the headlong retreat from the progressive and internationalist presidency created by Roosevelt and Wilson in a return to the "normalcy" of the passive party-line presidencies of Warren G. Harding and Calvin Coolidge. The onset of the Great Depression at the start of the Hoover administration revealed the inadequacy of the status quo approach to the executive office and made way for a new invention, the "personal presidency" of Franklin Delano Roosevelt. After dimming somewhat—but only somewhat—in the presidencies of Harry S. Truman and Dwight D. Eisenhower, both of whom made unique contributions to the office, the "personal presidency" reemerged vigorously in the unfinished presidency of John F. Kennedy.

Part 6, "The Imperial Presidency," investigates how Democrat Lyndon Johnson and Republican Richard Nixon pushed the constitutional envelope to create what critical historians have dubbed the "imperial presidency." This part explores the consequences of pushing the imperial presidency too far (Nixon is the only American president to resign his office) and how his successors, Republican Gerald Ford and Democrat Jimmy Carter—the first "outsider" president—each struggled to dismantle presidential imperialism and rehabilitate the tarnished office.

Part 7, "The CEO Presidency," starts with the election of another outsider president, Ronald Reagan, who embarked on a mission to "get big government off our backs," modeling the presidency on the private-sector corporate CEO. A controversial visionary, Reagan was succeeded by his vice president, George H. W. Bush, who introduced a vigorous "diplomatic presidency." Lacking his predecessor's charisma, Bush was defeated for reelection by yet another outsider, Democrat Bill Clinton, who struggled to overcome increasing partisan conflict by designing a "centrist presidency." Despite a troubled second term, Clinton bequeathed to his successor, George W. Bush, a country enjoying peace and prosperity. The final chapter of this part shows how Bush expanded executive authority, yet assumed inadequate personal responsibility for the consequences as the nation became mired in an unpopular war and was assailed by a massive economic meltdown. The 2008 election brought into the Oval Office its first African American occupant, Democrat Barack Obama.

At the back of the book, you'll find a chronological list of the presidents and vice presidents, a summary of presidential elections, and suggestions for further reading.

Extras

Throughout the book, you'll find the following four types of sidebars:

 What They Said

These are memorable statements from presidents, vice presidents, and others.

 Executive Event

Here you'll read about some of the most significant events in presidential history.

def•i•ni•tion

This feature defines the special words relevant to the American presidency.

 Tally

Here are the key statistics of the American presidency.

Trademarks

All terms mentioned in this book that are known to be or are suspected of being trademarks or service marks have been appropriately capitalized. Alpha Books and Penguin Group (USA) Inc. cannot attest to the accuracy of this information. Use of a term in this book should not be regarded as affecting the validity of any trademark or service mark.

Part 1

Presidential Precedents and Prototypes

The American presidency was invented for a new American government, but was not built from scratch. Part 1 explores the U.S. government before there were presidents, the constitutional specifications for the presidency, and the first presidents themselves, who laid the foundation and set the standards for the office. Here we trace the evolution of presidential party politics and also explore the vice presidency, a constitutional afterthought that has at times proved far more central to American government than the framers of the Constitution could have imagined.

America Before the Presidents

In This Chapter

- Why most colonists didn't think about government
- The American Revolution forces the creation of the first U.S. government
- America's fear of powerful government
- The Articles of Confederation—and its problems
- Government without a chief executive

Any group that assembles for a common purpose, whether it is to manufacture paper clips or live together as a nation, customarily divides itself into a leader and followers. How strange it seems that during all of the American Revolution the government of the United States had no president—a condition that would endure for five years after independence had been achieved. American government was headless for the first thirteen years of its existence, not because the people were absent-minded or thoughtless, but because they wanted it this way. Having violently broken with one king, the last thing they wanted to do was create another.

A Body Without a Head

The earliest English settlers of the country that would become the United States—the first permanent English settlement was Jamestown, Virginia, founded in 1607—were colonists. They set up various forms of local government, some headed by royally appointed governors, some by locally selected governors (often elected exclusively by the colony's property holders), others by councils of elders or other authorities, but everyone understood that all authority ultimately flowed from the king of England, who, according to the doctrine of *divine right*, had been anointed by no less a sovereign than God.

def•i•ni•tion

> **Divine right**, or the divine right of kings, is the doctrine that any rightful earthly monarch is God's sovereign representative to the people of his or her kingdom; therefore, the authority of a monarch to rule flows directly from God and cannot be challenged without committing mortal sin.

Liberty

For a long time, very little thought was given to the basis of colonial government. In effect, colonists thought of themselves as English men and women who, for practical purposes of survival and some degree of prosperity, voluntarily submitted themselves to governors and magistrates, who were not heads of state, but managers or administrators. For the colonists, the only head of state was the king—even if he sat on a throne across the Atlantic.

The colonists were content with this arrangement for a long time because, as British subjects, they enjoyed rights and privileges guaranteed by the Magna Carta signed by King John in 1215, and developed and amplified over the centuries since that time by the great body of English law and English common law. This prevented the king from ruling as a tyrant and therefore, kept all English men and women, colonists included, from descending to the contemptible status of slave.

Taxation Without Representation

From 1607 through the middle of the eighteenth century, the English colonists in North America had very little reason to think about government because crown and Parliament in the mother country were content, for the most part, to allow the colonies and the colonists to look after themselves. Historians call this policy *salutary neglect*, and it was practiced until the cost of defending the English colonies against the French colonies and their Indian allies during the French and Indian War (1754–1763) began to seriously deplete English government coffers. A host of taxes, tariffs, and duties on colonial exports and imports were on the books, but, in the spirit of salutary neglect, these went uninforced until about 1760, when British government officials began to get serious about collecting revenue from the colonies. The crown started issuing writs of assistance, which were orders to colonial officials, compelling them to cooperate with royal officers to curb customs and duties violations.

def•i•ni•tion

Salutary neglect is the historical term for the period of Anglo-American colonial history in which the mother country largely left the colonies to shift for themselves. The period applies to colonial history from the founding of Jamestown in 1607 to about 1760.

Now the long period of benign neglect by the British government and the corresponding epoch of colonial complacency reached its end. Nobody likes paying taxes, but it was not the taxes per se that galled the colonists. On February 24, 1761, James Otis, a highly respected Boston lawyer, articulated the growing colonial grievance. "Taxation without representation," he declared, "is tyranny."

It wasn't the newly enforced tax laws that prompted the colonists to begin thinking about the nature of government, it was the imposition of taxes in the absence of a colonial voice in the government that imposed them. The king of England has no power to tax. That is reserved to Parliament, which represents the people; therefore, it is the people who, through their representatives, agree to tax themselves for the common good. Taxes imposed by a parliament in which one is unrepresented is tyranny, and those forced to pay such unjust and illegal taxes are no better than slaves, denied the rights, the privileges—the liberty—English men and women living in England take for granted.

Now it was at this point that the colonists started thinking about government. *Fact:* Taxation without representation is tyranny, an unacceptable condition. *Fact:* Colonial representation in Parliament was impractical, perhaps impossible. For one thing, America was separated from England by a vast ocean, which made travel and communication by colonial representatives difficult, costly, and dangerous. Even more critical was the fact that colonial population was growing rapidly, which meant that proportionate representation in Parliament would require a large body of members, which would inevitably come to outnumber members representing districts in the mother country itself as the colonial population surpassed that of England.

Accept both facts, and there are only two alternatives: either the colonists had to resign themselves to slavery, or they had to claim independence from England.

A Government of Necessity

The dilemma of taxation without representation continued to fester and relations between England and America deteriorated, pushing the colonies to the brink of revolution, 12 of the 13 colonies sent delegates to a Continental Congress convened on September 5, 1774. After the American Revolution began with battles of Lexington and Concord of April 19, 1775, a Second Continental Congress was called on May 10. This time, all 13 colonies sent delegates.

The Second Continental Congress was the government of revolutionary America, a government not created as a matter of choice, but of necessity—to finance and fight the war and to present a united front to England and the rest of the world, a single voice with which the colonies might speak.

Power to the People

Because the people had not purposely set about to create a new nation, they did not formally endow the Second Continental Congress with legal authority to govern. Nevertheless, it assumed—*de facto* (as a matter of fact) rather than *de jure* (as a matter of law)—all the functions of a central national government. However, while the Continental Congress had authority to allocate and disburse funds, it lacked the power to levy taxes. Although the people were fighting against taxation without representation and not merely against taxation, they were unwilling to grant taxation authority even to a representative body—especially because the nature of the representation was inconsistent. Delegates were not chosen by direct election but, in some states, by popular conventions, and in others, were appointed by the state assembly. The ultimate source of the authority of the Continental Congress was self-bestowed in that the body had been created by members of the Sons of Liberty and "committees of safety" that had sprung into being throughout the colonies.

Executive Event _____

Continentals, the currency authorized by the Continental Congress, was theoretically backed by Spanish milled dollars, but in practice was nothing more than paper money printed in large quantity. It was practically worthless—a fact that gave rise to a once-popular expression applied to anything of little value: "not worth a Continental."

If the Second Continental Congress was the only government of the United States during the revolution, its authority derived not from law or even from truly democratic principles of popular representation, but, rather, from the unspoken acquiescence of the people. Stated more positively, the American government, as embodied in the Congress, existed by virtue of the will of the people. And, from 1775 to 1788, the year the Constitution was ratified, the people were unwilling to concede any authority to an executive—a president.

Bound by a "Rope of Sand"

As the war continued, the members of the Second Continental Congress increasingly felt the need for a stronger union and more centralization of authority in the government. These ends could not be achieved in an improvisatory, ad hoc manner, but required embodiment in a constitution. There were objections. Many believed that a central government would be unable to govern a large nation, that the legislators would lose touch with the people and would therefore fail to be true representatives, a circumstance that would ultimately lead to tyranny. Those who feared central government believed that the new nation should be nothing more than a loose federation of the 13 independent colonies. Nevertheless, even these individuals realized the need for more efficient constitutional order.

Try, Try Again

Benjamin Franklin tried his hand at drafting a constitution, which he presented to Congress in July 1775. It was read, but discarded without formal debate. Later in the year, Connecticut delegate Silas Deane submitted an entirely new draft. When it, too, was rejected, the entire Connecticut delegation submitted what was probably a revision of Deane's original. This gained no traction, either.

In June 1776, John Dickinson of Pennsylvania submitted a fourth candidate document. This time, a committee of Congress worked it over, producing three more drafts, which were discussed and debated by all of the delegates. They authorized the third draft to be printed so that each of the delegates could study it at leisure. After more debate, a final draft was approved, but because the Continental Congress lacked the authority to enact it, the document was submitted to the states in November 1777 for ratification.

The States Bicker

The Continental Congress continued to wrestle with the management of the war while the states pondered what was now called the Articles of Confederation—the word *constitution* having been avoided lest it imply too much centralization of power. Interstate wrangling and conflicting land claims delayed ratification and implementation of the Articles of Confederation until March 1, 1781.

Tax Troubles

Since 1775, the Second Continental Congress had been charged with managing the revolution, including its financing, but was compelled to do so without the authority to levy taxes. For Congress, one of the principal motives for the Articles of Confederation was to acquire taxation authority. Yet while ratification of the articles also ratified the authority of Congress to levy taxes, it left unresolved just how the taxes would be apportioned among the states.

As Dickinson had drafted the document, the states would contribute funds to Congress in proportion to their population, white as well as black, excluding only those Indians who did not pay taxes. Even after ratifying the articles, the southern states opposed this apportionment scheme because of their large slave populations. They held that taxes should be based on the white population only. When this failed to pass, Congress worked out an alternative basis for apportionment: Each state would contribute based on the value of its privately held lands and the improvements on those lands.

Just Friends

The authority to tax implied the centralization of governing power, but the Article III explicitly disavowed genuine nationhood by characterizing the confederation as "a firm league of friendship" for the sake of the states' "common defense, the security of their liberties, and their mutual and general welfare."

And the articles shied even further away from central government by, in effect, denying that the revenue Congress collected from the states—apportioned according to owned land—was even a tax. Instead, it was described as a *contribution*, and, beyond accepting this contribution, Congress could levy no other taxes or make laws regulating commerce. Each state retained its own "sovereignty, freedom, and independence."

An Uneasy Compromise

Even as the articles guaranteed the states sovereignty, freedom, and independence, they also gave the central government some important powers, such as jurisdiction over foreign relations, including the authority to make treaties and alliances. The central government was exclusively authorized to declare war and make peace, to establish an army and navy, to coin money, to create and administer a postal service, and to administer Indian affairs. The central government would also arbitrate disputes between the states.

All of these powers were exercised through Congress and only Congress, which was a unicameral (one chamber) body in which each state had one vote. The states were represented by delegates, two to seven per state (though each state had only a single vote), who were elected not directly by the people, but by the state legislatures. The Articles of Confederation made no provision for a judiciary or a chief executive. The government it created was a body without a head.

Many of the decisions Congress was authorized to make would be determined by a simple majority vote on the basis of one state, one vote, but decisions about declaring war, making treaties, and regulating coinage required the agreement of nine of the thirteen states. It was possible to amend the Articles of Confederation provided that the legislatures—not the delegates—of all 13 states agreed to do so. Twice, in 1781 and in 1786, the delegates attempted to amend the articles to give Congress the explicit power to tax. Both attempts fell short of the required unanimous ratification.

Meet Me in Philly

The bottom line for the government created by the Articles of Confederation was that Congress was given great latitude to pass laws, but it had no power to enforce them. Ultimately, it was up to each state to comply or not. Little wonder that many congressional delegates called the confederation under the Articles nothing more than "a rope of sand."

In 1786, a convention held in Annapolis, Maryland, to discuss problems of interstate commerce came to the conclusion that the issues the delegates had been tasked with deciding could be resolved only by a major revision of the Articles of Confederation. The Annapolis delegates called for a constitutional convention.

Thus, in May 1787, 55 delegates convened in Philadelphia to begin what they thought would be a major overhaul of the articles. Their first step was to elect George Washington, who had led the Continental Army to victory in the revolution, as president of the convention. Under his leadership, the delegates quickly transformed what they had conceived of as a project of remodeling into one of construction from scratch. All agreed that a genuine national government, not just a "league of friendship," was needed to create a viable and enduring republic.

Once again, the political leaders of the United States debated the nature of national government, but this time in addition to remolding the body of that government, they also lavished a great deal of attention to the creation of a head.

The Least You Need to Know

- As long as the king and Parliament left the colonies to govern themselves and refrained from imposing taxes—a policy historians have called "salutary neglect"—there was little concern about colonial government and no popular desire for independence.

- Taxation without representation ignited the American Revolution, which in turn, made creating a United States government urgently necessary.

- Having committed themselves to fighting for independence from the tyrannical power of a king and Parliament, most Americans were reluctant to create a new central government with much authority; they were especially fearful of creating a new head of state—in effect exchanging one king for another.

- The Articles of Confederation was the first constitution of the United States. It did not create a nation, but a loose "league of friendship" among the 13 states.

- Under the Articles of Confederation, the United States had no chief executive. The founding fathers who called for scrapping the articles in favor of a new constitution advocated for the first time establishing a chief executive.

2

Presidential Precedents

In This Chapter

- ◆ The three major proposals for a chief executive
- ◆ Why Americans feared the idea of a president
- ◆ How the founding fathers chose from among three forms of government
- ◆ What the Constitution says about the president and vice president

All 55 delegates who met in Philadelphia from May 25 to September 17, 1787, for what became a constitutional convention, agreed that the United States needed a document that would "render the constitution of government adequate to the exigencies of the Union," and most (though not all) agreed that such a document would have to be substantially different from the Articles of Confederation. But few came to the convention agreed on just how it should be different. The product that finally emerged, the Constitution of the United States, is a great synthesis of opposing views that grew from the boldest aspirations of democracy as well as the darkest fears of tyranny.

Priorities and Plans

The top priority of the convention was to design a national legislature. The Congress was considered the principal organ of republican government. Many—but not all—delegates also favored the creation of an executive office, but this was a secondary priority. Besides, having devoted nearly eight years of their blood and treasure to liberating America from the rule of a king, no one wanted to risk swapping one monarch for another.

The Virginians Propose a Plan

Discussion and debate at the convention was impassioned and complex, but from it emerged two major schemes of government and a compromise between them.

Edmund Randolph of Virginia introduced a plan largely created by fellow Virginian James Madison. This "Virginia Plan" called for a central government consisting of a legislature (a congress), an executive branch, and a judicial branch. Unlike the *unicameral* (one-chamber) legislature under the Articles of Confederation, the Virginia Plan proposed a *bicameral* legislature, consisting of a "lower house," with delegates proportional to the population of each state and elected by the citizens of each state, and an "upper house," whose delegates would be elected by the members of the lower house. The executive would be elected by the members of both houses of the legislature.

def•i•ni•tion

Whereas a **unicameral** (one-chamber) legislature contains a single deliberative body, a **bicameral** (two-chamber) contains two, usually an upper house (sometimes with appointed or even hereditary delegates) and a lower house (with popularly elected delegates). The idea is that the two chambers will compensate for one another's legislative limitations and excesses.

New Jersey Weighs In

Predictably, the Virginia Plan met with opposition from delegates representing the smaller states, which would have less representation in the proposed legislature—and that also meant a diminished voice in the election of the executive. To address this concern, William Paterson of New Jersey proposed the so-called "New Jersey Plan."

Less radical than the Virginia Plan, the New Jersey Plan embodied most of the Articles of Confederation and specified that all the states would be represented equally in the unicameral legislature, whose members were to be elected by the people. Like the Virginia Plan, it added to the legislative branch a judicial as well as an executive branch. The judiciary would consist of a supreme court, with judges appointed for life by the executive. That executive, however, would not be a single person, but a committee elected by the legislature for a single term. Moreover, the legislature could remove the executive committee if a majority of the governors of the states demanded it. Thus the executive was inherently weak, a structural provision designed to nip tyrants in the bud.

Compromise from Connecticut

Debate between advocates of the Virginia and New Jersey plans was heated and, apparently, intractable until Roger Sherman, a delegate from Connecticut, stepped in with a compromise designed to reconcile the two apparently irreconcilable plans.

Called the Connecticut Compromise—some admiring historians have dubbed it the "Great Compromise"—Sherman's proposal included the bicameral legislature of the Virginia Plan, but with an important difference. The lower house—called the House of Representatives—would consist of popularly elected representatives apportioned according to each state's population, whereas the upper house, the Senate, would afford each state equal representation. Unlike the representatives, elected directly by the people, the senators would be elected by the popularly elected legislatures of each state.

The Great Compromise incorporated the judicial branch of the New Jersey Plan. As for the executive, Sherman had originally advocated allowing the legislature to decide whether it should be unitary or plural, but in the final form of the compromise, he proposed a unitary executive, who, however, would be elected neither by the people nor by the representatives in the legislature, but by an entirely new invention Sherman called the Electoral College.

Executive Event

Although Roger Sherman's Electoral College was highly innovative, it did have historical precedents. The Holy Roman emperor, for example, had been chosen by prince-electors since the late Middle Ages, and the last election would take place a few years after America's Constitutional Convention, in 1792. The early Christian Church elected a bishop, a tradition that was institutionalized in the Catholic Church in 1059 as the College of Cardinals, who function as electors of the pope.

The Electoral College was designed to reconcile the conflicting demands of small states and large by ensuring that the election of the president would be only somewhat proportional to population, so that all states would be heard. As Sherman conceived it, the legislature of each state would chose electors equal in number to the state's representatives and senators. When it was time to vote for president, each elector would vote for two candidates, one of whom had to be from a state other than that of the elector. The candidate who received the most votes became president, and the runner-up vice president. (If no candidate received a majority, the House of Representatives would choose a president and vice president from among the three front-runners.)

The Benefit of Compromise

The beauty of the Connecticut Compromise was that it made strong central government more palatable, even to those who feared creating tyranny, by introducing what we now call the *system of checks and balances.* The legislative and executive branches counterbalanced each other.

def•i•ni•tion

> The **system of checks and balances** is the product of *separation of powers*, the principle of government by which governing authority is divided into branches, each with its own area of responsibility and power. The framers of the Constitution were well aware that the government of the Roman Republic—which most of them admired and looked to as a model of republican government—had been divided into three branches. This, combined with the thought of such French Enlightenment philosophers as the Baron de Montesquieu (1689–1755), inspired the Constitution's separation of powers into legislative, executive, and judicial branches.

Within the legislative branch, the absolute democracy of the popularly elected House of Representatives was balanced by the more republican Senate, and vice versa.

As for the executive branch, the structure of the Electoral College served as a check against the tyranny of the majority as well as monopolization of power by the big states.

With regard to the judicial branch, its full power, although implicit in the Connecticut Compromise and the Constitution based on it, would not be realized until Chief Justice John Marshall introduced the concept of judicial review in the 1803 case of *Marbury* v. *Madison.* By virtue of judicial review, the Supreme Court had the final word on the constitutionality (and therefore, the lawfulness) of an executive act or a law passed by Congress.

Selling It

Armed with the Connecticut Compromise, William Johnson (the convention's secretary), Alexander Hamilton, James Madison, Rufus King, and Gouverneur Morris drafted the actual Constitution, which was submitted for the delegates' approval then sent to the Confederation Congress, which in turn submitted it to the states for ratification. After New Hampshire became the ninth state to vote for ratification on June 21, 1788, the Constitution became law and was put into effect on March 4, 1789.

Models of Power

The framers of the Constitution had plenty of experience with executives, from the king to the royal governors of the colonies, and, for the most part, that experience had not been good. Given executive power, most executives did whatever they could, first, to preserve, and, second, to increase it. The Confederation Congress often found it impossible to get anything of substance accomplished. The need for an executive at the head of the government was often made apparent. Yet the evils and potential evils attached to executive power were daunting.

Political science, as the framers understood it in the 1780s, was largely defined by the three broad types of government the ancient Greek philosopher Aristotle had described:

♦ Monarchy—in which one person rules

♦ Aristocracy—in which an elite group rules

♦ Democracy—in which the people rule

Each form of government had its problems. Monarchs and aristocrats are vulnerable to the basic human fault of greed and selfishness; therefore, monarchies all too often become despotic tyrannies, and aristocracies become oligarchies. As rule by the people, democracy is liable to degenerate into the selfishness of the many instead of the one (monarchy) or the few (aristocracy). If this happens, anarchy ensues, and anarchy provides fertile ground for the growth of tyranny.

Monarchy: Been There, Done That

Although the Americans had rebelled against a monarchy, their dispute had not been with the king so much as with a government in which they had no voice but which nevertheless imposed burdens (taxes) on them. Except for a relatively small number of genuine radicals, of whom Thomas Jefferson was the most brilliant and articulate, the majority of Americans actually held the ideal—if not the actuality—of the English constitutional monarchy in high regard because this form of government managed to balance the rule of one against parliamentary safeguards of personal liberties. That is, Parliament's House of Lords tempered the monarchy with rule by an aristocracy, while the democratic House of Commons tempered both (and was tempered in return by) the monarchy and the aristocracy.

The bottom line? Strong executive power—and no executive power is stronger than that of a king—threatens liberty. The threat may be lessened by the countervailing presence of legislative power, but it probably cannot be eliminated entirely.

Prototype 2: The Royal Governor

Another executive prototype familiar to colonial leaders was the royal governor. In colonial practice, a governor, although appointed by the king, was more subject than the king to the countervailing authority of the legislature. Like Parliament, colonial legislatures generally consisted of an upper and lower house. The members of the upper house were appointed by the royal governor, whereas those of the lower house were elected by the colonists. Royal governors had the authority to *veto* any act of the legislature, and they could, in certain circumstances, *prorogue* (end) a legislative session or even dissolve the legislature; however, colonial legislatures possessed the power of the purse, controlling the funds necessary to finance colonial government, including the salary of the governor himself. Royal governors had weaker motives and less latitude than a king for the outright abuse of power; nevertheless, the potential for abuse was very much present.

def•i•ni•tion

> **Veto** is borrowed from Latin, in which it means "I forbid." It describes the power of an executive to override acts of the legislature. **Prorogue** comes from Middle English and Old French words meaning "to postpone"; as used in government, the word applies to a king or other executive's authority to end or discontinue a session of the legislature.

An Elected King or a President?

The most basic question the framers of the Constitution needed to resolve was whether the executive should be an elected king, with relatively few legislative checks on his power, or a president, whose executive authority was highly subject to a legislature.

As most colonial political leaders saw it, neither the constitutional monarch nor his governors could serve as fully adequate prototypes for the chief executive of a true republic. While the power of both was somewhat tempered by that of the legislature, it still, under normal circumstances, outweighed legislative authority. The solution was to define the nation's chief executive as a president—that is, a figure whose power was institutionally limited by the legislature, so that this limitation was a matter of normal routine and not extraordinary defiance.

Outline of Power

Having made the decision to create an elected presidency instead of an elected monarchy, the framers of the Constitution provided little more than a barebones description of their creation in Article II of the Constitution.

Section 1 of Article II specifies:

- The term of office (four years).
- The nuts and bolts of the College of Electors.
- The basic qualifications for office (born citizen, at least 35 years old, resident within the U.S. for at least 14 years).
- Circumstances under which the vice president succeeds the president.
- Provision for "compensation" (an unspecified salary).
- The oath of office.

Section 2 enumerates a handful of presidential powers:

- Serves as commander in chief of the army and navy
- "May require the opinion, in writing, of the principal officer in each of the executive departments, upon any subject relating to the duties of their respective offices"

♦ May grant reprieves and pardons

♦ Makes treaties, with the "advice and consent of the Senate," two thirds of which must approve

♦ Appoints ambassadors, public ministers, consuls, Supreme Court judges, "and all other officers of the United States, whose appointments are not herein otherwise provided for," subject to the same senatorial approval as applies to treaties

♦ May temporarily fill "vacancies that may happen during the recess of the Senate" without approval

Section 3 obliges the president "from time to time" to "give to the Congress information of the state of the Union, and recommend to their consideration such measures as he shall judge necessary and expedient." Additionally, the president:

♦ May call Congress into special session "on extraordinary occasions."

♦ May adjourn Congress when Congress fails to agree on a time of adjournment.

♦ Receives ambassadors and other public ministers.

♦ "Shall take care that the laws be faithfully executed."

♦ Commissions all "officers of the United States."

def•i•ni•tion

Impeachment is the proceeding undertaken by Congress to remove the president or vice president. It is not synonymous with *removal* from office, which is only one of two possible results of impeachment. The other is *acquittal*, in which case the executive remains in office.

Section 4 covers the *impeachment* and removal not only of the president and vice president, but of "all civil officers of the United States." Causes for removal from office are limited to "treason, bribery, or other high crimes and misdemeanors."

One of the greatest powers, and potentially the one subject to greatest abuse, is the authority to veto acts of the legislature. This power, however, is not addressed along with the other attributes of the president in Article II; indeed, nowhere in the Constitution does the word *veto* even appear. Almost certainly, this omission was by design. The framers did not want to set off alarm bells by using a word that the colonists had come to associate with the tyranny of the royal governors. Section 7 of Article I, the article devoted to the legislative branch, defines the president's role with regard to legislation:

Every order, resolution, or vote to which the concurrence of the Senate and House of Representatives may be necessary (except on a question of adjournment) shall be presented to the President of the United States; and before the same shall take effect, shall be approved by him, or being disapproved by him, shall be repassed by two thirds of the Senate and House of Representatives, according to the rules and limitations prescribed in the case of a bill.

Not only did the framers soft-pedal their expression of presidential authority by avoiding the word *veto*, they severely limited this particular presidential prerogative by giving the legislature a means of overriding it: repassing the vetoed legislation by a two-thirds vote rather than a simple majority vote.

Thus, in a single sentence in Article I, Section 7, and in the concise whole of Article II is the American president constitutionally described. The Constitution does not so much define the office as it merely outlines it, the framers having thereby left it to the presidents themselves to invent—and when necessary to reinvent—what would be, after all, *their* office.

The Least You Need to Know

◆ Most Americans were reluctant to create a strong executive branch of government, but they wanted even less to perpetuate the headless, weak, and inefficient government of the Articles of Confederation.

◆ The framers of the Constitution considered three types of executive: an individual elected by the legislature, an executive committee elected by the legislature to serve only during the legislative term, and an individual elected by a state-selected Electoral College.

◆ As the framers of the Constitution chose from among three basic executive models, so they chose from among three forms of government: monarchy, aristocracy, and democracy. The republic they finally designed draws on all three models.

◆ The Constitution does not so much describe the office of president and vice president as it outlines them, leaving it to the occupants of these offices to fill in the details.

Veep

In This Chapter

◆ An office both weak and poorly defined

◆ The VP—according to the Constitution

◆ VPs—political pawns and political dregs

◆ The effect of Theodore Roosevelt and Harry S. Truman on the vice presidency

◆ What about Dick Cheney?

In a letter of December 19, 1793, John Adams, the first vice president of the United States, bewailed his fate to his wife, Abigail: "My country has in its wisdom contrived for me the most insignificant office that ever the invention of man contrived or his imagination conceived; and as I can do neither good nor evil, I must be borne away by others and meet the common fate." Nearly a century and a half later, the thirty-second vice president, John Nance Garner, observed less elegantly, "The vice presidency isn't worth a pitcher of warm piss."

Except for the nine occasions (eight presidents died in office, one resigned) on which a vice president completed the term of a chief executive, the office has generally been to the American body politic what the appendix is to the body human—undeniably part of it, but usually an unnoticed part and one that can be dispensed with, if necessary.

Constitutional Orphan

Although the vice presidency has been the inexhaustible butt of political jokes, most Americans today believe the office is valuable. The modern world moves so quickly and the stakes of presidential-level decisions are so high, it seems both prudent and imperative to have at hand a designated successor (as the popular saying goes) "a heartbeat away from the presidency." Yet as Hugh Williamson, one of the framers of the Constitution, observed in 1788, "Such an office as vice president was not wanted. He was introduced only for the sake of a valuable mode of election which required two to be chosen at the same time." The vice presidency was to the builders of our constitutional government what a shim is to a carpenter—a thin scrap of lumber put in to make everything else fit together.

Early in the Constitutional Convention, after deciding that the government should have a president, the delegates considered giving Congress the job of selecting him. By the end of their debates, however, they embraced Roger Sherman's idea of an Electoral College, a body composed of electors chosen by the legislatures of each state who, in turn, would elect the president by majority vote.

The problem with this system was that the electors were likely to vote for local favorites, making it almost impossible to elevate to office a truly *national* choice of president. This shortcoming was remedied by obliging each elector to cast two votes, one of which had to be for a candidate who "shall not be an inhabitant of the same State with themselves." Since this would produce a winner and a runner-up, the framers were loath simply to discard the second-place finisher and therefore, invented the office of vice president.

Executive Event

Under Article II, Section 1, of the Constitution as originally written, in the event of a tie in the Electoral College, the election would be entrusted to the House of Representatives, whose members would choose the president by ballot. If the Electoral College gave a majority to no one, "then from the five highest on the list said house shall in like manner choose the President.... In every case, after the choice of the President, the person having the greatest number of votes of the electors shall be the Vice President. But if there should remain two or more who have equal votes, the Senate shall choose from them by ballot the Vice President."

Something for the Guy to Do

If the Constitution says remarkably little about the duties of the president, it says even less about those of the vice president. Article II, Section 1, specifies that, in "case of the removal of the President from office or of his death, resignation, or inability to discharge the powers and duties of the said office, the same shall devolve on the Vice President." That is all, and you must turn back to Article I, Section 3, which describes the Senate, in order to find the only other vice presidential duty mentioned in the Constitution: "The Vice President ... shall be President of the Senate ...." That sounds impressive, until you read further in the job description: "but shall have no vote, unless they be equally divided." That is, the "president" of the Senate can cast only a tie-breaking vote.

> **What They Said**
>
> The man with the best job in the country is the vice president. All he has to do is get up every morning and say, "How is the president?"
>
> —Humorist Will Rogers, circa 1930

The President's Understudy

The seventeenth-century English poet John Milton wrote, "They also serve who only stand and wait." This would be a perfectly adequate characterization of the vice presidency as described by the Constitution. As far as the framers seem to have been concerned, the vice president's job is "stand and wait" for the Senate to convene or for the president to be removed from office, get sick, or die.

In 1819, Supreme Court Chief Justice John Marshall wrote the majority opinion in *McCullough* v. *Maryland*, a case in which the state of Maryland in effect held that Congress had exceeded its constitutional mandate by establishing the Second Bank of the United States. Marshall wrote that, although the Constitution did not *specifically* give Congress the power to establish a bank, it did give that body the authority to tax and to spend, which implies the authority to create a bank, because a bank is an appropriate instrument for the collection and disbursement of funds.

The immediate effect of the McCullough decision was to overturn an attempt by Maryland to tax the Second Bank of the United States, but the more enduring effect was to create the doctrine of *implied powers* that give Congress powers for implementing those congressional powers expressly stipulated in the Constitution (*enumerated powers*) in order to create a functional government.

def•i•ni•tion

> Enumerated powers are those powers specified in the Constitution for a given branch or officer of government. Implied powers, while not specified in the Constitution, flow from the enumerated powers as powers necessary for their execution.

The implied powers doctrine, some have suggested, may be applied not only to Congress but also to the vice presidency. Since the Constitution assigns the vice president the duty of succeeding the president in certain extraordinary circumstances, some have argued that it is proper to assume that this duty *implies* that the vice president should serve as the president's active understudy, devoting his term to preparing for succeeding the president.

This is a logical interpretation, but, in practice, few vice presidents have deliberately prepared themselves, and the only "implied power" vice presidents have consistently enjoyed is the authority to discharge whatever assignments the president may give him. Historically, these have usually been of a minor, usually ceremonial nature. On eight occasions, vice presidents have been called to office by the sudden death of the president. Of these, perhaps only Lyndon Johnson, who succeeded John F. Kennedy after his assassination on November 22, 1963, was reasonably well prepared for the office. The others were obliged to learn on the job as best they could.

When the Vice President Is Called Mr. President

As mentioned, the single sentence the Constitution devotes to the vice president's role in the Senate gives him an impressive title—president—but severely limits his practical power to casting a vote on legislation and other Senate matters only in the event of a tie.

John Adams, the first vice president, tried to do for his office what George Washington did for the presidency—establish a model for successors to follow. This was especially true of his conception of the role of president of the Senate. Taking the word at its root, Adams sought to "preside" over the Senate, and he spent a great deal of time involving himself in debates among the senators, who generally resented his interference. It was thanks to Adams that the Senate devoted an entire month to debating just what the official title of the president of the United States should be. Adams argued for such titles as "His Majesty the President" and "His High Mightiness," whereas most senators favored, simply, "President of the United States." The matter was eventually settled by President Washington, who insisted on being called nothing more grandiose than "Mr. President." By this time, however, the Senate was fed up with the somewhat corpulent Adams, on whom the senators conferred a title of their own invention: "His Rotundity."

Adams actually did exercise considerable power during his tenure as president of the Senate, casting 29 tie-breaking votes—a record yet to be equaled, let alone eclipsed (although John C. Calhoun, vice president from 1825–1832, came close with 28). But no vice president following him has presumed to "preside" over the Senate in the sense of actually leading that body.

Meet Mr. Also-Ran

As originally conceived by the framers of the Constitution, the vice president was the candidate electors judged second best. He was a runner-up, an also-ran. That was demoralizing enough, perhaps, but, incredibly, there was no consideration given to the possible consequences of elevating political competitors—perhaps even political opponents—to high office. After all, the president and vice president did not run *with* one another, but *against* one another.

What were the framers thinking?

To begin with, they seem not to have imagined that candidates would regard each other as opponents. Even as the Constitution was being created, the delegates envisioned George Washington as the first president. No one dared oppose him, and John Adams, although he disdained the office of vice president, nevertheless regarded Washington as the best choice for chief executive and felt that it was an honor to serve him. The framers assumed that, in succeeding administrations, president and vice president would find similar ways of working together.

Of course, the notion of putting competitors together at the head of government may also suggest that the framers did not believe there would be much need for the vice president and president actually to *work* together. That the vice president's office was designed to be filled by the also-ran suggests that, as originally conceived, the vice presidency neither embodied nor implied many substantive powers. That is, the vice president had just two duties: (1) to assume the reins of authority if the president left office (from causes natural or not) or was unable to discharge the duties of office and (2) to cast tie-breaking votes in the Senate. The framers did not expect him, on an ongoing basis, to be an adviser or a presidential "teammate."

It's My Party

The most consequential development the creators of the Constitution failed to consider was the rise of opposing parties in American political life. When George Washington first took office on April 30, 1789, political parties did not exist in the

United States. Throughout his tenure in office, Washington passionately counseled his countrymen against emulating the British practice of forming political parties, which he believed would lead to destructive factionalism. Although Americans revered Washington as the father of their country, they did not follow his advice. Even before his second term had ended, the new nation's political life was dividing into two parties, the Federalists (who favored a strong central government) and the Democratic-Republicans (who wanted the bulk of power to be held by the states as well as the people themselves).

Jefferson v. Adams, Burr v. Jefferson

During the American Revolution, Thomas Jefferson and John Adams were close collaborators and cordial friends, but they drifted apart, both politically and personally, during the Washington presidency, when Adams was vice president and Jefferson secretary of state. After Washington declined to run for a third term in 1796, Adams ran as a Federalist against Jefferson, a Democratic-Republican. More precisely, both Adams and South Carolina governor Thomas Pinckney ran as Federalists against Democratic-Republicans Jefferson and Senator Aaron Burr of New York.

Under the Constitution as it then existed, Adams and Pinckney were not running mates, nor were Jefferson and Burr. Adams hoped that he would emerge with an electoral majority and Pinckney would be runner-up and therefore, vice president, whereas Jefferson hoped that he would get the most votes, followed by Burr. What actually happened was that Adams received 71 electoral votes to Jefferson's 68, which made Thomas Jefferson—his opponent—vice president.

It was a bitter and acutely uncomfortable arrangement, in which Vice President Jefferson worked anonymously to oppose most of President Adams's Federalist initiatives, the most important of which were the infamous Alien and Sedition Acts of 1798, which (among other things) gave the president extensive powers of arrest, imprisonment, and deportation during war and sharply abridged free speech, freedom of the press, and the right of assembly.

Thanks in large part to the unpopularity of the Alien and Sedition Acts, Adams failed to win a second term in 1800, but the election was a messy one. Adams the Federalist was voted out, but the Electoral College majority was tied between the two Democratic-Republicans, Jefferson and Burr. Per the Constitution, the election was sent to the House of Representatives, which broke the tie only after a marathon 36 ballots. Jefferson was named president, with Burr the vice president.

With president and vice president of the same party, it would seem that the Jefferson-Burr administration was bound for clear sailing; however, once again, the runner-up system created a problem. The Democratic-Republican strategy was for Jefferson to be president and Burr vice president, but disruptive Federalists in the House of Representatives repeatedly attempted to give the election to Burr, even as Burr, who promised Jefferson that he would settle for vice president, did nothing to discourage the Federalist agitation for his presidency. In the end, Alexander Hamilton—Jefferson's arch political foe, but Burr's bitter personal enemy—persuaded his Federalist colleagues to abstain, thereby finally nudging Jefferson to the narrowest of victories in the House. Jefferson therefore entered the White House (the construction of which had been completed during the presidency of John Adams) with a profound distrust of his vice president, whom he cut out of all governmental, political, and party matters.

> **What They Said**
>
> We are all Republicans—we are all Federalists. If there be any among us who would wish to dissolve this Union or to change its republican form, let them stand undisturbed as monuments to the safety with which error of opinion may be tolerated where reason is left free to combat.
>
> —President Thomas Jefferson, inaugural speech, March 4, 1801

The Twelfth Amendment

The Jefferson vice presidency under Adams and the Burr vice presidency under Jefferson were such miserable experiences, fraught at every turn with the potential for disaster, that legislators began looking for an alternative to naming the electoral runner-up as vice president. The obvious solution was a constitutional amendment requiring electors to vote separately for president and vice president.

The amendment was introduced in Congress in 1804, only to fail in both the House and the Senate. A new amendment was quickly substituted, which required the *electors* to "name in their ballots the person voted for as President, and in distinct ballots the person voted for as Vice President." Thus, no distinction was made between the presidential and vice presidential candidates who offered themselves to the electors, but in casting ballots, each elector would designate one of his votes as applying to the office of president, the other to vice president. If no presidential candidate received a majority, the House of Representatives would chose the president—on the basis of one vote per state—from among the highest three candidates. If no vice presidential candidate received a majority, the Senate would choose from the two highest, also on the basis of one vote per state. In both the House and the Senate, a two-thirds quorum was required for selection.

The proposed amendment also gave the vice president a new power. Anticipating the possibility of a deadlock, the amendment provided that if the House was unable to choose a president before March 4—at the time, the first day of a presidential term—the person elected vice president would act as president. The proposed amendment did not specify how long the vice president would act as president, nor did it stipulate whether or not the House could still choose a president after March 4. The Twentieth Amendment, ratified in 1933, addressed these issues and also changed March 4 to January 20, the new date on which a president was to be inaugurated. The proposed amendment was adopted and ratified as the Twelfth Amendment in 1804.

A Bad, Sad Bunch

The Twelfth Amendment was ratified just as political parties were becoming powerful. Through the state legislatures, the party leaders in effect chose the electors. Although the amendment required the electors to designate a separate vote for president and for vice president, in practice, the parties designated one nominee as their presidential candidate and another as their vice presidential candidate, and the electors were expected to designate their votes accordingly. Moreover, throughout the nineteenth century, it was party leaders—not the presidential nominee—who chose the vice presidential candidate.

The VP as Political Pawn

Most of the time, the preferences of the presidential nominee were neither consulted nor considered in selecting the vice presidential nominee. The choice was made for strategic political purposes, which had little or nothing to do with governing. If, for example, a party nominated a northerner for president, it might choose a southerner for vice president in order to avoid alienating southern voters. Or party strategists might choose a vice-presidential candidate capable of carrying a critical swing state that the presidential nominee could not carry on his own.

An Office Devalued

This kind of jockeying was called *ticket balancing*, and it tended to devalue the vice presidency, making the candidate for that office little more than a token. Throughout the nineteenth century, some of the nation's ablest statesmen flatly refused nomination as vice president because it could actually damage, even destroy a person's political standing. Indeed, many nineteenth-century vice presidents were either failed politicians or men too old to run for any other office.

def•i•ni•tion

Ticket balancing is the practice of choosing a vice presidential candidate for the strategic purpose of compensating for some purely political deficiency of the presidential candidate. For example, a party that nominated a northerner for president might tap a southerner as his running mate to avoid alienating that region of the country.

The reputation of the vice presidency improved dramatically at the start of the twentieth century with the elevation of the dynamic young Theodore Roosevelt in 1900. He was the first vice presidential candidate to campaign vigorously for the ticket— and he made a great impression that gave a tremendous boost to his running mate, incumbent William McKinley. That president's assassination in 1901 gave Roosevelt the opportunity to prove himself one of the great American chief executives.

After Theodore Roosevelt, vice presidential candidates were chosen with more care, which raised them at least to a level of respectability. Still, they rarely played major roles in an administration and were certainly not treated by the president as a partner.

 Tally

Eight vice presidents died in office at an advanced age, and two resigned—one, John C. Calhoun, because of political differences with his president, Andrew Jackson; the other, Spiro T. Agnew, in disgrace after pleading no contest to criminal charges of income tax evasion and bribery.

The FDR Revolution

Franklin D. Roosevelt came to office in 1932, in the depths of the Great Depression, and during his first term made extensive use of his vice president, John Nance Garner, as an adviser and as an unofficial liaison between himself and key members of Congress. Garner also sat in on critical cabinet meetings. Whereas FDR was the leader of the Democratic Party's liberal wing, Garner was an important figure among party conservatives, and during FDR's second term, the two men drifted apart ideologically—Garner going so far as to challenge Roosevelt's bid for an unprecedented third term in 1940. Nevertheless, the Roosevelt administration demonstrated just how useful a good vice president could be.

Presidential Coup

For his third-term bid, FDR needed a new running mate, and he decided this time to draw from the liberal wing with which he was comfortable. He picked Secretary of Agriculture Henry A. Wallace, an enthusiastic backer of the New Deal and an administrator in whom the president had great confidence. When the Democratic Party balked at this choice, party leaders insisting that they retain their traditional prerogative to choose the vice presidential nominee, Roosevelt threatened to refuse the Democratic nomination altogether. The party leaders yielded instantly.

The Lesson of Harry S. Truman

Wallace was a high-profile vice president, but, as his leftist political sentiments began to verge on socialism and even (as some saw it) communism, FDR looked elsewhere for a fourth-term running mate.

Harry S. Truman of Missouri had entered the Senate in 1935 and was fairly undistinguished in that body until early in his second term, when he assumed the chairmanship of a committee charged with exposing and correcting waste and fraud in the U.S. military and its suppliers. He quickly earned a reputation for ending corruption and vastly increasing efficiency. His leadership of the Truman Committee—as it came to be called—made him an appealing choice for vice president.

FDR had personally drafted Truman, but during the 82 days of Truman's vice presidency, he met with the president only twice. Roosevelt never formally briefed him, let alone counseled with, groomed, or in any way prepared him. Of the existence of the atomic bomb project, for instance, he was told absolutely nothing.

On April 12, 1945, Franklin D. Roosevelt suddenly died of a cerebral hemorrhage. Truman was summoned to the White House and immediately took the oath of office. The next day, at his first impromptu press conference as president of a nation still in the throes of a desperate war, its beloved leader of 12 years gone, Truman confessed to the reporters: "Boys, if you ever pray, pray for me now. I don't know whether you fellows ever had a load of hay fall on you, but when they told me yesterday what had happened, I felt like the moon, the stars, and all the planets had fallen on me."

As it turned out, Truman was a quick study, who rose to the occasion magnificently and saw the nation through to victory over Germany and Japan, even unexpectedly winning a term in his own right.

That is how it turned out. But everyone knew, it might have turned out very differently. And *that* was the great lesson of the Truman vice presidency. After him, no president dared keep his VP at arm's length. Although the office continued to be rather weak in itself, each man who occupied it was aware that he could, at any moment, be called on to occupy the Oval Office.

When's My Turn?

"In case of the removal of the President from office," Article II, Section 1, of the Constitution states, "or of his death, resignation, or inability to discharge the powers and duties of the said office, the same shall devolve on the Vice President ...." Seems clear enough—until something bad actually happens.

When William Henry Harrison was inaugurated on March 4, 1841, he delivered an 8,444-word speech in a frigid rain. It took nearly two hours—and, historians have traditionally argued, his life. The story goes that he caught cold, developed pneumonia, and died. Actually, he did not fall ill until three weeks after the inauguration, so the connection with that event is doubtful; however, his illness proceeded rapidly, and he succumbed on April 4, 1841, a month to the day after taking office. He was succeeded by his vice president, John Tyler—the first such succession in American history.

The deficiency of Article II, Section 1, now became painfully apparent. It did not specify whether the vice president was to serve out the dead president's entire term or to fill his place until a special election could be held. By 1841, all of the Constitution's framers were dead. So there was no one to ask concerning the intentions of the delegates to the Constitutional Convention. A very complete record of the convention existed, but politicians and scholars were unaware of it at the time. If they could have looked at it, they would have seen that the matter had been discussed, a number of the delegates had wanted a special election, and no one seems to have objected to this. That a provision for such an election was not incorporated into the Constitution was probably nothing more or less than an oversight. In default of law, Tyler laid claim to Harrison's entire term, and no one fought back. American law thrives on precedent, and the precedent Tyler set endured until ratification of the Twenty-fifth Amendment in 1967, which settled the matter by declaring, "In case of the removal of the President from office or of his death or resignation, the Vice President shall become President." End of story.

 Tally

Nine vice presidents have risen to the presidency, eight upon the death of the president, and one, Gerald R. Ford, after the president's resignation.

The Twentieth Amendment

In 1933, the Twentieth Amendment was ratified. It changed the date of the start of presidential terms to January 20, mainly to reduce the length of the awkward period in which the nation has both a sitting president and a president-elect. The new amendment also tied up the ends left loose by the Twelfth. The Twentieth specifies that if the president-elect should die before his inauguration, the vice president–elect would become president. If no president is chosen by January 20 or if the president-elect "shall have failed to qualify, then the Vice President–elect shall act as President until a President shall have qualified." If neither a president-elect nor a vice president–elect has qualified, then Congress, through legislation, is to determine "who shall then act as President" as well as set any necessary conditions of this person's term.

Twenty-Fifth Amendment

On November 22, 1963, John F. Kennedy became the eighth president to die in office and the fourth to die by assassination. The event stunned lawmakers into tying up two more constitutional loose ends.

Article II, Section I, of the Constitution states that in case of the president's "inability to discharge the powers and duties" of his office, "the same shall devolve on the Vice President." The clause does not specify what constitutes "inability," how the vice president should step in, or if "devolve" means that the vice president becomes president or merely serves until the president recovers. The Article also fails to address succession to the presidency in the absence of a vice president. Between 1789 and the Kennedy assassination in 1963, the nation was without a vice president 16 times—eight times because the president died, seven times because the vice president died, and once because the vice president resigned. It was sheer luck that a double vacancy—the lack of both a president and a vice president—had ever come about.

Ratified in 1967, the Twenty-fifth Amendment specifies that the vice president would become president on the death or resignation of the president. Whenever the office of vice president became vacant, for whatever reason, the president was to nominate a new vice president, who would assume office after confirmation by a majority of both houses of Congress.

So much was straightforward. The issue of presidential "inability" was thornier.

Section III of the amendment provides that the president may transmit to the president pro tempore of the Senate and to the speaker of the House a written declaration that he is unable to discharge his presidential duties. Until the president "transmits ... a declaration to the contrary," the vice president is to serve as acting president.

Section IV states: "Whenever the Vice President and a majority of either the principal officers of the executive departments or of such other body as Congress may by law provide" inform the president pro tempore of the Senate and the speaker of the House that the president is unable to perform the duties of his office, the vice president becomes acting president. When the president informs the president pro tempore and the speaker "that no inability exists, he shall resume the powers and duties of his office unless the Vice President and a majority of either the principal officers of the executive departments or of such other body as Congress may by law provide, transmit within four days to the President pro tempore of the Senate and the Speaker of the House of Representatives their written declaration that the President is unable to discharge the powers and duties of his office." In this event, Congress decides the issue. If a two-thirds majority of both houses determine presidential inability, the vice president continues to serve as acting president. If Congress fails to decide within 21 days, the president automatically resumes the powers and duties of his office.

The Cheney Challenge

Throughout most of presidential history, the office of vice president has been a quiet place, ranging in level of activity and influence from virtually dormant to active and influential, but always subordinate to the will and direction of the president.

In 2000, George W. Bush and his vice presidential pick, Richard Bruce "Dick" Cheney, prevailed after a hotly contested election. Cheney had served as a Republican representative from Wyoming and as secretary of defense in the cabinet of Bush's father, George H. W. Bush. Early in his vice presidency, he had a conversation with George H. W. Bush's vice president, Dan Quayle, who remarked to Cheney that the office of VP was largely ceremonial. Cheney replied: "I have a different understanding with the president."

It was an understatement.

New York Times reporter Eric Schmitt called Cheney Bush's "war minister über diplomat, political adviser and consigliere" (October 7, 2001). In *USA Today* (July 29, 2002), Susan Page reported that Bush always asked "What does Dick think?" before making any major decision.

A tight-lipped, even secretive man, his face to all appearances frozen in a perpetual scowl, Cheney was not a popular figure. Moreover, his highly ideological "neoconservative" orientation seemed sinister to many Americans, especially the growing majority who did not approve of the costly Iraq War and who accused Cheney of having prodded Bush (and other political leaders) into it with the aid of exaggerated and manipulated intelligence.

Many believed Cheney functioned as a "shadow president." In June 2007, the *Washington Post* published a four-part series on Cheney, based largely on interviews with administration insiders, concluding that he was not literally a shadow president, but that he did almost invariably have the final word as the president's counselor.

The controversial tenure of Dick Cheney, who served during both Bush terms (2001–2009), presents a challenge to future vice presidents—and the presidents they supposedly serve. Whether or not any future vice president will exercise influence of a magnitude approaching Cheney's remains to be seen, but it seems certain that he has, for better or worse, reconfigured the contour and limits of the office, pushing it beyond any question of ceremonial irrelevance.

The Least You Need to Know

- The Constitution says remarkably little about the office of vice president—a circumstance that, historically, has rendered the vice presidency vague and weak.

- Until the Twelfth Amendment was adopted in 1804, the vice president was the runner-up in the presidential election.

- The dynamism of Theodore Roosevelt—a VP who became a great president—and Harry S. Truman's fortunate capacity to learn on the job helped transform the vice presidency from an exercise in "ticket balancing" to an office of significant responsibility.

- Dick Cheney, vice president under George W. Bush, was such a powerful presence that his vice presidency stands as a challenge to future occupants of the office.

Chapter 4

Number One

In This Chapter

♦ The character of George Washington

♦ Shaping the office of president

♦ Inventing the cabinet

♦ The precedent of executive supremacy

♦ Washington's stance against political partisanship

Whatever else it is, the Constitution is a legal document: a contract. Of course, no lawyer today would approve of its broad, often vague language, which has left so much to be filled in by future interpretation. Perhaps no article in this sketchy document is sketchier that Article II, which outlines ("defines" is too strong a word) the presidency.

How could the framers have been comfortable with providing the merest outline of the single most important—and controversial—office of federal government? The answer is simple. They all knew who the first president would be, and they were entirely confident that his proven wisdom, courage, judgment, and, most of all, his character would define the office of president as no mere words could.

Roman Virtue in America

Most Americans are taught from an early age that *democracy* is our form of government and that it is derived, ultimately, from the example of the ancient Greeks. This is not terribly mistaken, but it is mistaken nevertheless. In truth, our form of government is a *republic*, and those who created it looked more to the ancient Romans than to the Greeks for precedents.

def•i•ni•tion

A **democracy** is government by the people, exercised either directly by them or through their elected representatives. Strictly speaking, a **republic** is any government whose head of state is not a monarch. The framers of the Constitution certainly created a republic, and they also included in it important elements of democracy, but they by no means gave the people direct power to govern, nor even the power to elect all of their representatives directly.

The most important feature of a republic is that its head of state is *not* a monarch. In republican Rome, the head of state was elected by the Senate, which (at least in principle) took care to choose a figure of wisdom and virtue, the kind of man to whom the Senate might give the most honored title it could bestow: Pater Patriae, father of his country.

Father of His Country

Even before General George Washington resigned as commander of the Continental Army on December 23, 1783, after having led the nation to victory in the American Revolution, he was being hailed as Pater Patriae.

In the Revolution, Washington showed himself to be a superb manager, a combat leader of remarkable courage that inspired courage in others, and a leader who commanded the adoring loyalty of the vast majority of his subordinates and troops.

What They Said

I am embarked on a wide ocean, boundless in its prospect and in which, perhaps, no safe harbor is to be found.

—George Washington, 1775, just after the Continental Congress commissioned him to lead the Continental Army

American Cincinnatus

Of all Washington's extraordinary attributes, the one that the framers found most compelling was his resigning command once his mission had been accomplished and returning to his beloved Potomac River plantation, Mount Vernon.

To the classically schooled builders of American government, the significance of the resignation and the retirement was unmistakable. They recognized it as a modern incarnation of the story of Cincinnatus, the noble Roman who left his farm in 458 B.C. when the Senate called on him to rescue a consular army besieged on Mount Algidus by the fierce Aequi, tribesmen of central Italy. In sending him on his mission, the Senate bestowed on Cincinnatus the powers of absolute dictator, which he wielded to defeat the invaders in a single day. His task completed, he resigned the dictatorship and returned to his farm.

To a convention of men given the monumentally difficult assignment of creating a powerful chief executive's office whose occupant would neither be tempted nor able to turn tyrant, the Cincinnatus myth represented the ideal.

The framers of the Constitution were confident that Washington would show similar self-restraint in occupying, shaping, and modeling the office of president of the United States.

"I Walk on Untrodden Ground"

Charles Thomson, secretary to Congress, arrived at Mount Vernon on April 14, 1789, to notify Washington of his election and to officially ask if he would serve. "I cannot give a greater evidence of my sensibility for the honor my fellow citizens have done me," Washington replied to Thomson, "than by accepting the appointment."

Yet Washington did not rush to New York. Unwilling to appear overeager to assume his office—lest he seem hungry for power—he waited two days before leaving Mount Vernon, and rode not in a grand carriage of state, but in his own plain coach. His progress was deliberately slow, as he alighted at every town and village through which he passed. His objective had been to assess the mood of the nation at his election. That mood, he found, was sheer adoration. He was inaugurated, in New York City, on April 30, 1789.

The stately pace of his journey, its humble nature, his deference to the people who greeted him—all of these things flowed from Washington's personal character. He was, however, keenly aware that his behavior had consequences far beyond his personal sense of decorum. Early in his first term, Washington said of his tenure, "I walk on untrodden ground. There is scarcely any part of my conduct which may not hereafter be drawn into precedent."

Conduct, Washington decided, not written proclamations or laws, would guide future presidents. He would shape the office by his actions, his deeds, as much as his words.

A Republican Monarch

Until 1789, the people of the United States had known only kings and royal governors as executives. Trying to imagine how they must have thought of Washington in 1789, the historian Joanne B. Freeman called him a "republican monarch." This oxymoron—remember, a republic is defined as a government without a monarch—suggests just how thin a tightrope Washington believed he had to walk. His role, as he conceived it, was to conduct himself as a chief executive, commanding respect, power, and authority, yet to do so without behaving like a king.

A Man of the People?

From day one, Washington had to resolve the most basic issues of executive conduct, beginning with the president's accessibility. Should he freely meet with virtually any and all callers, or should he be insulated by a staff? Those of Jeffersonian stamp, who distrusted centralized authority, wanted the office to be wide open, whereas others, such as Vice President John Adams, believed the chief executive should hold himself somewhat aloof in order to create an aura of dignity about the office.

Washington did not leave the resolution to chance. He established a strict schedule whereby, on Tuesday of each week, any "respectably dressed" man could call upon him between three and four o'clock in the afternoon without an appointment. Every Friday evening, he and his wife, Martha, would preside over a "tea party," freely open to men and women.

On Thursdays, the president held an invitation-only dinner at 4 P.M. These occasions were strictly limited to government officials and their families, but the president ensured impartial inclusiveness by consulting a list of officials and inviting them in an unalterable rotation, taking care to leave no one out.

Minding His Manners

From the beginning, a significant aspect of the president's role was to represent the United States socially. This entailed a good deal of entertaining. Thomas Jefferson, Washington's secretary of state, was again critical, judging the president's soirees too European, smacking of corrupt monarchy, whereas Adams thought they should be more formal and elaborate than they were, in order to put the environment surrounding the president on a par with the "courts" of Europe.

As mentioned in Chapter 3, Adams was particularly eager to establish a title and form of address for the president that would convey the dignity of the office. Adams favored "His Highness" or, even more grandly, "His High Mightiness, the President of the United States and Protector of Their Liberties." Congress disagreed and insisted on nothing more than "the President of the United States." Washington agreed enthusiastically.

In the end, Washington resolved the conflict between republican informality and monarchal formality by demonstrating that a president of high character and admirable conduct could carry off republican simplicity in a manner perfectly consistent with the dignity of high office.

Tally

George Washington still holds the record for number of constitutional amendments ratified during his term: 11. The first 10, constituting the Bill of Rights, were ratified in 1791, and the Eleventh Amendment, which bars the citizen of one state from suing another state or foreign citizens from suing any state, was ratified in 1795.

Washington the Cabinet Maker

The *cabinet* is one of the many things about the presidency that most of us today take for granted. The fact is that Article II of the Constitution says nothing about a cabinet and alludes to the existence of "executive Departments" only in its specification that the president can require "the Opinion, in writing, of the principal Officer in each of the executive Departments, upon any Subject relating to the Duties of their respective Offices." Concerning what these departments should be and how they should be established the Constitution is silent.

After Washington's first term was already under way, it was Congress, not the president, that created the first three executive departments: State, Treasury, and War.

def•i•ni•tion

A **cabinet** is a body of individuals chosen by a chief executive or head of state to lead the executive departments and to advise the chief executive. Both the word and the concept were imported into American government from the British government, but Washington did not refer to his advisers as a "cabinet" until the start of his second term.

In accordance with the Constitution, which gives the president authority to appoint government officers, subject to the advice and consent of the Senate, Washington nominated Thomas Jefferson as secretary of state, Alexander Hamilton to head up the treasury, and, as secretary of war, his own revolutionary comrade at arms, the general who had been in charge of the Continental Artillery, Henry Knox. The Senate approved all of the appointments.

In addition to his three-department cabinet, Washington took it upon himself also to appoint an attorney general, Edmund Randolph of Virginia. His office, as Washington conceived it, was not a cabinet-level department, but a legal advisory position.

Governing by Ear

Washington did not call his three department heads his cabinet until the beginning of his second term, in 1793, and he did not even convene regular, formal meetings with them until the very end of his first term.

Nor did the first president see his cabinet as resembling the British Parliamentary concept of a cabinet, which, as presided over by the prime minister, was often referred to as the "government" of the nation. Instead, the members of the cabinet and the attorney general were primarily presidential advisers.

Although he conceived the cabinet without great formality, Washington did devote great care to selecting his advisers, every one of whom was highly respected intellectually and had been instrumental in creating the United States. None of those he chose were mere yes men—not to the president or to each other. Indeed, Jefferson and Hamilton represented opposite poles of American political thought at the end of the eighteenth century, and their arguments were often heated. Washington was closer in political philosophy to Hamilton (who had been his adjutant during the revolution) than he was to Jefferson, but, even so, he was far more moderate than his secretary of the treasury, who was both personally ambitious and ambitious on behalf of the federal government, seeking to acquire more and more authority for it. In formulating policy, Washington saw his role as mediating between the extremes his cabinet offered.

Human Resources Manager

President Washington exercised as much care over the appointments he made to lesser government offices as he did to selecting his cabinet. Had he wanted, he could have handed out administrative plums to friends and anyone else he wished to out in his debt. But Washington scrupulously avoided political patronage, and he also generally avoided appointing friends and relations. The chief criteria by which he judged appointees included character, their standing in the community, and their manifest support for the Constitution.

Washington considered his function as what we might today call a human resources manager as one of the most important duties of the president.

Of Presidential Supremacy

Although Washington provided an example of self-restraint in the exercise of power, he also established the enduring precedent of the chief executive's supreme authority over the executive branch itself. Although his cabinet-level appointees were subject to Senatorial advice and consent, *he* was the man who nominated them, and they were answerable solely to *him*. Washington insisted that neither the Senate nor the cabinet was to play any executive role in the executive branch. The branch was sole province of the president.

Executive Supremacy Challenged

Colonial tradition had included strong legislative involvement in the administration of executive affairs, and during Washington's first term, Congress debated a bill that would give the Senate authority to approve or disapprove the removal from office of persons appointed by the president. The argument in favor of the bill rested on the theory that, because the Constitution gave the Senate the authority to approve or disapprove high-level presidential appointments, it also *implied* the Senate's authority to approve or disapprove removal of such appointees. Opposing this, advocates of a strong presidency argued that the bill severely compromised presidential authority by depriving the executive of power over his own domain. The bill was defeated in the House, but tied in the Senate. Vice President Adams broke the tie, defeating the measure, and preserving presidential supremacy over the executive branch.

Congress refrained from making further assaults on presidential supremacy until the Tenure of Office Act, passed in 1867, during the tumultuous administration of the highly unpopular Andrew Johnson (see Chapter 12).

Tally

Three new states were added to the union during President Washington's administration: Vermont in 1791, Kentucky in 1792, and Tennessee in 1796.

Executive Event

The Constitution imposed no limit on the number of terms a president could serve, and Washington would certainly have been elected to a third term in 1796 had he chosen to stand for reelection. Washington's decision to retire rather than offer himself for another term was motivated by three imperatives. First he longed to return to Mount Vernon and private life. Second, he wanted to ease Democratic-Republican fears (expressed by Thomas Jefferson) that the presidency could become an appointment for life. Third, Washington wanted to demonstrate to his fellow citizens that the Constitution and constitutional government would survive without him. In declining to run for a third term in 1808, Thomas Jefferson effectively ratified the two-term tradition, which endured until Franklin D. Roosevelt was reelected to a third term in 1940.

Supreme but Self-Restrained

Washington believed that presidential supremacy was essential to upholding the dignity and authority of the presidency, but he was careful to practice the utmost restraint in dealing with the legislative branch. He deliberately withheld his veto, using it only against bills he believed were unconstitutional. If he merely disagreed with a bill, he declined to exercise a veto of the bill. It was, he believed, the business of the legislature, not the executive, to make laws. As president, he did not so much as suggest legislation.

Foreign Policy

Washington also crafted a delicate combination of executive supremacy and deference to the Senate in the conduct of foreign policy. He always asserted his constitutional authority to function as the nation's chief diplomat, but he worked closely with the Senate in the spirit of the Constitution's stipulation that it was to provide "advice" and give (or withhold) its "consent" in the primary function of foreign policy, treaty negotiation.

Initially, Washington took the concept of "advice and consent" literally, seeking the Senate's advice on a given treaty before he signed it. This proved awkward, and Washington soon stopped the practice. He introduced instead the precedent of negotiating and signing treaties, then submitting the finished product to the Senate for consent—or not.

No Parties, Please

One precedent Washington wanted almost desperately to set failed to take hold. He disapproved of political parties because he believed that they introduced harmful factionalism in the administration of government. He did accept that Congress, especially the House, whose members were elected directly by the people, would likely fall prey to party politics, but since the president's primary duty, as Washington conceived it, was to "faithfully execute" the laws passed by Congress—and not to originate or sponsor legislation—there was no reason for partisanship to take hold at the executive level. The laws were the laws.

> ## 66 99 What They Said _____
>
> The common and continual mischiefs of the spirit of party are sufficient to make it the interest and duty of a wise people to discourage and restrain it. It serves always to distract the Public Councils, and enfeeble the Public Administration. It agitates the Community with ill-founded jealousies and false alarms; kindles the animosity of one part against another, foments occasionally riot and insurrection.
>
> —George Washington, Farewell Address, September 17, 1796

Despite the president's popularity and prestige, despite the reverential awe in which lawmakers and public alike held him, parties had become a fact of American political life as early as the beginning of Washington's own second term.

The Federalist Party was established by 1792 and remained important until 1816, although some isolated Federalists served in various offices through the 1820s. Closely associated with Alexander Hamilton and John Adams, the Federalists believed in the centralization of government authority and the creation and maintenance of a strong chief executive.

The Federalists were opposed by the Democratic-Republican Party, founded in 1792 by Thomas Jefferson and his political ally/protégé James Madison. The name "Democratic-Republican" was invented by historians because the members of the party variously referred to themselves as Democrats, Republicans, and sometimes Jeffersonians. The party is the origin of the modern Democratic Party. Democratic-Republicans favored decentralization of governing power—vesting it mainly in the states and in the people themselves—and, in consequence, a relatively weak executive.

George Washington could no more stem the tide of party politics than a man could contain the rushing waters of a great river. Political factionalism had an energy all its own. Yet even in Washington's unsuccessful attempt to keep the nation—or, at the very least, the presidency—above party politics, there is evidence of the enduring influence of his example. During the more than two centuries since Washington left office, all American presidents who aspired to greatness have attempted to rise above partisanship.

The Least You Need to Know

- ◆ The framers of the Constitution refrained from being too specific about the office of president, largely because they were certain that the first president would be George Washington, on whom they depended to shape the office both wisely and nobly.

- ◆ Among the most important presidential legacies of George Washington was the cabinet, which he, for all practical purposes, invented.

- ◆ Washington established the precedent of executive supremacy—the doctrine that the president exercises absolute authority over the executive branch (except for the Senate's role in approving or disapproving certain presidential appointments).

- ◆ Washington's most enduring contribution to the presidency was the tone of dignity, integrity, authority, and restraint he established for it.

Chapter 5

An Office Under Fire

In This Chapter

◆ How the Jay Treaty embroiled the presidency in a constitutional crisis

◆ The presidency becomes a partisan prize

◆ The election of 1796

◆ Alexander Hamilton attempts to hijack the presidency

◆ Alien and Sedition Acts

Partisan politics began to get ugly within Washington's own cabinet during the first president's second term, but his personal prestige was such that, had he chosen to run for a third term, open conflict would almost certainly have been avoided—or, at least, held at bay. John Adams, whom Washington effectively anointed as his successor, was widely admired but, unlike Washington, by no means revered. For this reason, the election of 1796, for the second president of the United States, was surprisingly bitter and hotly contested. Party politics, even at the presidential level, was here to stay.

A Question of Implied Powers

The one issue that brought party strife to a boil was a dispute over the so-called Jay Treaty (Treaty of London, 1794). Eager to improve strained relations with Britain, President Washington sent Chief Justice John Jay to London to negotiate a treaty with the British government to secure British evacuation of military forts and trading outposts in the Northwest (something promised in the Treaty of Paris, which ended the American Revolution, but yet to be carried out) and to negotiate important trading concessions. In return, the United States agreed to guarantee most private pre–revolutionary war debts Americans owed to British merchants. Jay did not push for the British to compensate southern slaveholders for slaves lost as a result of British action during the war, nor was he able to compel an end to the practice of *impressment*. There was little or no recourse in cases of arbitrary impressments or impressments on faulty or mistaken grounds. The Jay Treaty was signed November 19, 1794, and (per the Constitution) sent to the Senate for its "consent."

def•i•ni•tion

Impressment was the mostly British practice of intercepting U.S. merchant ships on the high seas, boarding them, seizing any sailors the officer of the boarding party deemed to be either a British subject or a naval deserter, and "impressing" (forcibly recruiting) these individuals into the Royal Navy.

The Democratic-Republicans argued that the treaty made the United States subservient to the British; they condemned the continuation of impressment as an ignominious surrender of national sovereignty; and southerners—most of whom were Democratic-Republicans—were outraged by Jay's failure to secure compensation for slaves lost (escaped or killed) during the revolution.

Senate vs. House

The Senate, a majority of which was Federalist, ratified the Jay Treaty, whereupon James Madison sought to undermine the Senate by challenging the treaty in the Democratic-Republican–dominated House of Representatives. The treaty called for international arbitration commissions to be established to survey and settle boundary issues that had been left unresolved by the treaty itself. Such commissions would require funding, which, in turn, would require passage of a "money bill." The Constitution stipulated that such bills were to originate in the House, not the Senate; therefore, Madison argued, although the Constitution explicitly gave the Senate the *enumerated* power to approve or disapprove treaties, it also gave the House the *implied* power to participate in the approval or disapproval because of the House's *enumerated* power to originate appropriations legislation. Acting on this theory, Albert Gallatin, a Democratic-Republican, prompted the House to pass a resolution requesting the president to furnish that body with all executive papers relating to the negotiation of the Jay Treaty. The resolution was based on the strength of Gallatin's assertion that, because the House would have to vote necessary funding to enable implementation of the treaty, it had the authority to obtain all information necessary to "assist … in deciding the question."

In short, the Democratic-Republicans were attempting to assert the right of the House to participate in the treaty-making process. They feared that a president, once he secured the compliance of two thirds of the Senate, could simply usurp all the powers of the House. To counteract this, they sought for the House the same degree of influence over the executive branch that the Senate enjoyed.

Tally _____

Implementation of the Jay Treaty required funding a boundary commission as well as an ambitious project to survey the disputed boundaries separating British Canada from the United States. Congress was called on to appropriate $90,000—a very considerable sum in the late eighteenth century.

Washington Stands Firm

If the House Democratic-Republicans expected that Washington's impending retirement would make him more compliant, they were sorely mistaken. The outgoing president issued a stern refusal to the request of the House, which he deemed unconstitutional.

The House stood as firmly as the president, which precipitated a constitutional crisis because the Democratic-Republicans threatened to withhold the funding necessary to put the treaty into effect. Madison and his allies hoped that this fight between the House (on one side) and the Senate and president (on the other)—pitting liberal democracy against conservative federalism—would be a compelling campaign issue in the upcoming presidential election. But in the end, the enduring prestige of Washington persuaded a sufficient number of representatives to cross lines of party and ideology and vote for the funds—by just three votes.

The First Presidential Campaign

Although they were defeated in their bid to challenge the combined power potentially represented by an alliance between president and Senate, the Democratic-Republicans recognized that the Federalist victory in this case had depended solely on the personal prestige of Washington.

And now he was stepping down.

Thomas Jefferson predicted that, without Washington, the Democratic-Republican philosophy of decentralized government would prevail.

Tough Act to Follow

That John Adams, designated by Washington as his favored successor, had to struggle for election revealed two things about the nature of the presidency after the departure of the Father of His Country.

First, Washington would almost certainly prove a unique case—the one figure in all of American history on whom virtually all Americans would agree as their choice to lead the nation. And this was a good thing. As Adams himself would repeatedly say, the strength of the United States depended on the American government's being a government of laws, not men. A chief executive who became the focus of a cult of personality was a short step away from becoming a dictator.

Second, the presidency would henceforth be regarded as a prize, for which more than one figure would compete.

Campaign 1796

More accurately, the partisans of one presidential hopeful would compete against the partisans of the other. Although political parties had made their unmistakable debut, Americans and the candidates themselves still judged party politics to be undignified, if not disreputable. Neither John Adams nor his chief rival, Thomas Jefferson, deemed it appropriate to campaign personally. Instead, both remained silent while their factions—the Federalists and the Democratic-Republicans—campaigned on their behalf.

The campaigns were ugly, the parties reveling in what today would be called "negative campaigning." The Federalists did not so much tout the virtues of their candidate, John Adams, as they attempted to smear the character and philosophy of the Democratic-Republican, Thomas Jefferson. He was an atheist who was determined to destroy religion in the United States. He was a radical democrat who embraced the French Revolution (1789), and whose idea of government was little more than anarchy—mobocracy. For their part, the Democratic-Republicans condemned Adams as a monarchist, so pro-British that he would throw away America's dearly won independence.

A Presidency Embattled

In vivid contrast to the unanimity that had elevated George Washington to office, John Adams achieved election by the narrowest of margins, winning 71 electoral votes to Jefferson's 68. In other words, nine states supported Adams, while seven favored Jefferson. This split was largely regional. The New England and Mid-Atlantic states (save Pennsylvania) went for Adams, whereas the South and West sided with Jefferson, a division that seemed to bode a regionalism incompatible with genuine nationhood.

Not only, then, did President Adams come to office without the full support of the country, he was saddled with his opponent as vice president. Recall from Chapter 3 that, before ratification of the Twelfth Amendment in 1804, the electoral front-runner won the presidency, and the closest runner-up became vice president.

 Tally

John Adams carried Connecticut, Delaware, Maryland, Massachusetts, New Hampshire, New Jersey, New York, Rhode Island, and Vermont, earning 71 electoral votes; Jefferson carried Georgia, Kentucky, North Carolina, Pennsylvania, South Carolina, Tennessee, and Virginia, for 68 electoral votes.

Adams vs. the Other Party

Thanks to the Jay Treaty, Anglo-American relations were improved at the expense of relations between the United States and its erstwhile ally France. French harassment of U.S. merchant shipping became so frequent that an undeclared naval war—historians call it the Quasi-War—erupted between the United States and France in 1798 and continued until 1800, all the time verging on an all-out declared conflict. Determined to avoid that eventuality, Adams dispatched three envoys, John Marshall, Charles Cotesworth Pinckney, and Elbridge Gerry, on a diplomatic mission to France in an effort to patch up relations. (The inclusion of Gerry, a Democratic-Republican, was Adams's gesture toward overcoming partisanship.) Napoleon's foreign minister,

Talleyrand, sent three of his own envoys to meet the American diplomats and inform them that the minister required loans to France as well as a personal bribe for himself as a condition of meeting with them. In their report to President Adams, the three Americans referred to the French emissaries as "X, Y, and Z," and when Adams and the Congress made the report public in 1798, the "XYZ Affair" exploded.

In the face of this insult to United States dignity and sovereignty, war loomed as inevitable, prompting Adams to authorize an expansion of the army and the creation of a U.S. Navy and to ask Congress for funding, including a tax hike to pay for it all. Opposition to the new taxes became a rallying cry for the Democratic-Republicans, and Vice President Jefferson worked behind the scenes to fan the flames of opposition to the president he supposedly served. Soon, the interparty fighting became so intense that some in the southern states—solidly Democratic-Republican—began grumbling about the possibility of seceding from the Union.

Adams vs. His Own Party

Adams faced increasing dissent not only from the opposition party but also from within his own, which had splintered into so-called "Arch-Federalists" (led by Alexander Hamilton) and more moderate mainstream Federalists (such as Adams himself).

Hamilton in particular urged Adams to go to war with France, largely because he believed a war would strengthen the central government, as would the necessary enlargement of the army and navy. Hamilton had persuaded President Washington, during his second term, to appoint Timothy Pickering secretary of state, James McHenry secretary of war, and, to replace himself as secretary of the treasury, Oliver Wolcott. Out of deference to Washington, Adams retained these three men in his own cabinet, failing to understand that they felt greater allegiance to Hamilton, the man who had gotten them their positions, than they did to Adams. Thus, from outside of the administration, the Arch-Federalist Hamilton worked through Adams's cabinet in an attempt to reshape the policies of the moderate Federalist president.

Rescuing the Presidency

By 1799, the Adams presidency was under siege—less by members of the opposition party than by a single powerful member of Adams's own party. And because Adams was only the second president of the United States, his actions, like those of Washington before him, would set precedents for the office for years to come.

Check ...

Adams was, in fact, slow to perceive what Hamilton was doing, but once Adams grasped the threat to the presidency, he acted promptly to check Hamilton and the other Arch-Federalists. In February 1799, without consulting his disloyal cabinet, he named William Vans Murray, at the time U.S. minister the Netherlands, *minister plenipotentiary* to France. He did this in the knowledge that Murray got on well with the French and the French government and that Talleyrand had signaled his readiness to negotiate. Napoleon, with a full plate, did not want war with the United States.

def•i•ni•tion

> A **minister plenipotentiary**, sometimes called simply a plenipotentiary, is a diplomatic representative who has full authority to act on behalf of the government he or she represents (a minister has more limited authority), but who ranks below an ambassador, who is considered the personal representative of the nation's chief executive. Throughout the eighteenth century and most of the nineteenth, only monarchies exchanged ambassadors—an office considered inappropriate for a republic. The United States did not appoint ambassadors until 1893.

This would be welcome news to the Democratic-Republicans, but, as Adams now knew, the Hamiltonian faction *wanted* war, and because the Senate was controlled by Federalists who leaned toward to Hamilton, Adams doubted that the Senate would confirm Murray's appointment. By acting unilaterally, however, the president caught the senators off guard, stunning them into offering a compromise in the form of a three-person mission. The president agreed.

... and Mate

By this time, Secretary of State Pickering stepped in with a request that the departure of the mission be postponed. Realizing that this was an attempt to undermine the mission, which needed to begin negotiations before the Franco-American Quasi-War could escalate into a "real" war, Adams indicated to Pickering that he had no objection to a delay. This done, he quietly bundled the three ministers onto a U.S. Navy warship and sent them sailing—immediately—to France.

The cabinet and Arch-Federalists were up in arms over the president's high-handed action, but Adams stood firm, and when the mission produced an equitable trade agreement and pledge of friendship with France, thereby both averting war *and* preserving American honor, not only was Adams vindicated personally, the integrity of the executive office and the authority of the chief executive were also confirmed.

Having rescued the presidency, Adams summarily fired Secretary Pickering and forced the resignation of Secretary McHenry, further asserting the precedent of executive supremacy Washington had established (see Chapter 4).

The Alien and Sedition Controversy

Adams's triumphal rescue of the office he occupied in a time of great disunity and other threats both domestic and foreign was the high-water mark of his administration. Professional historians remember him for it, but the nonspecialist American public remembers Adams more for something else he supported.

As would sometimes happen when the United States came under external threat, Congress rushed to enact legislation intended to protect American freedoms by severely limiting them. (Witness, for example, the passage of the controversial Patriot Act one month after the terrorist attacks of September 11, 2001.) In the summer of 1798, the Federalist-controlled Congress passed the Alien and Sedition Acts, which included the Naturalization Act (June 18, 1798), raising the residence prerequisite for citizenship from 5 to 14 years; the Alien Act (June 25, 1798), authorizing the president summarily to deport, without trial or hearing, all aliens he regarded as dangerous; and the Alien Enemies Act (July 6, 1798), authorizing the president, in time of war, to arrest, imprison, or deport subjects of any enemy power, again without resort to trial or hearing.

Both of these acts drew vehement objections from the Democratic-Republicans. The Naturalization Act, they objected, was clearly partisan. Many of the supporters of the Democratic-Republicans were recent immigrants; increasing the residency requirement excluded them from voting as well as running for office, thereby reducing the constituency of the Federalists' rival party. The Alien Act and the Alien Enemies Act, opponents believed, gave the president unconstitutional unilateral authority by abridging the right to due process of law. But it was the Sedition Act (July 14, 1798) that was most shocking. Its prohibition of assembly "with intent to oppose any measure of the government" and of printing, uttering, or publishing anything "false, scandalous, and malicious" against the government seemed a blatant affront to the Bill of Rights.

While it is true that President Adams had neither drafted nor supported passage of the Alien and Sedition Acts, he signed them without hesitation. His argument for doing so was that the president needed the authority to protect the nation against sedition and other threats and that the people had to trust that the character and integrity of the occupant of the White House would be sufficient to restrain him from abusing the powers granted.

> **What They Said**
>
> Power naturally grows. Why? Because human passions are insatiable. But that power alone can grow which already is too great; that which is unchecked; that which has no equal power to control it.
>
> —John Adams, letter to Roger Sherman, July 18, 1789

This argument might have carried the day had it come from the mouth of George Washington, whose character and integrity were accepted without question. But John Adams was no George Washington. He himself advocated a government of laws, not men, and the likes of Thomas Jefferson and James Madison were not about to trust government to the character of its principal administrators.

Once again, Vice President Jefferson worked behind the scenes to undermine his president. He and Madison took it upon themselves to draft resolutions on behalf of the states of Virginia (Madison in 1798) and Kentucky (Jefferson in 1799) opposing the Alien and Sedition Acts as unconstitutional.

In response to the Alien and Sedition Acts, James Madison and Thomas Jefferson anonymously wrote the Virginia and Kentucky resolutions, respectively. Both of these documents argued that if a state judged an act of Congress unconstitutional, the state was not bound by the act and could, in fact, nullify it. The Virginia and Kentucky resolutions helped to ensure that three of the four Alien and Sedition Acts would have very brief lives; however, the theory of nullification Jefferson and Madison put forth would resurface years later as a prelude to and a pretext for the secession of the southern states and the consequent Civil War.

Our First One-Termer

The unpopularity of the Alien and Sedition Acts virtually assured that John Adams, who had narrowly defeated Thomas Jefferson in 1796, would not defeat him again in 1800. And if Adams's support of the acts had galvanized Democratic-Republican opposition to his reelection, the moderate course he had pursued to avoid war with France alienated the Arch-Federalists, the extremist wing of his own party.

The one-term Adams presidency was the first test of how the office would fare in a political system quite suddenly and quite thoroughly dominated by parties. John Adams had demonstrated that a president of high character and integrity could resist the pitfalls of party loyalty as well as party opposition. Such a president could keep the office from becoming subject to party will. But that was just the point. The presidency was indeed vulnerable to party interests, which, on any given issue, might or might not correspond to the interests of the country. Adams's refusal to bend his office to the interests of either his own party or that of the opposition cost him a second term.

The Least You Need to Know

♦ The Jay Treaty, concluded at the end of Washington's second term, precipitated a constitutional crisis as the House of Representatives sought to encroach on the authority of the chief executive; Washington stood firm, but he bequeathed to his successor, John Adams, a presidency under siege.

♦ After George Washington retired, the presidency emerged as the plum in a rancorous contest between political parties; beginning with Adams, no president would ever enjoy the unanimous national support that had greeted Washington.

♦ The close-fought election of 1796 elevated John Adams to the presidency by a very narrow margin and put his political rival, the electoral runner-up Thomas Jefferson, into the office of vice-president.

♦ Adams successfully defended the presidency against the attempt of Alexander Hamilton to influence it—unduly.

Chapter 6

The Revolution of 1800

In This Chapter

- Jefferson the "revolutionary"
- The Federalist vs. the Democratic-Republican approach
- The first "people's president"
- Jefferson as leader of his party

Of the 56 presidential elections from 1789 to 2008, perhaps only 13 were referendums for truly significant change: Andrew Jackson over John Quincy Adams in 1828; Abraham Lincoln over Stephen A. Douglas, 1860; Woodrow Wilson over William Howard Taft, 1912; Warren G. Harding over James M. Cox, 1920; Franklin D. Roosevelt over Herbert Hoover, 1932; Dwight D. Eisenhower over Adlai Stevenson II, 1952; Richard Nixon over Hubert H. Humphrey, 1968; Jimmy Carter over Gerald Ford, 1976; Ronald Reagan over Carter, 1980; Bill Clinton over George H. W. Bush, 1992; Barack Obama over George W. Bush, 2008. At the head of this list is the fourth presidential election, the contest of 1800, which pitted the incumbent John Adams against his vice president, Thomas Jefferson. With the exception of the elections of 1860, 1932, and 2008, no United States presidential choice was more dramatic, more consequential, more revolutionary, or produced more mixed results.

Why Jefferson Won

Looking back at the 56 elections between 1789 and 2008, it is not always easy to understand why one candidate was chosen over another, but in 1800, nobody had the slightest difficulty telling the candidates apart. John Adams and challenger Thomas Jefferson, represented two starkly different paths to national maturity.

Adams, the Federalist

Adams offered the Federalist past and present, in which the government was dominated by the chief executive functioning as unmistakable head of state, and in which governing power was concentrated at the national, rather than the state and individual, level. The Federalists distrusted what Adams frankly described as "the mob," by which he meant the people given an excess of governing authority. Federalist government was still representative government, but the elected officers did not so much represent the perceived *will* of the people as they did the *best interest* of the people. And it was the officers—president, senators, and representatives—who decided what those "best interests" were.

 What They Said _____

> I have long been settled in my own opinion that neither Philosophy, nor Religion, nor Morality, nor Wisdom, nor Interest, will ever govern nations or Parties, against their Vanity, their Pride, their Resentment or Revenge, or their Avarice or Ambition. Nothing but Force and Power and Strength can restrain them.
>
> —John Adams, letter to Thomas Jefferson, October 9, 1787

Jefferson, the Democratic-Republican

Jefferson offered the Democratic-Republican future, in which the power of the central government, including the chief executive, was subordinated to the governing authority of the states and the people themselves. From our current perspective, the Jeffersonian governing philosophy seems more "American" than that of Adams because we are accustomed to thinking of candidates for all government offices as representing what we want. Adams's Federalist philosophy of government probably strikes most of us as a "we-know-what's-good-for-you" approach, whereas Jefferson's Democratic-Republican philosophy seems to operate on a "you-tell-us-what-you-want" model.

A Second American Revolution

That "you-tell-us-what-you-want" is more attractive than "we-know-what's-good-for-you" seems downright obvious. But in 1800 it was far from self-evident. Just consider: as it existed in 1800, the Constitution specified that, of the officers of the three branches of the federal government, only one category—the members of the House of Representatives—were to be chosen by direct popular election.

The president and vice president were chosen by the Electoral College, consisting of members appointed by each state "in such manner as the legislature thereof may direct," the number of each state's electors being "equal to the whole number of Senators and Representatives to which the State may be entitled in the Congress" (Article II, Section I). It was widely assumed among the delegates to the Constitutional Convention that the states would allow the people to vote for the electors, but they did not make even this degree of popular democracy constitutionally binding.

Senators, two from each state, were "chosen by the legislature thereof" (Article I, Section III). Direct popular election of senators had to await ratification of the Seventeenth Amendment in 1913, a full 125 years after the Constitution had been ratified.

Selection of the officers of the judicial branch was a process even further removed from popular election. Article II, Section II, gave the president the power to appoint judges to the Supreme Court, albeit subject to the "advice and consent" of the Senate.

Thus, as it existed in 1800, the Constitution gave the people only a modest direct voice in the federal government. The states had more of a voice because state legislatures chose senators and decided how to choose members of the Electoral College. Insofar as the citizens of each state elected the members of the state legislature, an indirect voice in the federal government was added to direct representation in the House of Representatives. But the Constitution left the regulation of *suffrage* to the states, many of which restricted the right to vote to certain classes of citizens, usually white male property owners, so that even the states themselves limited rather than broadened the scope of democracy.

def·i·ni·tion

> **Suffrage** is the right to vote. It is sometimes also called the "franchise."

The truth is that, in 1800, the Democratic-Republican emphasis on popular democracy was revolutionary, and the election of Thomas Jefferson was, in effect, a second American Revolution.

The President as Party Leader

If Thomas Jefferson incited the revolution of 1800, it was the Democratic-Republican Party, of which he was the leader, that brought the movement to fruition in the form of an electoral victory.

Party Discipline

On one level, a political party is nothing more than an organization of like-minded people who combine their efforts and influence to achieve the election of the candidate who best represents their collective interests. But there is also another party function. The Constitution says nothing about political parties, but the electoral process the Constitution set up made them almost inevitable. Recall from Chapter 4 that the Article II, Section I, awards the presidency to the candidate who garners the most electoral votes and gives the vice presidency to the runner-up. In 1796, the Federalists backed Adams and Thomas Pinckney, with the understanding—or perhaps "hope" is the more appropriate word—that Adams would get the majority, Pinckney would be the runner-up, and therefore, Adams would have a political ally as his VP. But as we know, that is not how the election turned out. Jefferson came in second, which made Adams's political rival his vice-president.

America's political leaders turned to the political party system to avoid another outcome like this. A party could enforce discipline among those who chose the electors and upon the electors themselves in order to ensure that the whole ticket—president as well as intended vice president—would receive the required majority and runner-up numbers.

Prelude to the Twelfth Amendment

Although the two opposing political parties existed in 1796, it was not until 1800 that they were sufficiently well organized to meet in formally constituted caucuses. Both the Federalists and the Democratic-Republicans convened caucuses consisting of the party's members of Congress. At this meeting, they agreed upon the party's presidential and vice presidential candidates, then communicated their decision to the party organizations of each state. These, in turn, ensured that members of the Electoral College were chosen, in effect, as agents of the party, each pledged to cast their two ballots for the party's candidates in such a way that the person designated as president would receive a majority of the votes, and the vice presidential candidate would be the runner-up.

Executive Event

Of all the world's nations that elect their chief executive, the United States is the only country that does so indirectly, through the Electoral College. When we vote for president, we are actually voting for our state's electors who, it is assumed, will cast their vote for the candidate who receives the majority of the popular vote. In some states, electors pledge to vote this way, and in others, they are bound by law to do so; however, in Arizona, Arkansas, Delaware, Georgia, Idaho, Illinois, Indiana, Iowa, Kansas, Kentucky, Louisiana, Minnesota, Missouri, New Hampshire, New Jersey, New York, North Dakota, Pennsylvania, Rhode Island, South Dakota, Tennessee, Texas, Utah, and West Virginia, electors are bound neither by pledge nor law to vote in any specific way. In these states, the system runs purely on good faith.

It all seemed like a pretty good system, but it depended on electors following party instructions precisely. And there was the rub.

As in the election of 1796, the northern states went for Adams and the southern states for Jefferson in 1800—with one critical difference. Jefferson also carried New York. This gave the Democratic-Republicans 73 electoral votes versus 65 for the Federalists. Now it was critically important that at least one of Georgia's electors cast one vote for Jefferson and one or two for someone other than Aaron Burr, the designated Democratic-Republican vice presidential candidate. This would give Jefferson the majority and make Burr the runner-up. Instead, the Georgia electors ended up tying the election between Jefferson and Burr.

A Tortured Election

Aaron Burr had accepted the Democratic-Republican nomination as the vice presidential candidate, not the presidential candidate. He could have spoken up to correct the electoral results and thereby quickly achieved the outcome he had promised the party. But he did not, and, so, in accordance with the Constitution, the election was sent to the House of Representatives to break the tie.

The 1800 elections sent a Democratic-Republican majority to the House, but, at the time of the elections, that body still had a lame-duck Federalist majority. It therefore fell to a Federalist-dominated House of Representatives to break the tie between two members of the rival party. And they were unable to reach a consensus on which candidate to select.

Many were inclined to choose Burr, because, having already declined to honor the pledge he had made to his own party, they reasoned that he was less dedicated to the Democratic-Republican ideology than Jefferson was. But a sufficient number of Federalist representatives so disliked and distrusted Burr that they voted with Democratic-Republican minority for Jefferson. In accordance with the Constitution, breaking the tie required a majority of representatives from 9 of the 16 states to vote one way or the other. This proved to be excruciatingly difficult to achieve. No fewer than 35 votes were taken, each one failing to be decisive.

In one of the great political ironies of American history, it was Alexander Hamilton, Jefferson's arch-nemesis when both served on the Washington cabinet, who tipped the balance against Burr.

Hamilton secured a promise from Jefferson that, once in office, he would not abolish the navy or purge all Federalists from the executive branch. Jefferson made the promise, and, whatever else he thought of him, Hamilton knew Thomas Jefferson to be a man of his word—something that Burr had revealed himself *not* to be. Hamilton persuaded a sufficient number of Federalist colleagues to vote for Jefferson, and the deadlock was broken on the thirty-sixth ballot.

But nobody wanted to go through this again, and the experience motivated the formulation, passage, and—in time for the election of 1804—ratification of the Twelfth Amendment, which, as explained in Chapter 3, required electors to vote separately for president and vice president.

The Democratic-Republican Agenda

Like most revolutions, Jefferson's was defined at least as much by what it opposed as what it espoused. Among the new president's first acts was to undo the Alien and Sedition Acts. Jefferson also acted quickly to ask Congress to abolish most of the taxes that had been imposed under the two Federalist administrations, including property taxes and, most significantly, the whiskey tax, which, in 1794, had triggered an uprising and a stern federal response to it. Jefferson also acted to reduce the size of both the army and the navy (though, true to his pledge to Burr, he did not completely scuttle it), largely to reduce the power and prestige of the central government.

There is an irony in the fact that Jefferson exploited and even magnified the authority and prestige of the presidency, not to aggrandize both the federal government and the presidency, but to contract both. Whereas both Washington and Adams had taken care to leave legislation to Congress, believing that the president should confine himself to faithfully executing the laws passed by Congress, Jefferson instructed the Democratic-Republican Congress in how to legislate in order to implement his agenda.

Contradiction or Flexibility?

As we are about to discuss, although Jefferson entered office with a clearly defined agenda, his actions during his two terms often departed from Democratic-Republican ideology. Critics of Jefferson have judged this inconsistent or even contradictory behavior, whereas admirers see it as evidence of Jefferson's pragmatic flexibility, a refusal to be rigidly doctrinaire. The fact is that Jefferson, whose ideology was based on diminishing central authority and defusing it through the states and the people, was the first president to push the envelope of executive power, setting precedents for increased rather than reduced authority.

Marbury v. Madison

The pushing began as soon as he took office. In the waning days of the Adams administration, the lame-duck Federalist Congress created many new federal judge-ships, which the outgoing president rushed to fill with Federalist judges through last-minute, so-called "midnight appointments." The incoming administration attempted to block as many of these as it could. In one case, that of William Marbury, whom Adams had named justice of the peace for Washington, D.C., the official com-mission papers had been signed and ratified but not "distributed" (delivered) before the Adams left office. Jefferson's secretary of state, James Madison, whose responsibil-ity it was to distribute signed commissions, held onto Marbury's, so that the appoint-ment would not become official. Marbury pleaded before the Supreme Court for a *writ of mandamus* to compel Madison to deliver the commission.

def•i•ni•tion

A **writ of mandamus**—the word is Latin for "we command"—is issued by an appellate court to order a lower court or official to perform a mandatory duty.

In truth, *Marbury* v. *Madison* became much more than a case of simple partisanship. John Marshall, the Federalist Adams had appointed as chief justice of the Supreme Court, faced a dilemma. If he honored Marbury's plea and forced Secretary Madison to issue the writ, he would put the Supreme Court in direct opposition to the pres-ident. If he decided against Marbury, however, he would diminish the power of the

Supreme Court by apparently caving in to the president's wishes. Marshall found a third course. He wrote a decision finding that Marbury had indeed been wrongfully deprived of his commission, but he also declared that Section 13 of the Judiciary Act of 1789, under which Marbury had filed his suit, was unconstitutional. The Constitution created the Supreme Court as a court of appeal—that is, a court with "secondary" jurisdiction only. Section 13 of the 1789 law violated the Constitution because it illegally assigned to the Supreme Court "original" jurisdiction by allowing it to hear a case that belonged in a lower court, which properly had original jurisdiction. Thus Marshall was able to throw out Marbury's suit and avert an immediate interbranch showdown, but, more important, in so doing, he defined the Supreme Court's power of *judicial review*.

def•i•ni•tion

Judicial review is the authority of the Supreme Court to hear and decide lawsuits in which the constitutionality of acts of Congress and executive orders are at issue. The court's decision in any particular case becomes legal precedent. Judicial review is the principal power of the judicial branch of government as embodied in the Supreme Court.

Jefferson and his secretary of state opposed the principle that the judicial branch should have the exclusive authority to overturn, on constitutional grounds, the acts of elected officials. Such authority, they believed, unconstitutionally deprived the people of important governing power. In creating the precedent of judicial review, Marshall defeated the Jefferson administration's very first attempt to push the executive envelope in a way that would have asserted the primacy of the elected government over the appointed government.

A Pastoral Vision and a Bold Decision

Virtually all American historians have agreed that the greatest triumph of Jefferson's presidency was the Louisiana Purchase.

After the French and Indian War ended in 1763, France ceded its vast Louisiana Territory in North America to Spain. In 1800, however, Napoleon Bonaparte reacquired the territory by secret treaty, only to fall into a subsequent dispute with Spain, which refused to relinquish the territory and, in effect, held the United States hostage to its dispute with France by closing the Mississippi River to American commerce in 1802.

President Jefferson believed the United States could tolerate neither an interruption of western trade nor the presence of Napoleon at its back door. He therefore sent James Monroe to France with an offer to purchase New Orleans and Florida, which would reopen access to key ports. Coincidentally at this time, one of Napoleon's armies was bogged down in the disease-infested Caribbean. Unwilling to lose an army to sickness, Napoleon decided to withdraw entirely from the hemisphere and confine his program of conquest to Europe. Thus Monroe's offer to buy New Orleans and Florida was met with a French offer to sell him all of the Louisiana Territory.

Tally _____

The Louisiana Purchase added 90,000 square miles of territory to the United States. Purchased at a cost of 60 million francs (about $15 million), it was a spectacular bargain at 4 cents an acre.

Constitutional Questions

Acquiring a vast western territory magnificently suited Jefferson's long-held vision of the United States as a pastoral nation, a kind of frontier utopia in which most Americans could live as self-sufficient, independent farmers, their lives centered not in big cities—which Jefferson saw as an Old World source of corruption—but in small villages, where true representative democracy was both possible and practical.

But he had a problem. The Constitution gave the federal government no authority to acquire territory by purchase in this manner. Jefferson resolved the constitutional problem by simply ignoring it, in effect asserting the president's right to purchase territory and to secure a congressional appropriation to fund the purchase. It was a bold expansion of executive power, which ran counter to his own Democratic-Republican doctrine by setting a precedent by which future chief executives might claim an array of powers.

The Embargo and Other Disasters

The Louisiana Purchase was an overwhelmingly popular move, which helped Jefferson sail to a second term. In the election of 1804, he won every state except two Federalist holdouts, Connecticut and Delaware.

The second term began with great promise as Jefferson, who had acted to reduce the U.S. Navy, used it boldly to defeat the so-called Barbary pirates of Islamic-rule Tripoli, Algiers, Morocco, and Tunis, who had targeted the merchant shipping of the United States (and other "Christian nations"), extorting protection money in return for unmolested navigation of the Mediterranean. In 1805, the Jefferson administration concluded a triumphant treaty that ended much of the piracy (more naval campaigns would be required through 1815) and the extortion.

Jefferson's war against the Barbary pirates, like the so-called "war on terrorism" that began after Islamic extremists attacked the United States on September 11, 2001, was an undeclared war. President Adams had used the navy against French aggression in the Quasi-War (see Chapter 5), but the precedent of granting the chief executive, as commander in chief, wide latitude in employing the armed forces was even more firmly established by the Tripolitan War (1801–1805).

But the rest of Jefferson's second term was blighted by a severe economic crisis that resulted from the failure of a foreign policy administered heavy handedly, albeit with the best intentions.

The wars of the French Revolution had given way to the Napoleonic wars, which led both England and France to harass the seagoing commerce of noncombatant nations in an effort to cripple one another's economy. Britain stepped up the practice of impressment (see Chapter 5) and even seized American ships attempting to enter French ports. Unwilling to go to war, Jefferson prevailed on Congress to pass the Non-Importation Act, a boycott of many English-made goods.

The boycott proved ineffective, and the nation was driven to crisis when, on June 22, 1807, the HMS *Leopard*, off Norfolk Roads, Virginia, fired on and boarded the U.S. Navy frigate *Chesapeake*, impressing four sailors claimed as Royal Navy deserters. Americans now spoiled for a fight. Jefferson, still looking look for a way to avoid war, framed and pushed through Congress the Embargo Act of December 22, 1807, which prohibited all U.S. exports to Europe and further restricted imports from Great Britain. The new legislation succeeded only in hobbling the American economy, while making little impression on the British or the French.

Enforcing the Embargo Act put Jefferson in the unwanted position of continually exercising strong executive authority to suppress smuggling. Worse, he also used his office in an attempt to suppress adverse commentary on the embargo in the popular press. Thus the man who had led the opposition to the Alien and Sedition Acts, which had been used largely against newspaper critics of the Federalists, now exercised similarly repressive power.

The President and the People

The largely failed second term of Thomas Jefferson made for a sad contrast with his overwhelmingly triumphant first term. In this, Jefferson established an unwanted precedent for what many historians and political pundits have identified as an all-too common characteristic of second-term presidencies. They almost never have been as successful as the first.

While Jefferson's second term somewhat tarnishes his otherwise lofty standing in presidential history, another even more important aspect of the Jefferson legacy remains undiluted and uncompromised. He was the first chief executive to consciously fashion himself as the people's president.

Neither Washington nor Adams thought of themselves as representatives of the people. That, they felt, was a role reserved to the directly elected members of the House of Representatives. They conceived of themselves as executives much in the sense that a modern corporate CEO is an executive. His or her job is not primarily to respond to the will of the company's employees, but to lead and manage the company. Jefferson, in contrast, held that the government should be, in effect, the collective will of the majority of the people, and that the role of the president was continuous with the role of Congress: to represent and manifest the popular will to the extent that it was possible to do so.

Executive Etiquette

Thomas Jefferson strove to establish a presidential image that resembled the Roman tribune of the people more than it did a "republican monarch" in the manner of Washington or Adams. He simplified the protocol and reduced the ceremony with which both his predecessors had endowed the office. As a young diplomat and ardent Francophile, Thomas Jefferson had dressed with European elegance, but as president, he appeared in simple garb, which some observers considered far too informal for the head of the American state.

Theory Collides with Practice

In theory, Thomas Jefferson saw himself as the people's president, but he often found this role impossible to play fully in practice. In particular, he could not bring himself in most matters to appeal directly to the people, over the heads of the representatives and senators. To do so he deemed an unacceptable—perhaps even unconstitutional—breach of the separation of powers. Many historians have pointed out that the unpopular Embargo Act might well have enjoyed more success had Jefferson taken the issues that had motivated it directly to the American public. Yet he felt so strongly that doing this would abridge the constitutional standing of the legislative branch, that he held back.

State of the Union

The title of historian Joseph J. Ellis's critical 1997 biography of Thomas Jefferson, *American Sphinx*, is an eloquent expression of the role this great, fascinating, and flawed figure played in American history generally and the presidency in particular. A man who expressed boundless faith in the people, he was nevertheless far more comfortable in the company of ideas than among those people. A leader who desired to be the "people's president," he was finally a remote figure. A president who wanted to limit the reach of the presidency, he left office having extended it far beyond what his Federalist predecessors had bequeathed to him.

It is typical of Jefferson's ambiguous legacy that he composed some of the most ambitious and detailed state of the union addresses of any president, yet, unlike Washington or Adams, he chose to convey these to Congress in writing rather than to address that body in person, lest he appear monarchical. In spite of himself and his Democratic-Republican convictions, Jefferson made the presidency a more powerful office than his predecessors had left it, and, what is more, planted the seeds of even greater power for any future chief executive who wished to cultivate them.

The Least You Need to Know

- In the name of diminishing federal government, Jefferson expanded the power of the presidency.

- The presidency of Thomas Jefferson has been called a "second American Revolution" because it introduced the idea of the people's presidency, defining the president as the representative of the popular will, in contrast to the more strictly executive role that had been carved out by Washington and Adams.

- Jefferson established the precedent (not always followed, but central today) of the president as the leader of his political party.

- Although Jefferson introduced into American government the idea of a people's president, his own legacy is an ambiguous combination of the deliberate restraint of executive powers and the simultaneous expansion of the office of president.

The Jefferson Legacy

In This Chapter

♦ Tangible achievements vs. intangible values of Jefferson's legacy

♦ How Madison diminished presidential power

♦ The speaker of the House emerges as the president's partner/rival

♦ The Monroe Doctrine

♦ The ambitious but unsuccessful presidency of John Quincy Adams

Thomas Jefferson is buried in a family plot at his own beloved home, Monticello, the grave marked by an obelisk he himself designed and for which he wrote the epitaph:

> Here was buried
> Thomas Jefferson
> Author of the Declaration of Independence
> Of the Statute of Virginia for religious freedom
> And Father of the University of Virginia

Conspicuous by its absence is "Third President of the United States." We cannot know why Jefferson chose to leave this—of all things!—out of his posthumous resumé, but that he did reinforces the impression of many, that he was greater as a political philosopher than as a president. Little wonder that his executive legacy is far from straightforward.

A Matter of Style

At least three tangible achievements mark Jefferson's presidency as vastly important:

♦ He swept away most of the vestiges of the Alien and Sedition Acts.

♦ He purchased the Louisiana Territory.

♦ He directed the victory over the threat to U.S. sovereignty posed by the Barbary pirates.

Yet it is also true that the errors of his second term threatened to overshadow the triumphs of his first. Intended to avoid war with England and France, his embargo badly crippled the fragile American economy and set the nation on a path toward the nearly ruinous War of 1812. Perhaps even worse were the repressive actions Jefferson, champion of individual liberties, took in an effort to suppress criticism of his government before and during the embargo crisis.

Yet the tangible achievements and failures of Jefferson's two terms are less significant for his presidential legacy than the intangible new values he brought to the office:

♦ A political idealist, he was the republican equivalent of what Enlightenment Europe called a "philosopher king," providing for future chief executives a model of enlightened, forward-looking government tinged with utopian thought.

♦ An intelligent democrat, he introduced the idea of American civilization as a *meritocracy*, a combination of government and culture that fostered the natural rise to power of the nation's best, brightest, and most capable.

def•i•ni•tion

A **meritocracy** is a government, society, community, or civilization in which the most capable naturally rise to power, regardless of their social position, family connections, wealth, and so on.

♦ Jefferson saw the presidency as promoting education, science, and civilization—and creating a degree of liberal democratic government that allowed free, creative, and bold thought to flourish.

♦ Whereas his immediate predecessor, John Adams, saw in democracy the dangerous potential of mob rule, Jefferson saw in it the potential for the emergence of the genius of the people.

Beyond the Constitution

Before he became president, Thomas Jefferson voiced serious suspicion, even fear of executive power. Once in office, however, he came to accept that presidential authority was a necessary ingredient for the success of the American government.

Rise of the Caucus

Before he became president, Thomas Jefferson was the principal architect of the Democratic-Republican Party. After he entered the White House, he led the party with the object of using it to rally support in Congress for his point of view and programs.

Whereas the Federalists, Washington and Adams, had been concerned with defining, exploiting, and expanding the role of the presidency as defined in the Constitution, Jefferson used the president's role as party leader to impose the executive will on the legislative branch through the exercise of party discipline. This required the development of the party caucus beyond what its inventors—the Federalist Party—had envisioned for it. By means of the *caucus*, party leaders from the executive branch collaborated with those from the legislative branch to formulate national policy and to unify party support behind that policy.

def•i•ni•tion

In American party politics, a **caucus** is a nonconstitutional legislative institution in which members of a party meet in closed session to decide questions of policy and leadership.

Decline of the Presidency?

The benefit of the party caucus as Jefferson developed it was that the executive and legislative branches could work together more strategically and more productively. The cost, however, was a diminishment of what the framers of the Constitution—and especially thinkers such as John Adams—had sought to establish in American government: separation of powers among three very distinct branches of government for the purpose of creating a system of checks and balances that would prevent any one branch (and any one leader or group of leaders) from usurping too much power.

By bringing key members of the executive and legislative branches together, the party caucus threatened either to aggrandize the presidency at the expense of the Congress, or to aggrandize the legislature at the expense of the executive branch. Which of these outcomes might occur would depend largely on the attitude, political philosophy, or even the relative strength or weakness of a particular president.

In either case, to this day, every president longs to have a congressional majority made up of members of his own party. Failing this, the prospects for a "successful" presidency are greatly diminished.

Jefferson's Progeny: Madison, Monroe, John Quincy Adams

History may color Jefferson's presidency in shades of gray, but there is nothing ambivalent about what he achieved for his political generation. Whereas the first two American presidents were Federalists, Jefferson and the next three were Democratic-Republicans. They were followed by a pair of Democratic presidents, Andrew Jackson and Martin Van Buren, even more closely identified with popular rule than the Jeffersonians had been. The Federalists? Extinct!

From Mr. Secretary to Mr. President

Often characterized as Jefferson's protégé—perhaps because he was eight years younger than Jefferson—James Madison appeared, if anything, even better prepared for the presidency than his mentor. Whereas Jefferson had drafted the Declaration of Independence, Madison was the principal author of the Constitution and then, with John Jay and Alexander Hamilton, wrote the *Federalist* essays in a successful effort to secure its ratification. As secretary of state during both of Jefferson's terms, Madison managed the nitty-gritty of the Louisiana Purchase, and, in becoming the second secretary of state to be elected to the presidency, he may be seen as having participated in the creation of an early tradition. Six secretaries of state—Jefferson, Madison, James Monroe, John Quincy Adams, Martin Van Buren, and James Buchanan—became presidents. Madison set an even more pervasive and enduring precedent by becoming the first former member of Congress to be elected president.

Tally

Sixteen senators and 18 representatives have gone on to become president; however, only James Garfield, Warren G. Harding, John F. Kennedy, and Barack Obama were sitting members of Congress when they were elected to the White House. Just one president, John Quincy Adams, reversed the customary chronology by gaining election to the House of Representatives in 1830, two years *after* he was defeated for a second presidential term by Andrew Jackson. He served 17 years in Congress.

The President Sits, the Speaker Rises

Madison's connection with the legislative branch proved to be critically important to his influence on the presidency. He had been a standout in the First United States Congress, authoring many early pieces of legislation and none of greater consequence than the first 10 amendments to the Constitution—the Bill of Rights.

In the end it was the very fact of his membership in the First Congress that certified Madison's belief in the primacy of the legislative over the executive branch, and it was with the support of Congress that he secured his party's nomination as presidential candidate. Madison vigorously courted his party's votes in Congress. Whereas Jefferson had used the party caucus to gain legislative support for his agenda, Madison began his ascent to the White House by subordinating the presidency to the party's congressional caucus. The caucus, therefore, emerged both as the president's legislative partner (rather than his servant) and, at times, a nexus of party power wholly independent of the president.

Even more dramatic during Madison's two terms was the rise of the speaker of the House. As speaker, Representative Henry Clay of Kentucky set precedents of significant authority for the office. Among the most important of these was the elevation of the speaker to party leader within the House. This meant, in effect, that the speaker shared party leadership with the president.

Madison and "His" War

Clay's most enduring legacy to Congress was his creation and management of the committee system. Although the Constitution makes no mention of House and Senate committees, thanks largely to the precedents set by Clay, these became basic institutions of the legislative branch. Committees organized the House by giving key representatives platforms from which to exercise specialized influence. As speaker, Clay oversaw and coordinated the work of the committees. This not only gave certain representatives a louder voice, it made the Congress as a whole a more effective and powerful legislative instrument, and it endowed the speaker with an extraconstitutional authority that sometimes rivaled the constitutional authority of the president.

The extent to which Clay's power actually eclipsed that of the president is evident in the War of 1812. Those who opposed it—mostly members of the increasingly marginalized Federalist Party—condemned it as "Mr. Madison's War," but, if anything, the war belonged to Henry Clay.

Ostensibly, the War of 1812 was fought over conflicts with Britain that Jefferson's embargo had failed to resolve, but the actual cause of the War of 1812 was American land hunger. As the country's population burgeoned, so did its lust for new territory, and the juiciest real estate in 1812 was Spanish Florida, which extended from modern Florida to the Mississippi River, the point at which the Louisiana Territory commenced. In 1812 Spain was allied with Britain against Napoleon; therefore, war with Britain would mean war with Spain, and victory in such a war would mean the acquisition of Spanish Florida. Speaker Clay spoke for the westerners, who were hungriest for the new territory, and around him rallied the *War Hawks* of Congress. Many recent historians believe that Clay made President Madison's renomination for a second term contingent on his pledge that he would support war with Britain.

def•i•ni•tion

The **War Hawks** were a group of U.S. representatives and senators, mostly Democratic-Republicans and mostly from the southern and western (frontier) states, who favored a declaration of war on Britain in 1812. They were opposed mainly by members of the moribund Federalist Party, mostly New Englanders.

Like Jefferson, Madison abhorred war, but, bowing to pressure from the congressional caucus, he delivered to Congress the first presidential war message in American history, asking on June 1, 1812, for a declaration of war.

Constitutionally, Madison was the commander in chief, but his leadership of the military was practically nonexistent and insofar as he can be said to have prosecuted the war, he prosecuted it poorly. For the most part—except at sea—the War of 1812 consisted of one American military disaster after another, culminating in the sack of Washington, D.C., by British forces under Robert Ross, in August 1814. The government, including James and Dolley Madison, fled before the invaders, who burned the White House, the Capitol, and other public buildings.

In the end, Britain, exhausted by its recently concluded wars against Napoleon, chose not to push the War of 1812 to the point of America's total defeat. Nevertheless, the nation, having entered the war with a crippled economy, emerged from it in even worse shape. This left Madison no choice but to support the establishment of the Second Bank of the United States, even though both he and Jefferson had opposed the Hamiltonian idea of a national bank because of the power it concentrated in the central government.

The bank, as Madison saw it, was not only essential to postwar economic recovery, it was important to financing any future federal initiatives, including war. The absence of a central source of stable currency had greatly impeded the war effort.

Monroe and His Doctrine

Despite the national divisions created by the War of 1812 and despite the war's high cost, most Americans managed to convince themselves that the nation had won a victory inasmuch as it had stood up against the most powerful military power on the planet and, if America didn't exactly triumph over Britain, at least it was still standing. Thus, the Democratic-Republicans did not emerge as casualties of Mr. Madison's War, but the already moribund Federalists did. For their opposition to the contest, they were branded as unpatriotic, and in the election of 1816, James Monroe landslided his Federalist opponent, New York senator Rufus King.

 Tally

In 1816, Monroe won 183 electoral votes to King's 34. Even more remarkably, Monroe sailed to a second term in 1820 unopposed—except for George Washington, the only presidential candidate to do so.

Some Good Feelings

In 1817, writing in the *Columbian Centinel*, a local newspaper, Benjamin Russell remarked that the goodwill visit of Democratic-Republican President Monroe to Boston, last bastion of Federalism, initiated in American political life an "era of good feelings" after the bitter rivalry between the two parties. The truth of the matter is that the good feelings came less from reconciliation between the parties than from the rapid extinction of the Federalists, which left the Democratic-Republicans as the nation's only party.

It was also true that the good feelings were more apparent than real. The nation was still groping for a way out of the postwar economic depression, and the Democratic-Republican Party, having defeated all Federalist opposition, was now suffering an internal split between the so-called "old" party members, who wanted to adhere to a strict Jeffersonian interpretation of the Constitution (that is, the only legitimate governing powers were those actually enumerated in the Constitution, not those purportedly implied by it) versus the reformers—called the National Republicans—who advocated a greater degree of authority in the federal government. Whereas Monroe was an "old" Jeffersonian, Speaker Clay was a "new" Nationalist.

As a Nationalist, Clay led the congressional movement to use federal funds to finance national projects, including such internal improvements as major highways and canals to open up commerce between the East and his constituency, the developing West. Monroe objected, informing Clay that the federal funding of improvements was not provided for in the Constitution and would therefore require an amendment. In open defiance of the president—the ostensible leader of the party—Clay led the congressional caucus in passage of a bill to repair and improve the old Cumberland Road, the nation's principal east-west artery. Monroe greeted it with a veto, which served to widen the developing gap between the factions of the party.

The veto is perhaps the strongest assertion of executive authority any president can exercise, but this instance was exceptional in Monroe's presidency. On almost every other major issue, Monroe followed Madison's precedent by deferring to the will of Congress. In part, this was in keeping with the "old" Democratic-Republican ideology of the primacy of the directly elected legislative government and states' rights, but it was also a product of Monroe's conviction that the proper focus of Congress should be on domestic matters, whereas that of the presidency was foreign affairs—not a surprising position for yet another secretary of state turned president.

The great precedent-making achievement for which James Monroe is best remembered is, of course, the Monroe Doctrine, an enduring definition of U.S. foreign policy. Between 1817 and 1822, the nations of Latin America gained independence from Spain. In 1823, Austria, Prussia, France, and Russia supported Spain in its declared intention of regaining control of the region. Wishing to nip in the bud a post-Napoleonic resurgence of French power, the British government proposed that the United States join with Great Britain in issuing a condemnation of any attempt by European nations to regain control of Latin American countries. Monroe's secretary of state, John Quincy Adams, persuaded the president not to act jointly with Great Britain, but to issue a declaration—which Adams drafted—on behalf of the United States alone.

The result was the so-called "Monroe Doctrine," contained in an 1823 address to Congress, proclaiming that the "American continents by the free and independent condition which they have assumed and maintain, are henceforth not to be considered as subjects for future colonization by any European powers." The president warned that any interference by a European nation with the affairs of an independent nation in the Western Hemisphere would be seen as a "manifestation of an unfriendly disposition toward the United States."

Executive Event

The Monroe Doctrine has defined much of U.S. foreign policy and has been invoked by everyone from William McKinley at the end of the nineteenth century as a rationale for the Spanish-American War, to twentieth-century presidents in defense of several wars, both within and beyond the Western Hemisphere. In 1823, however, the leaders of Europe dismissed Monroe's declaration as just so much talk from an infant republic with a small navy and a smaller army.

Some Bad Feelings

While the Monroe Doctrine was a powerful assertion of presidential leadership in the international arena, James Monroe's absolute silence on the single most important domestic issue of his administration, the question of whether the Missouri Territory would be admitted to the union as a free state or a slave state, was deafening. It was on this issue that the future of slavery in the United States depended, and consequently the future of the United States as an enduring union.

In the end, Congress enacted the Missouri Compromise without any input from the president. By admitting Missouri as a slave state but balancing it in Congress with the admission of Maine as a free state, then banning slavery in all western territories north of Missouri's southern border, the compromise staved off civil war—for a time. That was an achievement, at least of sorts, but it came at the cost of an almost breathtaking demonstration of executive passivity, which left the next president a very narrow ledge from which to presume to lead the nation.

What They Said

But this momentous question, like a fire bell in the night, awakened and filled me with terror.

—Thomas Jefferson on the divisive issue of whether to admit Missouri as a slave state or a free state, letter to John Holmes, April 22, 1820

The Bitter Election of '24

No one would mistake the election of 1824 for the product of an era of good feelings. Monroe had run unopposed for a second term in 1820, and there was, for all practical purposes, no Federalist Party to oppose the Democratic-Republicans in 1824. But the bitterness of partisan rivalry was more than replaced by that of personal and regional rivalry as the party of Jefferson, Madison, and Monroe fragmented.

The election was a divisive contest among Henry Clay of Kentucky, William H. Crawford of Georgia, Andrew Jackson of Tennessee, and John Quincy Adams of Massachusetts—son of John Adams, but, unlike him, a Democratic-Republican. Predictably, none of the four candidates received a majority of the electoral vote. Jackson received the most—99—to Adams's 84, but because this was not a majority, the election was sent to the House of Representatives for resolution under the Twelfth Amendment (see Chapter 3). Because the amendment requires the House to choose from among the three candidates with the most votes, fourth-place Clay was eliminated. This left 14 state delegations in which Jackson came in either first or second to Clay. Had all of these now voted for Jackson, he would have become president. Instead, Clay prevailed on his House allies to vote for Adams, who thereby became the only president elected with fewer electoral votes than his opponent. When President Adams turned around and appointed Clay his secretary of state, Jackson and his supporters cried foul, accusing Adams and Clay of having made a "corrupt bargain." It was a serious stain on the presidency.

Tally

In 1824, Andrew Jackson garnered 99 electoral votes to John Quincy Adams's 84. William Harris Crawford received 41, and Henry Clay, 37. Because a majority of electoral votes—131—was required to choose a president, the election was sent to the House.

The Second Adams: Last of the Jeffersonians

Adams proclaimed himself a Jeffersonian, who promoted to Congress the funding of a national university (in the Jeffersonian belief that education was indispensable to successful popular government), scientific exploration (in the spirit of the great Lewis and Clark Expedition, which Jefferson had sponsored in 1803–1806), a national astronomical observatory, and a variety of internal improvements of the kind Henry Clay had advocated and President Monroe had vetoed. Yet to achieve these philosophically Jeffersonian ends, John Quincy Adams embraced distinctly anti-Jeffersonian politics by his attempt to resurrect and reassert the power of the executive.

Presidential CPR

Adams tried. In sharp contrast to both Madison and Monroe, he prevailed upon Congress to enact his initiatives, becoming the first president to make an open and deliberate effort to lead the legislature toward the realization of his own national vision.

He tried, and he failed. The presidency of John Quincy Adams cannot be judged a success. Congress rejected all of his major proposals and initiatives, and the midterm elections of 1826 installed in the House and Senate an array of partisans dedicated to Jackson. By this time, the splintering of the Democratic-Republican Party had begun to resolve itself into two new parties, the National Republican Party, led by Adams and Clay (in 1833, it would become the Whig Party), and the Democratic Party, led by Jackson. Thus the midterm election of 1826 created in Congress for the first time in American history an opposition majority. President Adams understood he was a lame duck, and he offered himself for reelection in 1828, resigned to being defeated by Andrew Jackson.

John Quincy Adams, the first presidential son to become president himself, was, like his father, a one-term chief executive. Yet that term, bitter and frustrating though it was, must at the very least be appreciated for its aspirations. The second Adams was the first American president to attempt fully to exploit the constitutional provision enjoining the executive to "recommend to [the] consideration [of Congress] such measures as he shall judge necessary and expedient." The most important chief executives who came after him followed Adams's example with regard to this passage, the greatest of them with far more success than he.

The Least You Need to Know

- ◆ Jefferson initiated a Democratic-Republican dynasty that endured until 1829, wiping out the Federalist Party in the process.

- ◆ Under presidents Madison and Monroe, the power of the president diminished and that of Congress increased.

- ◆ During the Monroe administration, the Democratic-Republican Party decisively triumphed over the Federalists, but also splintered into two new, competing parties, the National Republicans (later, Whigs) and the Democrats.

- ◆ Although John Quincy Adams failed to realize any of his major initiatives, he restored lost authority to the presidency by his ambitious and aggressive attempts to influence the legislative agenda of Congress.

Part 2

Uncommon Common Men

Andrew Jackson, burst out of the frontier to create the presidency of the "common man" and to radically redefine the relationship between the chief executive and the people. We explore the ways in which Jackson pushed the envelope of the presidency and how he put the office squarely in competition with both the Congress and the Supreme Court for ultimate governing authority. His legacy was mixed, and the next eight presidents governed in Jackson's long shadow, ultimately with catastrophic results for a nation marching toward civil war. This part ends with the remarkable presidency of Abraham Lincoln, who once again reshaped the presidency in a fierce and majestic effort to restore the Union.

The Age of Jackson

In This Chapter

- ◆ Jackson as the "people's tribune"
- ◆ Expanding the power and the scope of the presidency
- ◆ The Kitchen Cabinet
- ◆ The spoils system

Following his inauguration at the Capitol, Andrew Jackson rode to the White House. Those who had gathered to see "Old Hickory" take the oath of office—"Country men, farmers, gentlemen, mounted and dismounted, boys, women and children, black and white," as Washington resident Margaret Smith wrote to a friend—all "pursued him to the President's house." They crowded in, "scrambling fighting, romping" to shake hands with Jackson, whom they nearly pressed "to death ... almost suffocated" and tore "to pieces." Mrs. Smith observed: "it was the People's day, and the People's President and the People would rule."

Old Hickory: The First Outsider

Jackson was the first candidate of the new American political lineup. By the time James Monroe left office, the Federalists were all but finished as a party, and the Democratic-Republicans had split into the National

Republicans—who shaded toward the Federalist end of the spectrum in favoring a genuinely national government—and the Democrats, who aligned themselves with the "old" Democratic-Republicans in calling for the government to reside primarily with the states and the people. Jackson was the standard bearer of this latter faction, whose adherents historians would call Jacksonian Democrats.

For the "Jeffersonian" presidents—Jefferson, Madison, Monroe, and John Quincy Adams—the idea of power rightfully residing with the people was remained more or less an ideal, whereas for Jackson and all but two of the pre–Civil War presidents who followed him, it was reality.

Andrew Jackson had risen from a humble log cabin birth in the Waxhaws district on the border of North and South Carolina—both states still lay claim to his birthplace—in 1767. It was, at the time, very much a frontier place, and Jackson would always identify himself as a "westerner." As such, he was by definition a political outsider, distant from the long-settled seaboard, the traditional center of power, wealth, and those who, in a republic, still passed for the aristocracy.

Jackson was an outsider in another important sense. The two Adamses, Jefferson, Madison, and Monroe, all highly educated men of means, had all served in the executive branch before becoming president. In contrast, Jackson had briefly served in the House and the Senate and, even more briefly, as territorial governor of Tennessee, but he was far more famous as a general in the War of 1812, the Creek War, and the First Seminole War, a *popular* hero who ascended to greatness entirely on his own guts and talent.

Executive Event _____

An unmistakable sign of Jackson's popularity was the ubiquitous and affectionate use of his nickname, "Old Hickory." It dated from the War of 1812, when he commanded Tennessee militia, imposing upon his unruly men discipline so strict that they pronounced him "tough as hickory." The sobriquet stuck, and Andrew Jackson was the first American president to be known as much by his nickname as his given name.

The President Becomes the People's Tribune

The Jacksonian drive to democratize America—at least white male America—was sincere. Even more than Jefferson, Jackson sought to limit the role of national government in the belief that this would spread opportunity to the expanding frontier.

He put his foot down on the issue of federal funding of internal improvements (roads and canals), insisting that such matters were for states to decide on and to finance. Although he had been a general, as president he reduced federal military spending, putting greater reliance on state militias. As for the nation's central bank, as we will see, the president dismantled it.

As supporters of George Washington had identified him with the ancient Roman example of Cincinnatus, who answered his country's call to power, dutifully used that power to serve the people, then dutifully relinquished it, so partisans of Jackson characterized him as the "people's tribune." Elected by the Roman plebeians (members of the common class), the tribune was charged with protecting their rights against abuse by the aristocratic magistrates. The tribune was the champion of the people. Not only did Jackson feel obliged to defend the rights of the people against the other two branches of government, he laid claim to a relationship with the people that was even more direct than that of the representatives and senators in Congress. Paradoxically, therefore, the president who advocated a diminished federal government also repudiated the traditional Democratic-Republican belief that the legislative branch was the means through which the will of the people was most clearly expressed.

What They Said _____

> It is to be regretted that the rich and powerful too often bend the acts of government to their selfish purposes. ... But when the laws under take ... to make the rich richer and the powerful more potent, the humble members of society—the farmers, mechanics and laborers—who have neither the time nor the means of securing like favors to themselves, have a right to complain of the injustice of their government.
> —Andrew Jackson, July 10, 1832

All Power *from* the People

Whereas Jefferson and the Jeffersonians believed that most governing authority should be vested in the people and the states, Jackson held that the ultimate source of governing power was neither federal nor state government, but the people. In no case was this more evident than in his response to the Nullification Crisis of 1832. In 1828, at the close of the presidency of Jackson's predecessor, John Quincy Adams, Congress passed a tariff designed to foster American manufacturing industries by levying a hefty duty on manufactured goods imported from abroad. The tariff was welcomed by the industrializing Northeast, but was denounced in the agricultural South as the

"Tariff of Abominations" because it made imported goods too costly for Americans to buy, which meant that European manufacturers would buy less of such southern exports as cotton and indigo.

In response to the tariff, South Carolina called a convention, which, on November 24, 1832, passed an Ordinance of Nullification declaring the tariff unconstitutional and forbidding state officials from collecting tariff duties. Jackson responded by denying the power of any state to block enforcement of federal law and threatened to use force of arms to compel the collection of duties.

Fortunately, a compromise tariff was passed in 1833, which South Carolina accepted, and a possible civil war was thereby averted. But Jackson had made his point: the people, acting through state conventions in 1787 and 1788, had created the Union, and neither the states nor Congress had the right to act against or dissolve it. Because the president was the direct representative of the people, it was upon him that the preservation of the Union most directly depended, and Jackson was determined to act accordingly.

"As God Rules over the Universe"

For Jackson, the president was the direct representative of the people. While this view aggrandized the presidency, in effect elevating it above the Congress, it also made the president the servant of the popular will.

> **What They Said**
>
> The people reign over the American political world as God rules over the universe. It is the cause and end of all things; everything rises out of it and is absorbed back into it.
>
> —Alexis de Tocqueville, *Democracy in America*, 1835–1840

Although Jacksonian democracy continued to exclude Indians (infamously, President Jackson championed passage of the Indian Removal Act of 1830, which authorized the forcible of relocation of eastern tribes to "Indian Territory" west of the Mississippi), African Americans (Jackson supported slavery), and women (who were still excluded from suffrage and whose civil rights—including property rights—were determined largely by the states), Jackson's policies were aimed at equalizing the white male segment of the American populace, principally by extending the *franchise* to more people and by making government generally more directly representative.

Until amended after the Civil War, the Constitution left setting qualifications for the franchise entirely up to each state. Nevertheless, Jackson used his popularity and the prestige of his office to set a compelling democratic tone for *all* governments, and during his administration all of the states dropped ownership of property as a qualification for voting. By the end of Jackson's first term, *universal white manhood suffrage* was law in every state.

Even before Jackson took office, the states were overwhelmingly prepared to receive his democratizing influence. By the 1828 election, most states had changed their electoral laws so that the people, not the state legislatures, chose the members of

def•i•ni•tion

The franchise is the right to vote. In Jackson's time, the franchise was exclusively determined by each state. Universal white manhood suffrage means that the franchise is extended to all adult white males without further qualification, such as ownership of property.

the Electoral College. By the end of Jackson's first term, every state except South Carolina had made this change. Jackson was elected to his second term more directly by the people than any president before him. This gave added weight to his conviction that his role as chief executive was to be the people's direct representative.

From Cabinet to Kitchen Cabinet

If the jubilant hordes who stormed and pillaged the White House on Inauguration Day 1828 symbolized for conservative Americans the dangers of hyperdemocratic mob rule, that scene might also have served to predict the turmoil that would mark the internal workings of the Jackson administration. In two presidential terms, he had no fewer than four secretaries of state, five treasury secretaries, two secretaries of war, three attorneys general, three Navy secretaries, and three postmasters general (until 1971, a cabinet-level position). In 1831, he even forced the resignation of the *entire* cabinet—the only time this has happened in presidential history.

High cabinet turnover did not endure as a precedent of the executive office. Most cabinet appointees serve through a president's entire term. However, the decline in importance of the officially appointed cabinet corresponded to the rise in importance of an informal coterie of unofficial advisers dubbed the *Kitchen Cabinet*. The members of this body had no official standing in government and were unregulated by law or the Constitution. Because they had not been appointed, they were not subject to the "advice and consent" of the Senate.

Jackson's Kitchen Cabinet included his private secretary, friends, friendly newspaper editors, and a political protégé named Martin Van Buren, who became Jackson's second-term vice president and his handpicked successor to the presidency. Ever since

Jackson, most presidents have regularly consulted with informal advisers. Franklin Roosevelt, Harry S. Truman, John F. Kennedy, Lyndon Johnson, and Ronald Reagan would become particularly notable for their reliance on Kitchen Cabinets.

def•i•ni•tion

A **Kitchen Cabinet** is an informal, nonappointed group of confidants and advisers some presidents, beginning with Jackson, have assembled. The term was intended by Jackson's enemies to satirically evoke an image of advisers sneaking into the White House via the back—"kitchen"—stairs. In modern usage, the term carries no negative connotation.

To the Victor Belongs the Spoils

Just as Jackson did not hesitate to hire and fire cabinet officers, so he took a radically new approach to the exercise of the presidential power of appointment throughout government. All of the presidents before Jackson strove to create continuity in the federal workforce, which meant making appointments on a party-neutral basis. Jackson decided that appointments could be more effectively used to reward and enforce party loyalty and discipline; therefore, in 1829, the first year of his first term, he removed thousands of federal employees and made no secret of doing so for political reasons. He then replaced them with loyal Democrats.

Sen. William L. Marcy, a Democrat from New York, observed on January 25, 1832, that his party found "nothing wrong in the rule that to the *victor* belongs the spoils of the *enemy*." From that moment on, Jackson's presidential patronage system—the policy of awarding government posts and offices in return for party loyalty and party service—was known as the *spoils system*.

The spoils system proved stubbornly resistant to the efforts of subsequent presidents to reform it, even after it had come to seem a corrupt policy damaging to the dignity of the office of president.

The President vs. the Government

For Jackson, the notion of the president as tribune had a powerfully literal force. He really did see his role as defending the interests of the "common man" against the republican equivalent of the aristocracy—the wealthy.

Jackson Battles the Bank

In 1832, Henry Clay and Daniel Webster led their fellow National Republicans—now renamed the Whigs—in passing a bill to recharter the Second Bank of the United States, the current charter for which was scheduled to expire in 1836. The two Whig leaders expected Jackson to veto the bill, and in fact they hoped he would, because they believed it would cost him votes in the upcoming election in which Clay would be the probable Whig candidate.

But the significance of the veto, issued on July 10, 1832, went far beyond partisan politics. George Washington established the precedent of reserving the veto for acts the president considered unconstitutional; it was not to be used to undo legislative acts the president simply did not like. Jackson vetoed the bill because it was incompatible with his concept of democratic government. This in itself raised the bar of executive authority, but there was more. In the message that accompanied his veto, Jackson complained that Congress had failed to consult him before passing the legislation. No president had ever before presumed to claim that Congress was obliged to consult the White House before drafting a bill.

But there was still more.

Even though Jackson's veto was not based on a constitutional objection, he sought to head off criticism that, in its 1819 decision in the case of *McCullough* v. *Maryland*, the Supreme Court had affirmed the constitutionality of congressional authority to create a federal bank. Jackson asserted that each branch of government "must each for itself be guided by its opinion of the Constitution." In other words, Jackson denied that the Supreme Court's opinion on the constitutionality of a given law was necessarily supreme.

Finally, Jackson turned the tables on his Whig adversaries by presenting his veto not as the political liability Clay and Webster believed it would be, but as a means of appealing positively to the electorate. He closed his veto message not by addressing Congress, but the people, remarking that if his action were "sustained by his fellow citizens," he would be "grateful and happy." In the end, it was Congress that backed down by failing to override the veto.

Jackson Battles the Congress

Jackson decided to exploit his 1832 reelection victory as, in part, a mandate against the Second Bank of the United States. The bank's charter still had four years to run, and Jackson decided to destroy it immediately by transferring from the federal bank to selected state banks all of the federal government's deposits. Under the 1816 law that had established the bank, only the secretary of the Treasury had the authority to remove federal deposits from it. Jackson wanted to avoid a power contest with Secretary Louis McLane, so he sought from Congress the authority to withdraw the funds. When Congress refused, the president turned to McLane, and when he also refused, Jackson kicked him upstairs, nominating him as secretary of state, and replaced him with William J. Duane as secretary of the treasury. To the president's consternation, Duane also declined to make the money transfer. Jackson fired him. He then yanked Roger B. Taney from his post as attorney general and slotted him into the treasury secretary spot, where he proved compliant to the president's wishes. (In 1836, Jackson would reward Taney by appointing him chief justice of the Supreme Court, and in 1858, Taney would hand down the majority opinion in the Dred Scott case, one of the triggers of the Civil War.)

The Senate responded with history's first and only vote of censure against a president, charging that Jackson had acted beyond the bounds of his constitutional authority. Jackson responded with a "Protest," in which he asserted that the "President is the direct representative of the American people," whereas the Senate, elected by state legislatures, was not. Then turning the tables on the Senate, he charged that it had no constitutional right to censure the president.

At issue now was a question beyond the particular case of the Second Bank of the United States. Congress, in 1816, had vested a certain authority in the secretary of the treasury, an officer of the cabinet. In 1836, the president sought to dictate how that authority would be exercised by dismissing treasury secretaries until he found one who would do his bidding. Clay and Webster asserted that Congress, through legislation, had the right, independently of the president, to endow a cabinet officer with a specific power. Jackson countered that the president and the president alone had authority over "the entire action of the executive department."

In the end, Jackson's "Protest" proved compelling. The Democrats took control of the Senate in the election of 1836 and voted to expunge the censure from the Senate journal. This affirmed Jackson's position on the exclusivity of the president's authority over the executive branch.

Jackson Battles the Supreme Court

Jackson never actually challenged the Supreme Court on any of its opinions, but he did defy the court nevertheless.

In *Worcester* v. *Georgia* (1832), the Supreme Court ruled against a Georgia law that expelled the Cherokees from the state because the *state* law violated a federal treaty with the tribe. Jackson, who had championed passage of the Indian Removal Act of 1830 in an effort to remove all Indians from the East and resettle them west of the Mississippi River in Indian Territory (modern Oklahoma and parts of adjacent states), disagreed with the decision. Yet instead of publicly exercising the right he claimed of disputing it, he steadfastly denied that the president or any other agent of the federal government had the authority or the means to enforce the Court's decision on a sovereign state. This president who had threatened during the Nullification Crisis to use arms against the state of South Carolina now asserted presidential will over a Supreme Court decision by conveniently denying the president's authority to interfere in the business of a state.

Invention of the Convention and the Party Press

The links Andrew Jackson forged between the president and the people not only enduringly revised the idea of the presidency in the collective American psyche—modern presidents more closely resemble Jackson than they do Washington or John Adams—they also changed in a permanent way the manner in which presidential candidates are chosen and how the chief executive actively shapes the public opinion to which he supposedly responds.

The Convention Replaces the Caucus

In the Age of Jackson, nomination of presidential candidates by congressional caucus came to seem undemocratic; therefore, in 1832, the Democrats introduced the party convention for the purpose of choosing their candidate. The Whigs followed suit four years later.

The delegates to the national convention selected party's presidential nominee. The delegates themselves had been selected by state conventions of local party members. In view of this, Jackson and his followers claimed that, in nominating the party's candidate, the convention delegates truly represented the will of the people.

The "Party Press"

But just what was the "will of the people"?

During the Jackson presidency, public opinion—the will of the people—was transformed from something to which the president responded into something the president and his party managed, influenced, and even created. This was achieved through the development of a "party press," newspaper editors who spoke for the party. Jackson was a master at recruiting allies among editors—some were included in his Kitchen Cabinet—and it was with the Jackson presidency that the partisan press was born.

Although today most television and print news outlets claim objectivity in reporting on government and politics, readers and viewers know where they can find commentators, reporters, newspapers, and TV news programs that advocate the Republican or the Democratic point of view. This media advocacy was a product of the Age of Jackson, which not only dramatically democratized the concept of the presidency, it infused presidential party politics into the very fabric of American culture.

The Least You Need to Know

♦ Jackson was the first president elected as a Democrat, which developed from the populist wing of the Democratic-Republican Party, and conceived of the president as the "people's tribune" and direct representative.

♦ Although Jackson advocated a reduced role for the federal government, he simultaneously greatly expanded the power and the scope of the presidency, fighting the other two branches of government for supremacy of authority.

♦ Jackson democratized the institution of the presidency by introducing the Kitchen Cabinet and the "spoils system."

♦ Influenced by Jackson, the states acted to broaden the electorate through universal white manhood suffrage and popular election of the members of the Electoral College.

Chapter 9

Jacksonian Twilight

In This Chapter

- ◆ Jackson's challenging legacy
- ◆ Birth of the modern presidential campaign
- ◆ The question of succession
- ◆ Polk: the first "dark horse"

No president since George Washington cast a longer shadow than Andrew Jackson. The democratic spirit of his administration continues to influence not only the presidency itself, but how Americans view the presidency. Yet, like Washington, Jackson possessed a personality so large that he made those who immediately followed look small by comparison.

Jackson's Anointed

Alexis de Tocqueville observed in his *Democracy in America* (1835–1840) that Jackson had "constantly" increased his power, making the "federal government ... strong in his hands." But Tocqueville predicted, "it will pass to his successor enfeebled."

The French political thinker penetrated to the paradoxical core of the Jackson presidency. In terms of doctrine and policy, it had introduced a concept of democracy that limited the scope of the federal government, but in Jackson's own bold and grasping hands, the president became very powerful. Tocqueville saw that this power *inhered* at least as much in the personality of the particular president as it *adhered* to the office of the president. Jackson provided a model for what a strong president could do, but he did not necessarily endow the presidency itself with that strength.

Little Van

At 5 feet, 6 inches, Martin Van Buren wasn't particularly short for the early 1800s, but coming after Andrew Jackson's rawboned and imposing 6 feet, 1 inch, his modest height earned him the nickname "Little Van." Active in New York State politics, a U.S. senator from New York (1821–1828), and briefly governor (1829), Van Buren was one of the architects of the Democratic Party and a proponent of the spoils system (see Chapter 8). He was an ardent supporter of Andrew Jackson and became an intimate member of the Kitchen Cabinet before he replaced Henry Clay as Jackson's secretary of state in 1829. The president tapped him as his vice presidential running mate when he ran for a second term in 1832.

Donning Jackson's Mantle

Jackson handpicked Van Buren as his successor and trusted him to carry on his policies. For his part, after he was elected, Van Buren vowed that he intended "to follow in the footsteps of his illustrious predecessor," and, to demonstrate that he was in earnest, retained Jackson's final cabinet intact, but for a single member.

Tally _____

In 1828, Jackson (Democrat) earned 178 electoral votes (647,292 popular) against National Republican incumbent John Quincy Adams's 83 (507,730 popular). Against National Republican candidate Henry Clay in 1832, Jackson took 219 electoral votes (687,502 popular) to Clay's 49 (530,189 popular); 18 electoral votes went to other candidates. Van Buren, in 1836, won 170 electoral votes against Whig candidate William Henry Harrison's 73 (three others also ran). Van Buren earned 762,678 popular votes versus 548,007 for Harrison.

The Big Panic

Van Buren inherited more than the spirit and philosophy of Jacksonian democracy. No sooner did he take office than the nation was swept by the Panic of 1837, the culmination of Jackson's radically decentralized economic policy.

Of 850 banks chartered in the United States at the time, 343 closed their doors during the Panic of 1837, and another 62 partially failed. The system of state banks that Jackson had nurtured never fully recovered from this catastrophe.

Triumph of the Whigs

The Whigs clamored for more federal intervention in the economic crisis, and, in this call, they were even joined by a sizable number of Democrat defectors. Van Buren held firm, but the financial panic drove many conservative Democrats into an alliance with the Whigs, whose candidate, William Henry Harrison, triumphed over Van Buren by a wide margin when he ran for reelection in 1840.

Promises, Promises

The Whig platform had rested on a pledge to undo the Jacksonian aggrandizement of the presidency. The party promised that there would be no "King Andrew II" enthroned in the White House, and the executive branch would be generally reined in. Harrison made two specific pledges. The first was to return the veto to its "proper" function. Henceforth, the president would use it only against legislation he sincerely believed violated the Constitution. The second of Harrison's promises was to limit his presidency to a single term.

Tally

Harrison claimed 234 electoral votes (1,275,017 popular) to Van Buren's 60 (1,128,702 popular).

Harrison labeled as "preposterous" the Jacksonian assertion that a president was in a position to understand the people more clearly than their representatives in Congress. The Democrats responded by questioning whether Harrison truly believed this or was merely parroting what Whig Party leaders had told him to say. They pointed out that the party had failed to nominate their most distinguished and seasoned statesman and politician, Henry Clay, and had instead chosen Harrison, whom they lambasted as politically inexperienced, implying that he was a pliable party hack.

Log Cabin and Hard Cider: Inventing the Presidential Campaign

Harrison had actually held a good many elected and appointed posts, and if he *seemed* politically inexperienced, the reason was the way the Whig Party chose to present him. The campaign of 1840 was the first major political campaign in the history of the presidency. Like virtually all of the campaigns that followed at least through the first two thirds of the twentieth century, the contest between Harrison and Van Buren employed songs, symbols, and slogans, including perhaps the most famous campaign slogan in American history: "Tippecanoe and Tyler Too." This excursion into trippingly alliterative verse exploited Harrison's nickname, "Tippecanoe," a reference to the former general's 1811 victory over the forces of the celebrated and much-feared Shawnee war leader Tecumseh at Tippecanoe Creek (present-day Battle Ground), Indiana. The Tyler of "Tyler Too" was vice presidential running mate John Tyler of Virginia.

> ❝❞ **What They Said** _____
>
> I pledge myself before Heaven and earth, if elected … to lay down at the end of the term faithfully that high trust at the feet of the people!
>
> —William Henry Harrison, campaign speech, Dayton, Ohio, September 10, 1840

While the slogan is memorable, even more significant was the central symbol of the campaign, the log cabin, which denoted Harrison's connection with the western frontier. The log cabin symbol set an enduring precedent used in a number of subsequent presidential campaigns, most notably that of Abraham Lincoln in 1860. In Lincoln's case, however, the log cabin was accurately emblematic of the candidate's humble birth and upbringing, which had in fact taken place in a log cabin in the Kentucky backwoods. Harrison had been born and raised in prosperity and comfort on a Virginia plantation.

A member of the Democratic "party press" (see Chapter 8) lambasted candidate Harrison's log cabin pretensions by predicting that, given "a barrel of hard cider and … a pension of $2,000," Tippecanoe would "sit the remainder of his days in his log cabin by the side of a … fire and study moral philosophy." Harrison's Whig promoters appropriated this intended barb and proudly labeled their man with it, pronouncing him the "log cabin and hard-cider candidate." It was the first instance of what modern political strategists would call "branding" a candidate.

Ironically enough, the precedent-setting campaign for the Whig candidate, in which the complexities of issues and political philosophies were smothered in jingles, slogans, emblems, and other hoopla, was born of a Jacksonian vision of America. That is, this "modern" political campaign was designed to appeal to the common man, the very figure Jackson had helped to enfranchise and to elevate. It was an appeal virtually every other presidential candidate that came after the campaign of 1840 would emulate, up to and including "Joe the Plumber" in the McCain-Palin campaign of 2008.

The Death of a President

Tippecanoe was not destined to long relish his victory over Little Van. He delivered on March 4, 1841, the longest inaugural address in presidential history, clocking in at an hour and 40 minutes, addressing his audience in an icy rain and without the benefit of an overcoat. He caught a cold, which was apparently made worse some days later when he was drenched in a downpour while taking a walk. His illness developed into pneumonia, his condition rapidly deteriorated, and, a half hour after midnight on April 4, 1841, just one month after taking the oath, William Henry Harrison became the first American president to die in office.

Setting a Precedent for Secession

The president's death raised a question apparently no one had anticipated. As mentioned in Chapter 3, Article II, Section 1, of the Constitution specifies that on the removal or death of the president, his "powers and duties ... shall devolve on the Vice-President." The document does not stipulate that the vice president *becomes* the president, so that it is unclear if the vice president assumes the full status of president or merely fills in for him (and if the latter is the case, for how long?).

John Tyler did not wait for Congress to finish scratching its collective head. He immediately took the oath of office and then promised to faithfully complete Harrison's entire term.

There were objections in Congress, but they did not stick, and an enduring precedent of succession was established, which would not be codified as law until ratification of the Twenty-fifth Amendment in 1967.

John Tyler Redeems the Presidency

While Congress finally accepted the legality of Tyler's presidency, he never fully overcame the stigma of having been an "accidental president," especially in view of his differences with his own party. A former Democrat, Tyler, unlike Harrison, was not a fully compliant Whig. His inclusion on the ticket was a classic example of "ticket balancing" (see Chapter 3), intended to placate the wing of the Whig Party that embraced the Democrats' position on *states' rights*. Party leaders never intended for him to become president and never dreamed that he would.

def•i•ni•tion

Strictly speaking, **states' rights** are those powers the Constitution does not assign to the federal government and which, therefore, devolve upon the states. In the evolution of American politics, especially leading up to the Civil War, the phrase came to describe a political philosophy that limits federal powers to those actually enumerated in the Constitution and gives every other power to the states, which thereby enjoy considerable autonomy from the national government.

Although Tyler pledged to serve out Harrison's term, he made no promise to carry out what he knew—or surmised—would have been Harrison's policies. He intended to create his own administration, and that meant governing more like a moderate Democrat than a Whig. Like Jackson, he opposed the federalizing efforts of the Whigs and vetoed one Whig bill after another. When he vetoed legislation that would have established a new national bank, Whig partisans burned him in effigy across the country, and for the first time on record, a United States president received threats of assassination. Tyler's own cabinet rebelled. All except Secretary of State Daniel Webster simultaneously resigned.

For all intents and purposes, Congress declared war on the president. In a bid to force Tyler's resignation, Henry Clay cooked up a scheme whereby the Senate would with-hold consenting to any new cabinet nominees. This surely would have crippled the presidency, perhaps goading Tyler into stepping down, but the plot came to nothing. In 1843, however, after Tyler vetoed the high tariff essential to the implementation of the Clay's American System (a program of federally funded internal improvements, such as roads and canals), the House of Representatives convened a committee chaired by Representative—and former president—John Quincy Adams to make rec-ommendations on an impeachment resolution. The Adams committee concluded that Tyler had in fact misused the veto, and an impeachment resolution was voted on— the first in U.S. history. When it failed to pass, an intensely frustrated Henry Clay suggested that Congress vote on a constitutional amendment to permit a presidential veto to be overridden by a simple majority vote rather than the constitutionally man-dated two thirds majority.

Tyler responded to the attempted impeachment by claiming that he represented "the executive authority of the people," and it was in the name of the people that he protested attacks by Congress on the "undoubted constitutional power" of the chief executive's office.

Tyler took some satisfaction when the Whigs were handed a sharp defeat in the midterm elections of 1842, but, understandably, the Whig Party declined to nominate him as its presidential candidate two years later. Nevertheless, he had kept the Jacksonian presidency alive despite Whig attempts to kill it.

Behold a Dark Horse

The death of William Henry Harrison and the political apostasy of John Tyler wrecked the Whig scheme to roll back the Jacksonian concept of the presidency. Conversely, Tyler's "accidental" quasi-Jacksonian presidency improved the prospects for electing a Democrat in 1844, and the party was prepared to give Martin Van Buren the nod—again.

But history intervened—again.

In 1836 Texas fought its way to independence from Mexico, proclaimed itself a republic, and sought annexation to the United States. This raised the grim specter of upsetting the congressional balance of members from slave states versus members from free states—for Texas would surely petition for admission to the Union as a slave state—and for years, therefore, presidents and Congress put off the annexation issue. In 1844, fearful that England or France or both were getting too chummy with the Republic of Texas, Tyler directed his secretary of state, John C. Calhoun, to conclude an annexation treaty. Texas was admitted to the Union on December 29, 1845, shortly before the nominating conventions of both the Democrats and the Whigs. Suddenly, potential candidates were forced to declare their position with regard to annexation.

The front-running Whig nominee, Henry Clay, did not hesitate to proclaim his opposition to annexation, and the Whig Party, which was populated mostly by northerners, had no objection to this position. When Martin Van Buren also announced his opposition, however, the powerful southern bloc of the Democratic Party moved to scuttle his candidacy. A nomination deadlock ensued and was not broken until James K. Polk, governor of Tennessee, was tapped as an acceptable compromise candidate between North and South.

def•i•ni•tion

A **dark horse** candidate is one who suddenly emerges from obscurity to prominence. The phrase was borrowed from the world of horse racing, in which a "dark horse" was a contender unknown to bettors and handi-cappers and there difficult to give odds on.

He was the first *dark horse* candidate in American presidential history. An obscure figure who had not been considered before the convention, Polk came up from behind on the convention's ninth ballot. After that, his nomination caught fire, and the party lined up behind him.

Polk proved to be a strong candidate who presented himself as a Jacksonian Democrat even as he deftly preempted what the Whigs thought of as their ulti-mate anti-Jackson weapon: the candidate's promise to rein in the presidency by pledging to leave office after a single term. Polk the Democrat made that very pledge.

Introducing the Fiscal Presidency

Polk gained his party's nomination through compromise, and he won election in part through his willingness to gain power by pledging a term limit to his power. Once in the White House, he took a similar compromise approach in his project of reinstating the chief executive's office to something approaching the scope Andrew Jackson had claimed for it. Instead of asserting presidential

Tally

Polk took 170 electoral votes to Clay's 105. He polled 1,337,243 popular votes against 1,299,068 for Clay.

authority by fighting other branches of government, as Jackson had, Polk concentrated most intently on taking complete and detailed control of the executive branch. He oversaw and directed all of the executive departments closely, but, most of all, he took charge of the Department of the Treasury.

Prior to Polk, the secretary of the treasury had assumed considerable autonomy, thanks to the Treasury Act of 1789, by which Congress tasked the treasury secretary with creating annual estimates of government expenditures and reporting these to Congress. The act did not require the treasury secretary to formulate a federal budget, nor did it give the president the authority to require a budget or direct the creation of one. But neither the Treasury Act nor the Constitution *barred* the president from formulating, directing, requiring, or managing a budget, and so Polk seized upon this lack of prohibition to carve out a new key function for the chief executive: directing the government's fiscal policy.

The president's role in formulating the budget for the executive departments and providing direction for the creation of the federal budget as a whole is taken for granted today as one of the chief executive's basic duties. Yet none of Polk's nineteenth-century successors—except for Lincoln, who, like Polk, was a wartime president—followed his example. Little wonder, considering the storm of Whig protest that greeted Polk's approach to fiscal policy.

> **What They Said**
>
> I prefer to supervise the whole operations of Government myself rather than entrust the public business to subordinates and this makes my duties very great.
>
> —James K. Polk, 1847

In his last message to Congress, shortly before leaving office, Polk amplified the doctrine that both Jackson and Tyler had promulgated. He asserted that, through the Constitution, the people of the United States had enjoined the president as well as Congress to execute their will. He went a step further for the presidency, however, asserting that whereas each member of Congress represents only a portion of the American people, the president represents the whole of the American people.

Commander in Chief

Another reason that Polk was able to assert executive authority without provoking a bitter battle with Congress was that the people and the government naturally tend to rally around a president in war time. The U.S. annexation of Texas in 1845 provoked Mexico to declare war on the United States. Although a significant minority, mainly New Englanders, condemned the war as imperialist (it was, they said, a barely disguised pretext for robbing Mexico of territory) and immoral (because it would bring into the Union at least one slave state—perhaps more), most Americans enthusiastically embraced the conflict.

In the War of 1812, James Madison, who lacked military understanding and leadership skills and whose commitment to the war was half-hearted at best, had set a very poor example of the president as commander in chief. Polk delivered the first positive example. He was not a military man, but he worked well with them. He also formulated an overall strategy and a clear set of war aims and ably administered the nation's military resources in war. He personally chose all high-ranking commanding officers, and he coordinated his actions closely with his secretaries of war and the Navy. Most of all, he was unafraid to assert and maintain his complete and final authority over all aspects of the war.

Underappreciated

James K. Polk did what the Panic of 1837 made it impossible for Martin Van Buren to do. He affirmed and sustained the Jacksonian "strong" presidency. Even more important is that he managed to do this without as much of the disruptive and destructive drama the pugnacious Jackson brought to the White House. Polk provided an example of a strong *presidency* rather than an overbearing *president*. The authority that he claimed was claimed for the office, and not for himself personally. For this reason, some historians—and at least one president, Harry S. Truman—have judged Polk and "underappreciated" chief executive.

If James K. Polk did not bring the Jacksonian presidency blazing back to its full contentious glory, he revived it as a lingering twilight that continues to linger to this day.

The Least You Need to Know

- ◆ Jackson's presidency created a very difficult legacy for those who followed because he put the executive branch in perpetual conflict with the other two branches.

- ◆ The 1840 contest between Democratic incumbent Martin Van Buren and Whig challenger William Henry Harrison ("Tippecanoe") was the first "modern" presidential campaign.

- ◆ Harrison's sudden death just one month after he took office exposed the vagueness of the Constitution's rules of vice presidential succession to the presidency.

- ◆ Democrat James K. Polk, the first "dark horse" candidate, did much to reestablish the Jacksonian presidency and also established two demanding precedents: the president as a true commander in chief and the president as "budgeter" in chief.

Found Wanting

In This Chapter

- When leadership is lacking
- The Whigs: Taylor and Fillmore
- The Democrats: Pierce and Buchanan
- Buchanan brings down the presidency

The four men who followed Polk to the White House failed to provide the kind of leadership that might have averted the cataclysm of Civil War. Doubtless, this failure was in part due to their being men of middling ability at best; however, their deficiencies were not entirely personal, but were also the products of a general retreat from the presidency as practiced by Jackson.

Four "Do-Nothing Presidents"

In an essay (unpublished during his lifetime), retired president Harry S. Truman wrote that all of the nation's presidents were "willing and anxious to do what was right, if they knew what it was." Some, however, "didn't know … and some had an inkling or real knowledge but were just too lazy or too timid to do the work involved or take the flak that would come from opponents or the opposition press." Presidents who knew what was right and were able to do it and to get others to do it, Truman deemed "great." Those who knew what was right and acted in accordance with that knowledge were "near great," even if they could not always persuade others to do the right thing. The rest, according to Truman, were "do-nothings."

It is a provocative way to evaluate the presidents, but by focusing exclusively on the personal qualities of a given president—his insight, courage, and capacity for hard work—Truman's criteria leave out political philosophy and historical circumstance.

Zachary Taylor and Millard Fillmore were Whigs, by definition opposed to the "strong" executive as exemplified by Andrew Jackson. Although both Franklin Pierce and James Buchanan were Democrats, their conception of the presidency was shaped—deformed is perhaps the better word—by the slavery controversy, which was rapidly mounting to its ultimate crisis in civil war. In all four cases, political philosophy and historical circumstance, at least as much as personal character, weakened the presidency.

Old Rough and Ready

Zachary Taylor was a career military officer who fought in conflicts from the War of 1812 (1812–1815) to U.S.-Mexican War (1846–1848). During his days fighting the Seminoles (1835–1842), Taylor's rumpled uniform and broad-brimmed straw hat—practical protection against the Florida sun—earned him the nickname "Old Rough and Ready," which would serve him well in his 1848 presidential campaign. Although the Whig platform included its usual promise to limit executive power, a big part of Taylor's appeal was that, like Old Hickory, Old Rough and Ready seemed the very embodiment of popular democracy as first dramatized by Andrew Jackson.

Tally

In the first presidential election in which voting took place on the same day throughout the nation, Taylor, the Whig, polled 1,360,101 popular votes and 163 electoral votes. Democrat Lewis Cass polled 1,220,544 popular and 127 electoral votes. Martin Van Buren, who ran as the candidate of the smaller Free Soil Party, drew 291,263 popular votes but no electoral votes.

As we are about to see, history, in the form of the Compromise of 1850, forced Taylor to deviate from the Whig conception of the executive. Worse—for Taylor—his presidency was cut short by his death on July 9, 1850, apparently from cholera.

Fillmore

Vice President Millard Fillmore took the oath of office at noon on July 10, 1850, the day after Taylor's death. He reasserted Taylor's Whig pledge to restrain executive power, yet, like Taylor, he used his authority as president in an effort to move Congress, but in precisely the opposite direction from the way Taylor had wanted it to go.

Whereas Old Rough and Ready opposed the Compromise of 1850, Fillmore spoke out just as persistently in favor of it. After the compromise was carried in Congress in September 1850, Fillmore, with singular absence of insight, hailed it as the "final settlement" of the slavery controversy and, therefore, the resolution of the conflict between the North and the South.

Pierce and Buchanan

Taylor was elected on a Whig platform pledging restraint in the exercise of executive powers. The one notable act during his 16 months in office was an attempt to exercise executive power to thwart passage of the Compromise of 1850. On his death, Millard Fillmore, also a Whig, exercised genuine executive authority just once—to undo what Taylor had begun. Fillmore *supported* the Compromise of 1850.

Tally

Democrat Franklin Pierce polled 1,601,474 popular votes and 254 electoral votes. Winfield Scott, running as a Whig, garnered 1,386,578 popular votes and 42 electoral votes.

If the electorate expressed a desire for stronger executive leadership by electing a Democrat, Franklin Pierce, in 1852, what they got was a chief executive even weaker than his two Whig predecessors.

In the run-up to the Civil War, eight of the most critical years in United States history, Pierce and Buchanan functioned as little more than placeholders, whose only effect on the office of president was to enfeeble it by making it appear powerless.

Presidential Politics in the Shadow of Slavery

Taylor and Fillmore were the last of the Whig presidents. Their party faded and died, not so much because of its opposition to the still-popular legacy of Andrew Jackson as because of its focus on national unity. With the slavery issue tearing the nation apart, unity was coming to seem impossible. Even worse for the Whigs, their unity message came from a party rooted almost entirely in the North.

The legislative package known as the Compromise of 1850 was intended to resolve the crisis brought on by the annexation of southwestern territory acquired as a result of the U.S.-Mexican War. The compromise sought to placate both southerners (who wanted to extend slavery into the territories) and northerners (who wanted slavery barred from the territories) by admitting California to the Union as a free state, but making all other territories acquired as a result of the war subject to popular sovereignty, the people of each territory deciding whether to seek statehood as a free or a slave state. To appease northerners who objected to thus taking the slavery question out of federal hands, the slave auction market in the nation's capital would be closed, and to appease southerners, a much stronger Fugitive Slave Law was passed, strictly forbidding anyone to grant refuge to escaped slaves.

Taylor Fights the Compromise

President Taylor found that the slavery issue made it impossible for him to relinquish executive power. He was a slaveholding Virginian, but he had no desire to see the Union dissolve, and he believed that the Compromise of 1850, although it was intended to stave off civil war, would have just the opposite effect by increasing exacerbating national disunity. He therefore announced his opposition to the pending compromise and informed Congress that he himself would, if necessary, lead an army to put down any rebellion.

Fillmore and the Fugitive Slave Law

Taylor's sudden death prevented his doing battle either with Congress or would-be secessionists. As already mentioned, Fillmore threw his support behind the compromise his predecessor had opposed, and after it passed, he was all the more determined to promote its success. He discovered, however, that abolitionist sentiment was so strong in New England that local authorities simply refused to enforce the new Fugitive Slave Law. This put Fillmore in the uncomfortable position of echoing

Andrew Jackson's condemnation of South Carolina's attempt to "nullify" the "Tariff of Abominations" in 1832 (Chapter 8).

President Fillmore announced that he would permit "nullification" neither in the North nor the South, only to find himself powerless to enforce compliance with the Fugitive Slave Law. Whereas Jackson had been willing to use federal troops to compel recalcitrant revenue agents in South Carolina to collect the required tariff duties, it was neither practical nor desirable for Fillmore to use federal troops in an attempt to force obedience to the Fugitive Slave Law.

> **What They Said**
>
> The government of the United States is a limited government. It is confined to the exercise of powers expressly granted, and such others as may be necessary for carrying those powers into effect ….
>
> —Millard Fillmore, 1850

Pierce and the Kansas-Nebraska Bill

The Compromise of 1850 staved off the eruption of civil war sparked by the territory acquired after the war with Mexico, but the application of Nebraska and Kansas for statehood four years later triggered a new crisis, which Sen. Stephen A. Douglas, Democrat of Illinois, proposed to head off by once again advancing the doctrine of popular sovereignty. Because applying this doctrine to a pair of plains states would violate the Missouri Compromise of 1820, which prohibited the extension of slavery to these territories, Congress would have to repeal the 1820 law and replace it with a piece of popular sovereignty legislation, the Kansas-Nebraska Act.

The fight over the Kansas-Nebraska Bill was fierce, monopolizing Congress for three months. In the only action for which his presidency is remembered, Franklin Pierce used his office to enforce sufficient party discipline to finally pass the bill. Although he appealed to party loyalty, he also exploited the spoils system (see Chapter 8) to further cajole Congress by offering certain constituents of key members lucrative federal jobs.

> **What They Said**
>
> A Republic without parties is a complete anomaly. The history of all popular Governments show [sic] how absurd is the idea of their attempting to exist without parties.
>
> —Franklin Pierce, 1825

Although Pierce exploited a feature of the Jackson presidency, political patronage, he did not exercise the far grander Jacksonian doctrine that asserted a direct relationship between the president and the people. Instead of appealing to the people—that is, instead of presuming to lead the nation—Pierce appealed exclusively to party loyalty and party discipline. This narrow appeal, combined with the whiff of corruption in his quid quo pro distribution of political spoils, not only tainted Pierce but cast the American presidency itself into cynical disrepute.

Worse yet, if Pierce sold the presidency, he made a very poor bargain indeed. Far from bringing stability to the nation, the Kansas-Nebraska Act served only to exacerbate the slavery crisis as Kansas exploded into a bloody guerilla war between pro-slavery and free-soil factions.

Buchanan's Inaugural Charade

Democrat James Buchanan entered the White House less committed to resolving the slavery crisis than to finding a way to tamp it down in the hope that it would somehow just go away. The tool by which he intended to accomplish this was neither a Democratic assertion of Jacksonian executive authority nor a recourse to a Whiggish reliance on Congress, but a retreat behind the Supreme Court. In his inaugural address, delivered on March 4, 1857, Buchanan acknowledged the crisis created by the status of the extension of slavery—the *territorial question*—but then dismissed it as "happily, a matter of but little practical importance" because the Supreme Court was about to deliver an opinion that would settle the issue "speedily and finally." He told his audience that he would "in common with all good citizens ... cheerfully submit" to the court's decision, "whatever [that decision] might be."

def•i•ni•tion

The **territorial question** in antebellum politics was the issue of whether slavery would be extended into the western territories. The South adamantly favored such expansion, whereas the North just adamantly opposed it.

Buchanan's listeners were well aware that the high court was hearing arguments in the case of Dred Scott, a slave suing for his freedom on the grounds that, because his late owner had taken him to live for extended periods in free-soil territories where slavery was illegal, he had become, legally, a free man. Of course, those who listened to the president did not know what the court's decision would be, but if they assumed that the newly sworn president was also unaware, they were almost certainly mistaken.

Chief Justice Roger B. Taney, Buchanan's friend and fellow alumnus of Dickinson College, was seen whispering in the president-elect's ear just before the inauguration. It was later widely assumed that Taney was conveying to him in advance that the court would decide the Dred Scott case in the way he had wanted, a way that would resolve the territorial question. To ensure this outcome, Buchanan also lobbied Associate Supreme Court Justice Robert Cooper Grier, a fellow Pennsylvanian, and persuaded him to vote with the majority in the Dred Scott case.

Tally _____

Democrat James Buchanan captured 1,838,169 popular votes and 174 electoral votes. John C. Frémont, the first candidate of the Republican Party, came in second with 1,334,264 popular votes and 114 electoral votes. Millard Fillmore ran on the ticket of two parties, the American Party (popularly called the Know-Nothings) and the moribund Whigs. He garnered 874,534 popular votes and 8 electoral votes.

The decision was made public two days after Buchanan's inauguration. The Supreme Court dismissed Dred Scott's suit on the grounds that, as a slave and "Negro," he was not an American citizen, and therefore, had no standing in federal court and could not bring suit. This alone would have been sufficient to decide the case, but Taney, who wrote the majority opinion, continued. He held that the Missouri Compromise, which banned slavery from the territories in which Scott had lived, was unconstitutional in that it violated the Fifth Amendment, which bars the government from depriving an individual of "life, liberty, or property" without due process of law. Congress, therefore, had no power to exclude slavery in the territories.

Presidential Abdication

Buchanan tried simply to wash his hands of the slavery controversy by reducing the "territorial question" to a matter of law as decided by the Supreme Court. This abdication of executive authority, he hoped, would end the matter by putting it beyond dispute.

Instead, the Dred Scott decision made Civil War inevitable by galvanizing the abolitionist movement. By defining slavery as an issue of property, a Fifth Amendment right, the decision required that slavery had to be protected in all the states. Far from resolving the slavery issue, the decision put it beyond any further compromise and beyond any law short of a constitutional amendment abolishing slavery. Since the South would never voluntarily ratify such an amendment, war was the only alternative to acquiescence in slavery.

Although he was a member of the party Andrew Jackson had helped to found, James Buchanan was the antithesis of Old Hickory and the presidency he had created. Whereas Jackson had built up the presidency, Buchanan tore it down. The consequence of his abdication of executive authority was the Civil War.

Fortunately, Buchanan was succeeded by a very different president. Abraham Lincoln, who took the oath on March 4, 1860, was a new kind of president and the standard bearer of a new party with a fresh moral and national resolve.

The Least You Need to Know

◆ As a Whig, Zachary Taylor pledged to rein in the power of the presidency, but the only memorable act in his 16 months in office was his attempt to persuade Congress not to pass the Compromise of 1850 for fear that it would bring civil war.

◆ Millard Fillmore succeeded the short-lived Taylor and tried to undo what little Taylor had managed to accomplish.

◆ Franklin Pierce attempted to govern through party discipline rather than through genuine national leadership.

◆ James Buchanan abdicated executive power to the Supreme Court's decision in the Dred Scott case; this accelerated the approach of Civil War and nearly wrecked the presidency in the process.

Presidential Greatness

In This Chapter

♦ Creating a "team of rivals" cabinet

♦ Defining the role of commander in chief

♦ The president as national moral leader

♦ Public opinion and the presidency

After a succession of four presidents most historians rate among our worst, Americans elected the president just about everyone ranks as the greatest.

He had to be. Torn over slavery, the Union had begun to fall apart, which meant that the United States was dying as a nation and required nothing less than a rebirth. But studying Abraham Lincoln not as a particular president but in the context of the history of the presidency requires examining more than his personal greatness. More than any president before him, except for Washington, who started it all, Lincoln shaped the presidency, taking it in directions not even imagined by Andrew Jackson, America's boldest chief executive before 1860.

Birth of the GOP

By coaxing passage of the Kansas-Nebraska Act in 1854, Democrat Franklin Pierce did not reduce sectional strife as he had meant to do, but he did make himself an accessory to the murder of the Whig Party. Northern voters and antislavery western voters were outraged over the Whig acquiescence to the repeal of the Missouri Compromise to allow the expansion of slavery through popular sovereignty. The Republican Party rushed in to fill the vacuum left by the Whigs' rapid demise, establishing itself in a series of political meetings in the upper Midwest. Made up of members of the short-lived Free Soil Party, so-called "Conscience Whigs" (Whigs for whom abolition was a central issue), and others opposed to the expansion of slavery into the territories, the Republican Party was the first party founded west of the Mississippi that spread eastward, taking especially strong root in New England, where *abolitionist* sentiment ran strong.

def•i•ni•tion

An **abolitionist** was an advocate of outlawing—abolishing—slavery everywhere in the United States. Not all opponents of slavery were abolitionists; Lincoln, for example, aimed only at barring the extension of slavery beyond the states in which it already existed.

Emergence of a Statesman

By 1858, the Republicans were well established on the American political map, and ran former Illinois state legislator and United States representative Abraham Lincoln against the formidable incumbent Stephen A. Douglas for a Senate seat. The centerpiece of the campaign was a series of debates focused on the overwhelming issue of the day: the expansion of slavery. The brilliance of the debates riveted the attention of the national press, and although Lincoln lost the Senate race to Douglas, the newcomer came across as a statesman to be reckoned with. The North was swinging heavily toward the new party.

66 99 What They Said

I agree with [my opponent, Stephen A. Douglas, that a black man] is not my equal in many respects—certainly not in color, perhaps not in moral or intellectual endowment. But in the right to eat the bread, without the leave of anybody else, which his own hand earns, he is my equal and the equal of Judge Douglas, and the equal of every living man.

—Abraham Lincoln, during the Lincoln-Douglas debates, 1858

"Team of Rivals"

Despite the attention Lincoln had attracted by his performance against Douglas in the 1858 senatorial campaign, many in the Republican Party were appalled by the prospect of offering a "prairie lawyer" as the party's presidential candidate in 1860. New York senator William Seward, former Missouri representative Edward Bates, Pennsylvania senator Simon Cameron, and former Ohio governor Salmon P. Chase all thought of themselves as far more qualified candidates, but the party convention nevertheless nominated Lincoln as its standard bearer for 1860.

Lincoln would not forget his rivals. Once elected, he drew upon them to create his cabinet. Seward became secretary of state, Bates attorney general, Cameron secretary of war, and Chase secretary of the treasury. Another prominent figure, Democrat Edwin McMasters Stanton, attorney general in the cabinet of President Buchanan, had voiced vehement opposition to Lincoln during the election, but, at the request of the president, agreed to serve as legal adviser to Secretary of War Cameron, who proved both inefficient and corrupt. When Lincoln asked Stanton to replace Cameron at the start of 1862, the Democrat agreed, but only, he said, to "help save the country."

In 2003, Doris Kearns Goodwin published a popular history of Lincoln and his cabinet, *Team of Rivals*, in which she argued that Lincoln's "political genius" and success as a president depended in part on his having placated and neutralized potential enemies by incorporating them into his administration and on the boldly creative manner in which he used their opposition to himself and one another as an aid in making key decisions. Lincoln's cabinet appointments created a precedent followed by some chief executives, most notably Barack Obama, who appointed New York senator Hillary Rodham Clinton, his bitter adversary in the Democratic primaries, as secretary of state.

Another Log Cabin, a Very Different Candidate

Lincoln was sold to the electorate as an impressive statesman who was nevertheless a "common man" in the mold of Andrew Jackson. Much was made of his frontier origin; like Tippecanoe (see Chapter 9), he had been born and raised in a log cabin.

While Lincoln's popular image was key to the 1860 campaign, the candidate did not take to the stump, but remained quietly in Illinois. In contrast, his Democratic opponent, Stephen A. Douglas, became the first candidate in presidential history to make a national campaign tour.

He was driven to it because the slavery issue had splintered the Democratic Party along the Mason-Dixon Line. Southerners formed the National Democratic Party and nominated their own candidate, James C. Breckenridge, the sitting vice president. The expected Democratic vote was further fragmented by another candidacy, that of Tennessee senator John Bell, who ran on the ticket of the Constitutional Union Party, consisting mainly of Whigs unwilling to join the Republicans plus the remnants of the short-lived American ("Know-Nothing") Party. In contrast, Lincoln and his supporters relied on the newborn strength of the Republican Party, which dominated the northern states and therefore potentially commanded a majority of electoral votes.

Tally

In 1860, Lincoln (Republican) polled 1,866,352 popular votes, capturing 180 electoral votes. Douglas (Democrat) earned 1,375,157 popular votes, which netted him just 12 electoral votes. Breckinridge (National Democrat), the southern splinter candidate, took 845,763 popular votes, which earned him 72 electoral votes among the southern states. Breckinridge's southern competitor, Bell (Constitutional Union), opposed to secession, polled 589,581 popular votes, which earned him 39 electoral votes. Lincoln's was a plurality victory; he received 40 percent of votes cast, whereas Douglas received 29 percent, Breckinridge 18 percent, and Bell 13 percent. That is, 60 percent of the American electorate preferred another candidate to Lincoln.

Slavery: Lincoln Redefines the National Debate

Abraham Lincoln did not run as an abolitionist, but he was opposed to the extension of slavery into the territories and disagreed with the Supreme Court's decision in the Dred Scott case. He also believed that the Constitution protected slavery where it already existed and that, absent a constitutional amendment ending slavery, the federal government had no authority to abolish slavery in the slave states. On this constitutional point, Lincoln agreed with his principal opponent, Douglas, but Lincoln could not stomach the manner in which the Kansas-Nebraska Act of 1854—authored by Douglas—had sanctioned the extension of slavery into the western territories, implying that slavery was not the "necessary evil" the framers of the Constitution had deemed it, but was actually desirable.

Lincoln tried to avoid civil war by using his candidacy to redefine the national debate on slavery not as a case of irreconcilable alternatives, but as an opportunity for the North and South to come together to restore the compromise on slavery that had existed in the United States even before the Constitution. Lincoln argued that the founding fathers had intended to preserve slavery without extending it, and the Missouri Compromise of 1820 had been enacted in the spirit of this compromise. Lincoln did voice agreement with what he said was the belief of the founding fathers, that slavery would die a "natural death" if it were not extended but was otherwise left alone.

It was certainly the first time that presidential *candidacy*—as opposed to presidential *office*—had been used not merely to reflect public opinion, but in an effort to shape it.

The President and Secession: The First Inaugural Address

Even if Lincoln could hold his nose in the spirit of compromise, the leaders of the southern states could brook no compromise and announced that if "black Lincoln" were elected, the Union would be dissolved.

And so it was. On December 20, less than a month after Lincoln's plurality victory, South Carolina seceded, followed by Mississippi, Florida, Alabama, Georgia, and Louisiana in January and Texas in February. On March 4, 1861, Lincoln was inaugurated as president of a broken country. (Virginia, Arkansas, Tennessee, and North Carolina would secede in April and May 1861, after Lincoln had taken office.)

In his inaugural address, the president declared, "I have no purpose, directly or indirectly, to interfere with the institution of slavery in the States where it exists. I believe I have no lawful right to do so, and I have no inclination to do so." Opening his presidency by reaffirming his understanding that the executive's central duty was to faithfully execute the laws of the United States, he pledged to abide by the Constitution—and expected the states to do so as well.

Unmistakably casting himself in the constitutional role as the nation's "Chief Magistrate," Lincoln argued from the basis of self-evident law: "It follows from these views that no State upon its own mere motion can lawfully get out of the Union … and that acts of violence within any State or States against the authority of the United States are insurrectionary or revolutionary, according to circumstances."

The New President Defines the Presidency

In his inaugural address, an incoming president typically outlines his principles and plans. Lincoln, however, used the address to define his understanding of the presidency itself, which existed to uphold the Constitution. Lincoln announced his intention to do this, subject to a single limitation: the lawful will of the American people, "my rightful masters."

President Buchanan yielded his executive authority to that of the Supreme Court in the belief that its decision on constitutional matters was final and would be accepted by the nation as final. Like Jackson before him, Lincoln sought to reduce the authority of the Supreme Court by challenging the finality of its decisions. In his inaugural address, Lincoln conceded that the court's decisions "must be binding ... upon the parties to a [particular] suit ... but may be overruled and never become a precedent for other cases ...." He reasoned "that if the policy of the Government upon vital questions affecting the whole people is to be irrevocably fixed by decisions of the Supreme Court, ... the people will [cease] to be their own rulers, having ... resigned their Government into the hands of that eminent tribunal."

Having challenged the finality of decisions of the Supreme Court, Lincoln reduced the issues dividing the nation to one: "One section of our country believes slavery is right and ought to be extended, while the other believes it is wrong and ought not to be extended. This is the only substantial dispute." Because the sections cannot physically separate—"A husband and wife may be divorced and go out of the presence and beyond the reach of each other, but the different parts of our country can not do this"—"intercourse, either amicable or hostile, must continue between them." Secession therefore offers no advantage: "Is it possible, then, to make that intercourse more advantageous or more satisfactory after separation than before? Can aliens make treaties easier than friends can make laws? ... Suppose you go to war, you can not fight always; and when, after much loss on both sides and no gain on either, you cease fighting, the identical old questions, as to terms of intercourse, are again upon you."

Having suggested a motive for remaining united, Lincoln defined a sharp limitation of the presidency. "The Chief Magistrate derives all his authority from the people," who have not asked him to "fix terms for the separation of the States." The president's "duty is to administer the present Government as it came to his hands and to transmit it unimpaired by him to his successor." It is up to the people, not the president, to use the government to resolve their differences. "Why," Lincoln asked, "should there not be a patient confidence in the ultimate justice of the people? Is there any better or equal hope in the world?"

The president's role was to defend the Constitution and preserve the Union so that the people's justice could, in the fullness of time, prevail.

Beyond the Definition: Greatness

In his inaugural address, Abraham Lincoln defined the presidency narrowly, but acting on that narrow definition, he would assume more power than any president before him. Yet, for Lincoln, the presidency was more than the sum of its defined authority and assumed power. It was also leadership, leadership that took the form of compassion—love, really. Lincoln ended his first address as president with words of nearly heartbreaking beauty, pregnant with human understanding that no mere definition of "president" can express:

> We are not enemies, but friends. We must not be enemies. Though passion may have strained it must not break our bonds of affection. The mystic chords of memory, stretching from every battlefield and patriot grave to every living heart and hearthstone all over this broad land, will yet swell the chorus of the Union, when again touched, as surely they will be, by the better angels of our nature.

Commander in Chief or Military Dictator?

Lincoln's inaugural message did not succeed in preventing war. Southerners could not bring themselves to believe that the president's power was as limited as he claimed it to be. Despite a succession of weak presidents, the spirit of Andrew Jackson continued to shape popular perceptions of the presidency. The people, including the people of the South, believed that the nation's chief executive could do pretty much as he pleased, and they believed that Abraham Lincoln intended, one way or another, to end slavery. Assuming he would resort to force, the South responded with preemptive force on April 12, 1861, by firing upon Fort Sumter.

Presidential War

The war began when Congress was in recess, and Lincoln did not call it into special session until July 4. This meant that the president exercised executive authority, unchecked by Congress, from April 12 to July 4. To preserve the Union and defend the Constitution, he boldly stepped outside of the Constitution by imposing a naval blockade on the South and expanding both the army and the navy. Even more boldly, Lincoln suspended habeas corpus in regions still under federal control. Acting on presidential authority, a whole range of civilian and military officials was empowered to make arrests at will, not only without warrant but even without specific charge.

Executive Event _____

The Constitution does not give the president authority to impose a blockade on any part of the nation, and it reserves to Congress the exclusive authority to raise an army and navy. Although the Constitution does provide for the suspension of habeas corpus "in cases of rebellion," this power is stipulated in Section 9 of Article I, the article devoted to the powers of the legislative branch, not the executive.

Challenges

While many in the North accepted the president's actions and rallied around him as the commander in chief, accusations that Lincoln had transformed the presidency into a military dictatorship were uttered frequently. To those who attempted to counter such charges by claiming that, in the absence of Congress, the president had no choice but to act, Lincoln's critics pointed out that the president has the authority to call Congress into special session at any time but had not done so. Did he delay so that he could prosecute the war unfettered by Congress? Or did he delay in the hope that executive action would end the rebellion without the necessity of asking Congress for a declaration of war (which, Lincoln believed, was tantamount to recognizing the Confederacy as a nation)?

> **What They Said** _____
>
> If I wanted to paint a despot, a man perfectly regardless of every constitutional right of the people, I would paint the hideous, apelike form of Abraham Lincoln.
>
> —Sen. Willard Saulsbury (Dem., Delaware)

The most cogent challenge to the legality of Lincoln's assumption of extra-Constitutional wartime authority were the *Prize Cases*, decided by the Supreme Court in 1862. Lincoln had imposed a naval blockade on the South without a declaration of war. Many vessels, American and foreign, were seized as "prizes" while attempting to run the blockade. Seeking the release of the prize ships and compensation for seized cargo, shipping interests sued the United States, arguing that, in the absence of a declared war between nations, the seizures were acts of piracy.

The court found that a state of war could exist even if the belligerents were not sovereign nations and that the president possessed the authority to impose a blockade as a lawful means of waging war.

Lincoln used the decision in the *Prize Cases* to justify wide latitude for the exercise of wartime executive authority, and Lincoln's broad definition established a precedent other commanders in chief have followed.

Limits

Emboldened by the *Prize Cases* and by congressional ratification of many of his executive acts, President Lincoln issued executive orders establishing *military tribunals* to try those suspected of insurrection and other rebellious activity. Unlike either civilian trials or military court martials, military tribunals, designed to try enemy combatants during war, operated according to very loose rules of evidence and provided few protections for defendants. As such, they were expedient and almost ensured whatever outcome prosecutors desired. Lincoln was the first American president to order them, and his actions set precedents acted on by Franklin Roosevelt acted on during World War II from 1941 to 1945 and George W. Bush during the so-called "War on Terror" beginning in 2001.

def•i•ni•tion

A **military tribunal** is a military court intended to try enemy combatants during wartime. The military tribunal operates without many of the rules and constitutional guarantees that govern and constrain both civilian courts and military court martials.

1864: Election in Time of War

President Lincoln established a precedent for far-reaching executive authority in wartime, but he also established a precedent of self-restraint in the actual exercise of that authority. The most dramatic example of this was the election of 1864. With the war ongoing, the president who had suspended habeas corpus might well have suspended the election as well. That he did not—even though he and other Republicans believed a Democratic victory was likely—is a testament to the integrity of the restraint Lincoln himself imposed on his office and his belief in the supremacy of constitutional government.

The Power of Presidential Proclamation

Until the early twentieth century, presidents, including Lincoln, issued executive orders almost exclusively to particular executive departments or executive officers. Presidents also occasionally issued proclamations, which were more public in their application than executive orders, but which were almost always merely ceremonial in nature. Lincoln, however, used the proclamation format to execute one of the most important acts in American history, the Emancipation Proclamation, issued in preliminary form on September 23, 1862.

It was a cautious document which did not free any slaves, but only warned slave owners living in states "still in rebellion on January 1, 1863," that their slaves would be declared "forever free." The proclamation did not apply at all to slaves in the border states or to those living in areas of the Confederacy occupied by Union forces; Lincoln did not want to incite slaveholders in such areas to violence against the occupying army.

Only after the deadline passed did Lincoln issue the Final Emancipation Proclamation. Since it excluded the border states and occupied areas of the Confederacy, the only slaves to which it applied lived in those areas over which Lincoln's government had no control. Thus the proclamation set no one free, but it did serve to galvanize northern abolitionist sentiment by elevating the war to a lofty moral plane. As it elevated the war effort, so the Emancipation Proclamation enshrined Lincoln as the "Great Emancipator" and greatly enhanced the prestige of the presidency. From this point forward, the president was expected to be a national moral leader and champion of social justice.

The President and Public Opinion

Although Lincoln had barely campaigned in 1860, he went to extraordinary lengths during his presidency to take the pulse of the public and respond to it. His White House was open to a wide range of visitors; indeed, Secretary of War Stanton repeatedly cautioned the president that his openness unnecessarily exposed him to possible assassination. Lincoln gave little weight to such warnings and explained that he needed his daily "public-opinion baths"—by which he meant conversations with ordinary people—to keep him in touch with the national mood. In this respect, his was a Jacksonian presidency, based on the idea that the president was the direct representative of the American people and was therefore, required to maintain direct contact with them.

> **What They Said**
>
> Public sentiment is everything. With public sentiment, nothing can fail; without it nothing can succeed. Consequently he who molds public sentiment, goes deeper than he who enacts statutes or pronounces decisions. He makes statutes and decisions possible or impossible to be executed.
>
> —Abraham Lincoln, during the Lincoln-Douglas debates, 1858

Lincoln also devoted careful attention to managing public opinion. On a regular basis, Lincoln wrote open letters to newspapers, typically in response to specific questions from actual correspondents. These open letters may be seen as a precedent for the celebrated fireside chats of Franklin Roosevelt (see Chapter 19).

Blood Moon

On the evening of April 14, 1865, John Wilkes Booth, matinee idol and self-proclaimed champion of the South, walked into the Ford's Theatre, where the president, his wife, and two guests were enjoying a performance of a popular comedy, *Our American Cousin*. Booth entered the president's box through a rear door, pointed a derringer between Abraham Lincoln's left ear and spine, squeezed off the pistol's single shot, mounted the railing of the box, leaped onto the stage, and declaimed to a stunned audience "Sic semper tyrannis!" ("Thus ever to tyrants!") It was the state motto of Virginia.

Later, Midwestern farmers would claim that the moon turned blood red at precisely the moment Booth's bullet tore into the president's skull.

The first American president to be assassinated, he would not be the last. Since Lincoln, assassination and the specter of assassination have stalked the American presidency.

Tally _____

> After Lincoln (1865), James A. Garfield (1881), William McKinley (1901), and John F. Kennedy (1963) were murdered. Theodore Roosevelt (running as a Progressive Party candidate in 1912) and Ronald Reagan (1981) were wounded by would-be assassins, and assassination attempts were made against President-elect Franklin D. Roosevelt (in 1933, resulting in the death of Chicago Mayor Anton Cermak), Harry S. Truman (1950, resulting in the deaths of a Secret Service officer and one of the assassins), and Gerald Ford (two attempts in 1975). Assassination plots or attempts against Jimmy Carter (1979), George H. W. Bush (1993), Bill Clinton (1994, two attempts), and George W. Bush (2001, 2005, and possibly 2008) were abortive, miscarried, or foiled. Prior to Lincoln's assassination, Andrew Jackson used his cane to beat down a would-be assassin in 1830.

The Lincoln Legacy

Abraham Lincoln is the standard against which all succeeding presidents have been measured. His most enduring legacy has defined the presidency as a combination of a faithful stewardship—of the Constitution, the Union, and the American people—and a quality of leadership that transcends politics and even government itself, requiring the president to be compassionate and possessed of an unerring instinct for knowing the right thing to do and the will to do it. Beyond this, there is even a quasireligious coloring to the Lincoln heritage. He is widely seen as the president-savior, on whose infinitely expressive face were etched the sorrows of his people, as if he had taken them upon himself, in the end suffering Christ-like martyrdom.

Although some of President Lincoln's successors have approached his legacy, none has fully lived up to it. Compounded of the sixteenth president's actual achievements and nearly a century and a half of accumulated lore and mythology, it is a legacy no one could ever fully satisfy.

The Least You Need to Know

♦ Lincoln incorporated his fiercest rivals into his cabinet, setting a precedent several chief executives have followed to the extent of appointing to cabinet positions one or two members of the opposition party.

♦ Lincoln defined the presidency narrowly as existing to defend the Constitution (which required the preservation of the Union), but within the confines of this definition, he claimed unprecedented executive powers, which prompted some critics to condemn him as a dictator.

♦ The Civil War forced Lincoln to define the president's role as commander in chief very boldly. Subsequent chief executives have followed his lead.

♦ The Lincoln presidency forever defined the American president as the moral leader of the nation, the embodiment as well as the molder of public opinion, sentiment, and resolve.

Part **3**

Retreat and Advance

Although most Americans regarded the presidency of Abraham Lincoln as redemptive, Congress recoiled from the tremendous governing power the martyred sixteenth president had claimed for his office. Under Lincoln's successor, Andrew Johnson, the presidency and the Congress were locked in mortal combat, culminating in the impeachment of the chief executive. A single senator's vote saved Johnson from removal and rescued the presidency from permanent irrelevance. Nevertheless, for the next three decades, until the beginning of the twentieth century, the presidency was a badly damaged and greatly diminished office.

Chapter 12

Impeached and Corrupted

In This Chapter

- The character of Andrew Johnson
- President vs. Congress
- The path to impeachment
- Grant's surrender

In his sublime poem on the murder of Abraham Lincoln, Walt Whitman wrote of "the great star early droop'd in the western sky in the night," the "powerful, western, fallen star" that symbolized the sixteenth president for whom he "mourn'd." In 1865, the year of Lincoln's assassination and of Whitman's "When Lilacs Last in the Door-Yard Bloom'd," neither the poet nor any other American could have imagined how long the mourning would last not alone for Lincoln, but for the presidency itself. Lincoln proved to be not only the last great president of the nineteenth century, but the last strong and fully effective chief executive until early in the next century.

Power Abhors a Vacuum

As the Civil War approached its close and the North became confident of victory, President Lincoln and Congress turned their attention to the postwar restoration of the Union—*Reconstruction*. Because most of the Democratic representatives and senators resigned when their states seceded, the Civil War Congress was overwhelmingly dominated by Republicans; however, these were sharply divided between a moderate faction that favored a lenient and conciliatory attitude toward the South and the so-called Radical Republicans, who regarded secession as an act of treason and therefore, advocated sternly punitive treatment of the South.

def•i•ni•tion

Reconstruction describes both the process by which the seceded southern states were restored to the Union and the period (1865–1877) during which the former Confederate states were occupied by U.S. troops and administered by U.S. military governors.

In his Second Inaugural Address, delivered on March 4, 1864, Lincoln made clear what side he took, declaring his intention to address the former Confederacy "with malice toward none, with charity for all" and with the intention of "bind[ing] up the nation's wounds." The president had already translated his words into deeds by his choice of his second-term running mate, Democrat Andrew Johnson of Tennessee. The only senator from the seceded states who demonstrated his loyalty to the Union by remaining in Congress at the outbreak of the war, Johnson was appointed military governor of Union-occupied Tennessee in March 1862. That Johnson was a southerner, a Democrat, *and* a fierce loyalist moved Lincoln to put him on the 1864 ticket. To further signal his desire for reconciliation between North and South, the president and his running mate agreed to submerge their traditional partisan identities, Republican and Democrat, in a new unity organization, the National Union Party.

❝❞ What They Said

Damn the negroes, I am fighting those traitorous aristocrats, their masters.

—Sen. Andrew Johnson, 1861, explaining his reason for remaining in the United States Congress after the secession of Tennessee

The War over Wade-Davis

Even before reelection, Lincoln had taken a bold step toward national reconciliation. By 1863, three southern states, Louisiana, Arkansas, and Tennessee, were occupied by the Union Army and under U.S. government control. Lincoln proposed that these states be reincorporated into the United States after just 10 percent of each state's voters swore a loyalty oath. The Radical Republicans rejected this by passing the Wade-Davis Bill, which permanently disenfranchised Confederate leaders and high-ranking military officers and, as a condition of readmission to the Union, required a loyalty oath from 50 percent of each state's citizens as well as formal acceptance of abolition.

Reconstruction, the legislators argued, was the province of Congress, not the president. Lincoln responded with a *pocket veto*, refraining from signing the Wade-Davis legislation before Congress adjourned, thereby killing it until it could be taken up again in the next session. Lincoln also sent a message to Congress, asserting that Reconstruction should be a matter for the executive, not the legislature. The pocket veto and the message provoked Radical Republicans to issue the Wade-Davis Manifesto, assailing Lincoln's lenient plan for Reconstruction and reasserting the primacy of the legislature in Reconstruction.

def•i•ni•tion

When a president receives a bill for signing within 10 days of congressional adjournment and holds the bill unsigned, he has issued a **pocket veto.** The bill may be reconsidered by Congress when it reconvenes.

Lincoln's solid reelection in 1860 (by a margin of 55 percent) came as a blow to the Radical Republicans, who resigned themselves to the conclusion that a majority of the American people would support whatever Reconstruction program the president advocated. It looked as if Congress had the lost the war.

Some Celebrate

April 14, 1865: Enter Booth, assassin.

While the nation mourned Lincoln's "martyrdom," the most radical of the Radical Republicans quietly celebrated. It appeared that they would win after all—especially, they thought, because Congress would now be working with Andrew Johnson.

Although Johnson was both a Democrat and a southerner, he had already amply proved his loyalty to the Union. As a senator, he had been a member of the Joint Committee on the Conduct of the War, the congressional body that, in effect, looked over Lincoln's shoulder throughout the Civil War, often criticizing his conduct of strategy and military policy. The very existence of this committee compromised and threatened to usurp the president's constitutional authority as commander in chief.

Since the committee was dominated by Radical Republicans, they had some reason to assume that, Democrat or not, Johnson would be on their side in the struggle over Reconstruction.

But even if he should prove less pliable than anticipated, the Radical Republicans took comfort in the fact that Andrew Johnson was no Abraham Lincoln. The graceless Johnson was a heavy drinker, but, even during his rare stretches of sobriety, he was a cantankerous loudmouth.

Lincoln's presidency was persuasive evidence that the power of the office was ultimately inseparable from its occupant's charisma—or absence thereof. Johnson's presidency was about to prove this beyond a doubt.

Congress Attacks the Presidency

The congressional Radicals counseled Johnson to purge the cabinet of Lincoln loyalists. Instead, he retained the cabinet intact. As if that weren't sufficient indication of his intention not to yield presidential authority to Congress, Johnson chose not to call Congress into special session. Thus, from April until December, when Congress was regularly scheduled to convene, he conducted Reconstruction by issuing executive proclamations.

Johnson Defies Congress

Not only did Johnson thus trespass on congressional territory, he modified the Wade-Davis Reconstruction program in the manner of an old-fashioned Jacksonian Democrat, seeking to protect states' rights above all else. He issued a blanket amnesty to anyone who took an oath pledging loyalty to the Union now and in the future. As conditions for reentry into the Union under their own elected governments, Johnson required the states to ratify the Thirteenth Amendment (which freed the slaves), to explicitly abolish slavery in their own state constitutions, to repudiate debts incurred while in rebellion, and to formally declare secession null and void. By the end of 1865, all of the secessionist states, except for Texas, had complied.

Compromise Spurned

But Congress, having convened in December, objected. Many representatives and senators feared that the president's policies restored power to the very individuals who had brought rebellion in the first place. Moreover, it was clear that while Johnson concerned himself with states' rights, he had no desire to pursue the Radical Republican program of securing legal equality for the freed slaves. It was apparent that the readmitted states were intent on keeping the former slaves in subservience, and this was fine with the president.

" " What They Said

> The attempt to place the white population under the domination of persons of color in the South has impaired, if not destroyed, the kindly relations that had previously existed between them: and mutual distrust has engendered a feeling of animosity which leading in some instances to collision and bloodshed, has prevented that cooperation between the two races so essential to the success of industrial enterprise in the Southern States.
>
> —Andrew Johnson, State of the Union Address, 1868

To correct this problem, Congress passed in 1866 the Freedman's Bureau Act, which created an agency to provide food, clothing, medical care, and rudimentary education to the former slaves to assist them in making the transition to their new lives. It was a humane and reasonable program, sponsored not by Radical Republicans but by Republican moderates.

Lincoln would surely have approved. Johnson vetoed it. Johnson wanted to prevent Congress from taking Reconstruction out of executive hands, but by vetoing a moderate Republican measure, Johnson spurned all compromise. His veto succeeded in uniting the moderate Republicans and the Radical Republicans against him.

The Final Break

Johnson next plied his veto pen against the Civil Rights Act, designed to ensure that African Americans would have full citizenship rights. In his veto message, Johnson expressed his belief that blacks were not qualified for citizenship and that the act would "operate in favor of the colored and against the white race."

Like the Freedman's Bureau Act, the Civil Rights Act was endorsed by all congressional Republicans. Congress responded on April 9, 1866, by overriding the veto, the first time in American history that the legislative branch had overridden the executive branch on a truly momentous item of legislation. With this override, Reconstruction passed from executive to congressional control.

Andrew Johnson, Marked Man

On June 13, 1866, the Fourteenth Amendment was proposed in Congress—again, under moderate, not Radical, Republican sponsorship. It was intended to make the provisions of the Civil Rights Act part of the Constitution, but it went well beyond that act by injecting federal authority into voting rights, which had been the exclusive province of the states, by reducing the congressional representation of states that withheld voting rights from African Americans. In addition, the amendment federalized a set of civil rights so that these could be protected by federal—not state—courts. This time, Johnson did not veto the measure in Congress, but used his influence as a president and a Democrat to block ratification in the southern states to prevent its achieving the three-fourths approval required.

Dismantling the Presidency, Phase 1

Johnson had made himself a marked man. After the southern states refused to ratify the Fourteenth Amendment, Congress passed the Military Reconstruction Act of 1867, which undid Johnson's executive Reconstruction by placing the entire South under military occupation, nullifying the civilian state governments. Johnson vetoed the act, and Congress overrode the veto.

Additionally, Congress attached *riders* to the 1867 military appropriations bill requiring the president as well as his secretary of war to convey all orders through General of the Army Ulysses S. Grant and forbidding the president to relieve or transfer Grant without Senate approval. Johnson's protest of these riders on constitutional grounds—they usurped executive authority—was simply ignored.

def•i•ni•tion

Riders are clauses added to a legislative bill that bear little direct relevance to the substance of the bill; that is, they go along for the ride, becoming law by virtue of the passage of the main bill.

In a final move to outmaneuver the president, Congress voted to remain permanently in session. This not only deprived Johnson of the power of the pocket veto, but even took away his constitutional authority to call or refrain from calling Congress into session.

Dismantling the Presidency, Phase 2

Congress next invaded the executive branch itself. The Tenure of Office Act barred the president from removing from office anyone whom he had appointed with the advice and consent of the Senate unless the Senate also consented to the removal. Such an encroachment on executive authority had been tried before, during the administration of George Washington no less (see Chapter 4), but now Congress meant to make it stick, and when Johnson vetoed the act, Congress overrode the veto on March 2, 1867.

The President Appeals to the People

Stripped of his ability to influence legislation through Congress, Johnson took his case to the people. On Washington's Birthday, February 22, 1866, the president, quite possibly drunk, addressed a group of citizens who had gathered outside of the White House to show their support for the veto of the Civil Rights Act. Johnson declared that the Radical Republicans were *northern* rebels and that Thaddeus Stevens of Pennsylvania, leader of the Radicals in the House, and Charles Sumner, Radical Republican leader in the Senate, were traitors as guilty of treason as the leaders of the Confederacy had been.

The rhetoric crossed a line few were willing to cross, and when Johnson embarked on a speaking tour to broadcast his message that the Radical Republicans were no better than rebels, he alienated the public all the more.

❝❞ What They Said

> Johnson is an insolent drunken brute in comparison with which Caligula's horse was respectable.
>
> —Sen. Charles Sumner of Massachusetts, 1865
>
> I look upon him [Andrew Johnson] as a patriot and as a statesman who for twenty-five years has been distinguished in the service of his country in the various offices that he has filled .... I look upon him as patriotic, wise, and prudent.
>
> —Former President Martin Van Buren, 1865

A Political Corpse

Undeterred by his failure with the American public, Johnson decided to defy Congress by forcing the Tenure of Office Act to a test. In May 1868, he dismissed Secretary of War Edwin M. Stanton—an openly disloyal cabinet member—without consulting Congress. His expectation was that this would result in the Supreme

Court's ruling the law unconstitutional. Instead, the House voted articles of impeachment, and the Senate tried Johnson in a proceeding that dragged on for a month and a half. In the end, he was acquitted by a single vote.

One of the seven Republican senators who voted for acquittal was Lyman Trumbull of Illinois, sponsor of the Freedman's Bureau Bill, which Johnson had vetoed, and author of the Thirteenth Amendment. He explained why he deemed it his duty to commit political suicide by breaking party ranks: "No future president [would] be safe who happens to differ with a majority of the House and two-thirds of the Senate on any measure deemed by them important, particularly if of a political character. ... What then becomes of the checks and balances of the Constitution ...?"

Andrew Johnson was an inept politician and an offensive person, which makes all the more admirable the refusal of seven principled men to undermine the presidency and assail the Constitution for the sake of political expediency. Yet *this* presidency, the presidency of Andrew Johnson, was dead, and he served out his term a political corpse while Congress conducted the daily business of government.

The Disappointment of Ulysses Simpson Grant

Ulysses Simpson Grant, the commander who led the Union armies to victory after years of loss and heartbreak under other generals, was a popular figure after the Civil War, and the nation had high hopes that he would restore the presidency to honor, authority, and effectiveness.

Grant was an extraordinary military leader, but his genius did not translate into civilian life. During the Tenure of Office Act controversy, from 1867 to 1868, Grant served as interim secretary of war, then accepted the Republican nomination for president, for all intents and purposes making a direct transition from general to presidential candidate. He had never held elective office and embarked upon the presidency as a babe in the woods, bearded though he was.

Bold General, Shrinking President

Grant entered office assertively enough, warning Congress that he considered the Tenure of Office Act an unconstitutional encroachment on executive authority and that he would refrain from making any federal appointments below the cabinet level until the legislature repealed it. Bowing to Grant's prestige and popularity, the House quickly voted to repeal, but the Senate responded with what it called a "compromise," an amendment to the act, which effectively maintained it unchanged. Had Grant exploited his popularity and stood firm, the Tenure of Office Act would doubtless have disappeared, and he would have commenced his presidency with the office strengthened and the constitutional balance of powers largely restored. Instead, he folded. It was as if Grant had opened the door of the White House, walked in, then turned over the keys to Congress.

Grant's capitulation probably had less to do with his character than with his conception of the presidency, which was very different from that of Jackson or Lincoln—or Andrew Johnson, for that matter—and instead harked back to the defunct Whigs. Like them, he believed that the chief executive's role was primarily to "faithfully execute" the laws enacted by Congress, the governmental body that was (Grant said) "the authoritative expression of the will of the American people."

The Veto Paradox

During Grant's two terms in office, Congress enacted an unprecedented torrent of legislation. The president neither instigated, championed, nor guided this legal downpour, but he did vigorously exercise the veto—no fewer than 93 times, which was more than all 17 of his predecessors combined. Moreover, the vast majority of Grant's vetoes stuck; just four were overturned.

Except in this negative sense, the presidency in Grant's hands was remarkably disengaged from the ongoing formulation of domestic policy and was only moderately more influential in shaping foreign policy. In Whig fashion, Grant regarded domestic policy as the responsibility of the legislature.

An Administration Amok

If Grant disengaged himself from the management of domestic affairs, he at least did so from ideological motives, but there was no ideological justification for turning his back on the conduct of the executive branch itself. The Grant administration was so riddled with larceny and fraud that it stands as an emblem of corruption at the highest levels of government.

Some of the corruption consisted of straightforward criminality, as in the notorious Whiskey Ring scandal, in which the federal collector of internal revenue in St. Louis conspired with officials of the U.S. Treasury and the president's own private secretary to skim millions due the government in federal taxes. But most was the product of the "spoils system" (see Chapter 8) run amok. Political patronage spawned crooked quid pro quo federal appointments and appointments purchased with outright bribery. This prompted Grant to create an executive board that became the basis of the Civil Service Commission and to make one of his rare appeals to Congress for legislation to codify civil service reform.

Instead of producing viable legislation, the president's call for legislation incited Sen. Roscoe Conkling of New York to rally the so-called "Stalwart" faction of the Republican Party in a fight to preserve and defend political patronage. Feeling himself outnumbered and outgunned, Grant yet again surrendered. When the Stalwart-controlled Congress declined to fund the newly created Civil Service Commission in 1874, Grant simply bowed out of the fight.

Although Grant's personal integrity remained almost miraculously intact, his administration established a precedent for institutionalized federal corruption that would endure throughout the nineteenth century and would recede early in the twentieth, only to reemerge with a vengeance during the administration of Warren G. Harding (1921–1923; see Chapter 17).

Where There Is No Vision

Historians have debated the causes of the disappointment that was the administration of the eighteenth president. Doubtless, part of it was the result of Grant's lack of civilian administrative and political experience or aptitude; part was surely due to his Whiggish view of the executive branch as subordinate to the legislative; part was a product of the ascendancy of Congress during the Johnson administration; and no small part was the result of an overabundance of politicians for whom public service ran a distant second to personal gain.

But beyond these particular causes of the failure of the Grant presidency was the chief executive's absence of political vision. Defining the presidency as an essentially administrative job, Grant offered no vision for a country still shattered by the Civil War. It was a failure of leadership as old as the Book of Proverbs (29:18): "Where there is no vision, the people perish: but he that keepeth the law, happy is he." As different as were the Johnson and Grant administrations, both were deeply marked by an absence of vision, and therefore, fostered a government that unhappily failed to "keep the law."

The Least You Need to Know

- ◆ Andrew Johnson was a graceless figure, whose loyalty to the Union was compromised by racist views and a belief in states' rights.

- ◆ The president and Congress went to war over the nature of Reconstruction—whether it should be lenient to the South (even at the expense of the continued subjugation of African Americans) or essentially punitive.

- ◆ Responding to the president's unwillingness to compromise on any part of Reconstruction, Congress sought to strip the presidency of much of its authority and to remove Johnson from office.

- ◆ Grant abdicated to Congress much of the constitutional authority of the presidency, further weakening the institution.

13

Prelude to the Progressive Presidency

In This Chapter

- ◆ The "stolen election" of 1876
- ◆ The fight for civil service reform
- ◆ Cleveland introduces the "centrist" presidency
- ◆ McKinley establishes the American president as a world leader

The Grant left the presidency at a low point of prestige and power. The only Americans pleased by this state of affairs were senators, who felt that, in cowing President Grant, they had permanently asserted the primacy of the Senate over the chief executive. What they had not counted on was the eagerness of Grant's successor, Republican Rutherford B. Hayes, to rehabilitate the damaged office.

"His Fraudulency"

Under the best of circumstances, the new president's ambition would have been difficult to fulfill, and Hayes's entrance into the White House was hardly under the best of circumstances. On the contrary, it was the product of a backroom political deal so brazen that President Hayes was mockingly referred to as "His Fraudulency."

The Loser and Next President ...

Although Grant had been elected to two terms, his eight years in office had left such a bitter taste that it was universally assumed that the American electorate would not install another Republican. The Democratic candidate was a strong one, New York governor Samuel J. Tilden, who had earned national fame as a fighter of corruption for his successful efforts to purge graft from the administration of the state's canal system.

Tally

Democrat Samuel J. Tilden polled 4,284,757 votes to Republican Rutherford B. Hayes's 4,033,950, a margin of 51 versus 48 percent. The election was disputed by the Republicans and was decided by a congressional commission, which awarded Hayes 185 electoral votes to Tilden's 184.

Although the popular returns on election night gave Tilden a quarter of a million vote lead over Hayes, Republican Party leaders determined that the fate of their candidate could be determined by contesting electoral votes in Oregon, Louisiana, South Carolina, and Florida—the three southern states were still under Reconstruction military rule, which in itself was sufficient to cast doubt on the results. If these disputed electoral votes could be delivered to Hayes, he would win, despite the popular vote.

The dispute that resulted raged wildly and with no end in sight before the looming March 4 inauguration date. With just two days left before the inauguration deadline, Congress authorized a bipartisan electoral commission while legislators hammered out a behind-the-scenes deal: the South would give the election to Hayes in return for his pledge to bring full home rule to the southern states and an immediate end to the military-enforced Reconstruction governments. The southern legislators agreed to a commission composed of eight Republicans and seven Democrats, who voted straight down party lines in favor of Hayes.

The Cost of the Bargain

The cost of the backroom bargain was the legitimacy of the election process, the perceived integrity of the presidency, and, worst of all, the rights of African Americans in the South. With the soldiers gone, the Fourteenth and Fifteenth Amendments—the former guaranteeing civil rights to all citizens of whatever color, the latter affirming the right to vote, regardless of color—became little more than ink on paper.

Yet, at this exorbitant cost, a reform-minded Ohio governor was ushered into the White House, determined to bring about the federal civil service reform Grant had proposed and then given away to Congress, and to create a cabinet of the highest distinction.

> **What They Said** _____
>
> The great fraud of 1876–77, by which, upon a false count of the electoral votes of two States, the candidate defeated at the polls was declared to be President, and for the first time in American history, the will of the people was set aside under a threat of military violence, struck a deadly blow at our system of representative government.
>
> —from the Democratic Party platform of 1880

The Cabinet Reborn

The senatorial Republican *Stalwarts*—the champions of machine politics who had even tried to get Grant to run for a third term—planned to populate the Hayes cabinet with Republican Party faithful. The incoming president, however, delivered a shot across their bow by independently selecting his own cabinet officers, all distinguished by their integrity and competence. Most notable was Carl Schurz as Secretary of the Interior; a militant civil service reformer, Schurz was the sworn enemy of the spoils system (see Chapter 8).

Outraged Senate Stalwarts dragged their feet on confirmation of each and every cabinet appointment. The Senate's intransigence backfired. The public demonstrated unprecedented support for the president against the Senate, deluging both the White House and the Congress with letters and telegrams expressing approval of Hayes's cabinet choices. Faced with the prospect of alienating voters, the Senate ultimately approved everyone Hayes had chosen. It was the first victory of the executive over the legislature since the Lincoln administration.

def•i•ni•tion

The **Stalwarts** were the Republican Party faction, led by New York senator Roscoe Conkling, that supported machine politics fueled by political patronage (the spoils system) and opposed merit-based civil service reform.

"Now for Civil Service Reform"

Having restored at least some balance between the executive and the legislative branches, Hayes recorded in his dairy on April 22, 1877, "Now for Civil Service reform."

The Custom House Fight

Hayes created a commission to investigate port-city custom houses, which had been staffed with patronage appointees. The commission made headway in most of the custom houses, except for the largest, at the port of New York. Hayes moved to replace top New York custom house management, which consisted of three Stalwarts, among them future vice president and president Chester A. Arthur. Senate Stalwarts hung up Hayes's nominations, and Republican boss Roscoe Conkling brought to bear the infamous Tenure of Office Act. Although it had been amended after the failure of the Johnson impeachment, so that it no longer empowered the Senate to overturn a presidential nomination, it did stipulate that the official who was to be replaced would remain in office (he could be suspended, but not removed) until the Senate approved the new nominee. The Senate withheld consent.

Executive Event _____

Federal duties payable on goods imported into the United States were assessed and collected at custom houses maintained at all major American ports. In the days before income tax (introduced in 1913 by ratification of the Sixteenth Amendment), import duties represented the largest single source of all federal revenue.

But the fight wasn't over. After the Senate adjourned in 1878, Hayes fired the three again, replacing them with recess appointments. When the Senate reconvened in December, the recess nominees had to step down, and the original three Stalwarts replaced them—ostensibly until the Senate voted on the president's nominations. Conkling, however, overplayed his hand by making a speech in which he divulged passages from the private correspondence of cabinet members. Widely perceived as a grave breach of protocol, this gaffe prompted the Senate to approve the nominees in spite of Conkling early in 1879.

Victory's Price

Hayes not only won another power struggle against the Senate and partisan self-interest, he also succeeded in reforming the New York custom house and, through this, provided the nation with proof that a merit-based civil service system was possible. The cost to Hayes was heavy, however. Locked in mortal combat with the Senate for a year and a half, the president was essentially powerless to suggest, let alone promote, any legislative agenda, and because he could not hope to receive the endorsement of his own party, he did not even offer himself as a candidate for reelection.

The Surprising Character of Chester A. Arthur

In 1880, the Republican Party nominated Ohio representative James A. Garfield, a candidate who aimed to please everyone in his party by offering something to the Stalwarts as well as to the moderates, who were known derisively as *Half-Breeds*.

The Battle Renewed

Once in office, Garfield found that concili-ation and compromise would only go so far. New York's Conkling renewed the Senate's battle against the presidency by coercing the president into installing New York banker Levi P. Morton as secretary of the treasury, which prompted Garfield to retaliate by installing one of Conkling's arch political enemies as collector of the port of New York. Working through Chester A. Arthur—Garfield's Stalwart vice-president— Conkling pressured the president to withdraw the nomination. When this failed, he maneuvered the Senate to approve all of Garfield's nominees *except* for the collector. The president responded by withdrawing every other nominee to federal posts in New York state. This forced the Senate to capitulate, and, in desperation, both Conkling and his fellow New York senator, Thomas Platt, resigned, confident that the New York legislature (popular election of senators would not become law until ratification of the Seventeenth Amendment in 1913) would reelect them, thereby forc-ing Senate Republicans to align behind them rather than the president. The ploy failed when state legislators sent two others to the Senate.

def•i•ni•tion

In the late nineteenth century, moderate Republicans, who favored civil service reform and opposed the party's Stalwart fac-tion, were dubbed **Half-Breeds**.

Tally _____

Republican James A. Garfield polled 4,454,416 popular votes in 1880, defeating Democrat Winfield Scott Hancock, who received 4,444,952 votes. The margin of victory was a razor-thin 48.3 percent to 48.2 percent.

Assassination

Garfield did not long savor his victory. On July 2, 1881, Charles J. Guiteau, described in newspapers as a "disappointed office seeker," shot the president in the back in a Washington railroad station. Although Guiteau was clearly psychotic, his declared motive was political. Arrested, he exclaimed, "I am a Stalwart, and Arthur is president!" The president lingered through the summer, his physicians unable to locate and remove the bullet lodged in his back. He succumbed to infection on September 19, the second American president to fall to an assassin.

... And Arthur Is President!

The Stalwarts had every reason to expect that Chester A. Arthur would undo the reforms Garfield had begun. But responding to a tidal wave of public opinion condemning the spoils system—many saw the slain president as literally a martyr to patronage—Arthur became at least a tentative advocate of civil service reform, supporting passage of the Pendleton Act, which introduced a form of the civil service examination system and barred political affiliation as a requisite for civil service appointment.

Grover Cleveland, the Bourbon Democrat

As the public went to the polls in 1884, their disgust with hardcore party politics was apparent. The Republicans accordingly nominated a Half-Breed, House speaker James G. Blaine, and the Democrats ran a member of their own moderate faction, New York governor Grover Cleveland, a *Bourbon Democrat*, so called because the sipping of Kentucky bourbon connoted old-fashioned conservatism, as did the Bourbon dynasty of France.

The Centrist Presidency

Cleveland's was the first self-consciously "centrist" presidency, a political philosophy that tended toward the conservative end of the spectrum and upon which most Democrats and most Republicans found common ground. Like moderate Republicans, the Bourbon Democrats saw themselves less as representatives of the masses than of the establishment, siding with big business against the "radical" demands of immigrants, industrial workers, and small farmers. The Bourbon presidency deemed the best government to be the least government.

Centrism, the Presidency, Congress, and Reform

As a centrist, Cleveland not only attempted to cooperate with Congress, he held as an article of political faith the belief that the president had no legislative role to play other than to recommend measures from time to time. As for reform, he faithfully enforced the Pendleton Act, partly because he believed that civil service reform was a good idea and partly in the belief that the chief duty of the presidency was to faithfully execute the nation's laws. Cleveland also carefully evaluated candidates for appointments not covered by civil service reform, but generally limited his choices to Democrats. The Republican-dominated Senate repeatedly invoked the modified Tenure of Office Act and often declined to approve his appointments.

The conflict came to a head over the removal of the Republican U.S. attorney for Alabama and his replacement by a Democrat. The Senate demanded to review all executive documents relating to the Democrat's appointment and the Republican's removal. Cleveland deemed it appropriate to furnish the documents relevant to the appointment because the Constitution specified the Senate's responsibility to "advise and consent," but he withheld the documents relating to the dismissal, because he did not believe the Constitution gave the Senate the power to approve removals from office.

The issue was rendered moot in the case in question by the expiration of the Republican's term, but, later, Congress, in a bipartisan vote, repealed the Tenure of Office Act, an action Cleveland heartily approved.

Tally

In the election of 1884, Democrat Grover Cleveland polled 4,911,017 votes (49 percent) to Republican James G. Blaine's 4,848,334 (48 percent). In 1888, Cleveland received 5,540,329 votes (49 percent) to Republican Benjamin Harrison's 5,439,853 (48 percent), but earned fewer electoral votes—168 to Harrison's 233—and therefore lost his reelection bid. Four years later, in 1892, Cleveland became the only U.S. president to win a nonconsecutive term, defeating Harrison 46 to 43 percent— Populist candidate James B. Weaver taking 9 percent of the vote. Cleveland polled 5,556,918 popular votes and 277 electoral votes; Harrison, 5,176,108 popular and 145 electoral; and Weaver, 1,041,028 popular and 22 electoral votes.

"The President Should 'Touch Elbows with Congress'"

The election of 1888, like that of four years earlier, was nearly a dead heat. Cleveland outpolled his Republican opponent, Indiana senator Benjamin A. Harrison (grandson of short-lived President William Henry Harrison; see Chapter 9), 49 to 48 percent, but Harrison captured more northern states, along with their hefty complement of electoral votes, and won.

What They Said

The President should "touch elbows with Congress." He should have no policy distinct from his party and this is better represented in Congress than in the Executive.
—Sen. John Sherman to presidential candidate William Henry Harrison, 1884

Without pressing to expand the presidency, Cleveland had gone a long way to bringing it into equity with the legislature, which, however, remained dominant in government. But whereas Cleveland fought Congress when he believed the executive's constitutional standing was at stake, Harrison always yielded, conceiving of the presidency not as a position of political leadership but as the office of the largely symbolic head of state.

Presidential Power Resurgent

As it turned out, the American public may not have wanted a strong Jacksonian president, but they wanted a mere figurehead even less. In 1892, Cleveland ran against Harrison and defeated the incumbent by the significant margin of 46 to 43 percent.

To this day, Cleveland remains the only U.S. president to win election to nonconsecutive terms, making him both the twenty-second and twenty-fourth chief executive.

A catastrophic financial panic during his first year in office, 1893, in which more than 15,000 firms, including 500 banks, failed and as much as 19 percent of the workforce became unemployed, spurred Cleveland to the vigorous exercise of executive power as he called Congress into special session to repeal the Sherman Silver Purchase Act. The 1890 legislation had been intended to make more credit available by increasing the amount of silver the government was required to purchase every month using treasury notes redeemable for either silver or gold, but it created severe inflation when investors redeemed their notes not for gold rather than silver dollars.

Cleveland prevailed, and the Sherman Act was repealed, but at the price of giving the president the appearance of an anti-populist dictator. This image was darkened even more by Cleveland's response to the massive Pullman Strike of 1894. Taking the position that he was enabling the unimpeded delivery of the U.S. mails, the president used his executive authority as commander in chief to send federal troops to break up the strike—without consulting Illinois governor John Peter Altgeld. Altgeld objected to what he deemed a violation of state jurisdiction, and many people were outraged by the exercise of executive authority to support big business at the expense of the working majority.

McKinley: *Almost* an Activist

Cleveland's unpopular resurrection of vigorous executive authority should have put the Democratic candidate for 1896, *populist* William Jennings Bryan, in a strong position; however, Bryan was identified not with small farmers rather than urban labor, whereas Republican candidate William McKinley appealed to voters in industrial cities and won.

def•i•ni•tion

> A **populist** is a politician or leader who appeals to the interests of the common people rather than the "special interests" of big business and the wealthier classes. The term is generic; however, a Populist Party was active in American politics from 1884 to 1908 and was defined mainly by its opposition to the gold standard.

The Partnership Presidency

The McKinley presidency was far more active than that of Benjamin Harrison, but, instead of competing with Congress, as Cleveland had in his second term, McKinley worked through the congressional Republican caucus to influence legislation.

Tally

Republican William McKinley defeated Democrat William Jennings Bryan in 1896 by a margin of 51 percent to 47 percent. McKinley won 7,035,638 popular votes and 271 electoral votes; Bryan, 6,467,946, for 176 electoral votes. In 1900, McKinley again defeated Bryan, 7,219,530 (52 percent) to 6,358,071 (46 percent), earning 292 electoral votes against Bryan's 155.

The President as Commander in Chief

Where McKinley did take the presidency unmistakably into the lead was in the conduct of diplomacy, foreign affairs, and war. During his administration, the United States became increasingly engaged in world affairs. McKinley saw a certain degree of American imperialism as necessary to ensure that the United States would remain economically competitive in international commerce.

The most dramatic demonstration of this was the Spanish-American War of 1898 and the associated annexation of Puerto Rico and the Philippines, the acquisition of Hawaii and lesser Pacific islands, and the establishment of Cuba as a nominally independent American client state. It may be argued that McKinley actually weakened the presidency by bending to public pressure and the will of Congress to go to war with Spain over Cuban independence instead of pursuing the course of diplomatic negotiation he clearly preferred. But what McKinley's secretary of state John Hay called the "splendid little war" was so brief and so resoundingly triumphant that it made the president, in his role as commander in chief, very popular. From McKinley forward, the American president was expected to be an able war leader, capable of rallying the nation to the support of military action. More important, the president was also now expected to be a world leader.

The Least You Need to Know

- The presidencies of Hayes, Garfield, and Cleveland were marked by efforts to promote civil service reform while restoring the presidency itself to a level of authority consistent with the Constitution.

- James A. Garfield became the second American president to suffer assassination; his successor, Chester A. Arthur, stunned fellow Stalwart Republicans by taking up Garfield's crusade to curb political patronage.

- Bourbon Democrat Grover Cleveland introduced the "centrist" presidency.

- William McKinley expanded the president's role in foreign affairs, establishing the American presidency as the office of a world leader.

Part 4

The Progressive Presidency

When Theodore Roosevelt came to office in 1901 after the assassination of William McKinley, he launched a program of national reform that put the presidency at the epicenter of American government in a way that had not been seen since the presidencies of Abraham Lincoln and Andrew Jackson. When his handpicked successor, William Howard Taft, failed to expand the legacy he created, TR came closer than anyone before or after him to making a "third-party" presidency a reality. Taft, the conservative Republican, was succeeded by a Democrat, Woodrow Wilson, whose approach to his office was as innovative and consequential as Roosevelt's had been. With Wilson, the nation got its first glimpse of the Oval Office as the center of world leadership.

Chapter 14

T. R.

In This Chapter

♦ Reversing the decline of the presidency

♦ The president as public opinion molder in chief

♦ The environmental presidency

♦ Roosevelt as progressive and world leader

"Now look!" Sen. Mark Hanna of Ohio moaned when he heard that William McKinley, twenty-fifth president of the United States, had died of gunshot wounds sustained in an assassination attempt a week earlier, on September 6, 1901, while attending the Pan American Exposition in Buffalo, New York. "That damned cowboy is president of the United States."

Hanna's exclamation was at least fractionally accurate. Theodore Roosevelt did own—and personally worked—a ranch in the Dakota Territories. But he was much more than a cowboy. Born and raised in Manhattan wealth, he served in the New York State Assembly, was a reformist member of the U.S. Civil Service Commission and a reformist president of the New York City Police Board, had been assistant secretary of the navy, made himself into a military hero as colonel of the "Rough Riders" in the Spanish-American War, and was governor of New York before he became McKinley's second-term running mate in 1900. He was also a pioneering naturalist and a highly successful author. Roosevelt was thrust into the White House as the most energetic and engaged president since Andrew Jackson.

An "Accidental President" Breaks Through

Republican Party leaders had plucked Roosevelt from the governor's chair in Albany because his reformist opposition to political patronage cramped their style. The vice presidency would shoo this gadfly out of the way. But the bullet of a self-proclaimed anarchist converted the state Republican Party's problem into a national party problem.

def•i•ni•tion

From about 1890 to 1920, **progressive** described any politician who favored social, economic, political, and (sometimes) moral reforms, including the restoration of a just balance between the interests of business and the interests of labor.

As a *progressive* Roosevelt believed that big business was the great engine of the American economy, but he also saw the long-time Republican policy of uncritical support for business at the expense of labor and consumers as fatal both to the future of the party and the nation. Capitalism, yes—but regulated by the faithful stewardship of good government. If government surrendered to business, it would lose all connection with the ordinary citizen, and American democracy would become American oligarchy.

From Executive Inertia to Presidential Leadership

To translate progressive ideology into policy, Roosevelt understood that he would have to reverse the long decline of the presidency relative to the ascendancy of the legislature. Harking back to Andrew Jackson, Roosevelt defined the president as the "steward of the people," implying at the same time that the Congress had failed in this role because too many of its members represented special interests—those of business—rather than the people who elected them.

Beyond Old Hickory

For Roosevelt, the Jacksonian presidency was a means rather than an end. Starting from it, Roosevelt promulgated what he called a "New Nationalism," by which he intended to refashion and expand the executive—and, with it, the entire administrative machinery of the federal government—to promote the public welfare. In the service of the people, *the nation* would be superior to *the states* and therefore, the federal government would be dominant over state governments. Within the federal government, the president, as the representative of all the people, would guide the Congress, curbing its tendency to represent special interests.

Beyond the Federalist Vision

As Roosevelt simultaneously looked back to Jackson and beyond him for his model of the presidency, so he returned to the old Federalist view of executive power but, at the same time, positioned the president less as an executive than as a popular representative. His view of executive power owed much to Alexander Hamilton: The president could lawfully claim all governing authority not otherwise specifically barred by the Constitution.

Thomas Jefferson and other Democratic-Republicans had opposed the hyper-Federalism of Hamilton and his definition of presidential authority as autocratic, but as Roosevelt saw it, the presidency had to be made sufficiently powerful to oppose the oligarchic direction in which Congress had taken the government. By expanding the scope of the presidency, Roosevelt sought to expand democracy, not curb it.

What They Said

The welfare of each of us is dependent fundamentally upon the welfare of all of us.

—Theodore Roosevelt, speech, New York State Fair, September 7, 1903

The Return of Vision

Roosevelt had in abundance what most of his predecessors had conspicuously lacked: vision—vision based on his interpretation of the nation's founding principles.

Roosevelt knew that historians regarded Hamilton and Jefferson as the two great philosophical poles of American government, the one espousing a strong executive presiding over a strong central government, the other eager to ensure that both the central government and its executive would remain inferior and answerable to the will of the people. Roosevelt proposed synthesizing the two poles. A strong central government led by a powerful executive was necessary, he argued, to assert the will of the people.

Tally

After serving out the term of the slain McKinley, Theodore Roosevelt ran for election in his own right in 1904, earning a solid victory with 7,628,834 popular votes (56 percent) and 336 electoral votes. Democrat Alton B. Parker received 5,084,401 votes (38 percent) and 140 electoral votes. Eugene Debs, running as a Socialist, polled 402,714 votes (3 percent).

Building the Bully Pulpit

For Hamilton, the ideal president was essentially a republican monarch. For Jefferson, he was the servant of the will of the people. Although some accused Roosevelt of monarchal ambitions—much as many had condemned Jackson as "King Andrew"—he insisted that the people were the ultimate governing authority. Yet, he insisted, the president's duty to represent and implement the will of the people did not prevent him from influencing, inspiring, shaping, and even creating that will.

Reportedly, T. R. called the presidency a "bully pulpit," a phrase that put the office on a par with the clergy in guiding the people to "right thinking."

In an America that has lived through such administrations as those of Theodore Roosevelt's fifth cousin Franklin Delano Roosevelt (see Chapter 19) and Ronald Reagan (see Chapter 25), the idea of the president as molder in chief of public opinion is hardly radical. When Theodore Roosevelt introduced it, however, the concept was heavily freighted with risk. The last president who had made a concerted effort to appeal directly to the people over and in spite of Congress was Andrew Johnson (see Chapter 12), with disastrous results. The difference, of course, is that whereas Johnson was a crude and abrasive man, Roosevelt was a powerful speaker, passionate if not always supremely eloquent, who exuded a masculine charisma that many found appealing. Indeed, during McKinley's 1900 bid for reelection, it was Roosevelt, not the president, who had been the chief campaigner.

Still, the risk of demagoguery was real and, at the very least, threatened to undermine the majesty of the office. Roosevelt avoided this by shaping the will of the people and then enlisting the people in a partnership with him to persuade Congress to pursue the course the president and the people had agreed upon.

Recruiting the Press

President Roosevelt did not rely exclusively on his oratorical skills to move the public. He recognized that he was living in the midst of an explosion in the growth of the popular press, including newspapers as well as a plethora of weekly, biweekly, and monthly magazines, and he became the first American president to exploit the mass media.

His principal journalistic partners were the very journalists on whom he bestowed the name by which they are still known, the *muckrakers*. Theodore Roosevelt established a symbiotic relationship with these avatars of the progressive press. The most familiar example surrounds passage of the landmark Pure Food and Drug Act and the Meat Inspection Act, both in 1906. Roosevelt advocated passage of these regulatory laws after reading Upton Sinclair's muckraking 1906 novel, *The Jungle*, a harrowing tale of the horrors of the unregulated Chicago meatpacking industry. In turn, Roosevelt enlisted the cooperation of the progressive and muckraker press to secure passage of the bills.

def•i•ni•tion

> The **muckrakers** were crusading journalists active at the end of the nineteenth century and beginning of the twentieth, who exposed social, political, and economic injustice, malfeasance, and scandal. Coined by Theodore Roosevelt, the term was inspired by a character in John Bunyan's allegory of Christian life and values, *The Pilgrim's Progress* (1678), who labors with a "muckrake" to clean the filth he finds on the stable floor.

Domestic Agenda

Roosevelt was the first president to package his domestic policies under a single compelling label—the Square Deal. The package consisted of legislative initiatives and policy directives designed to curb the abuses of big business—especially the trusts—while also shielding big business from the demands of what he identified as the radical fringe of labor. Trusts were the massive corporate monopolies that populated the corporate American landscape at the end of the nineteenth century and beginning of the twentieth.

Following Theodore Roosevelt's precedent, Woodrow Wilson bundled his chief domestic initiatives under the label of the New Freedom; Franklin Roosevelt offered the New Deal; Harry S. Truman, the Fair Deal; John F. Kennedy, the New Frontier; and Lyndon Johnson—so far the last of the packager-labeler presidents—proposed the Great Society.

Labor Leadership

Theodore Roosevelt was the first president to articulate a set of the legal rights of labor, and in this he created a precedent for the involvement of the chief executive in labor disputes and other industrial issues. Arguably, Grover Cleveland had thrust the presidency into the labor-capital struggle when he dispatched federal troops to bring

Tally _____

Theodore Roosevelt issued 1,091 executive orders during his nearly two terms in office. The combined total of executive orders issued by the 25 presidents who had preceded him was 1,259.

an end to the Pullman Strike of 1894 (see Chapter 13), but it is important to note that Cleveland sought to avoid the suggestion that he was intervening either on the side of labor or management by justifying the use of troops only to protect the processing and delivery of the U.S. mail. After Roosevelt, it became increasingly commonplace for presidents to intervene in major labor disputes, especially those deemed to involve the national interest.

Environmental Leadership

Roosevelt regarded America's forests and wilderness as national treasures to be preserved for the enjoyment of all as well as for their own intrinsic value. He used his bully pulpit to spread the gospel of "conservation" (what we would today call environmentalism) and to promote a program of conservation legislation, including laws that set aside some 43 million acres of national forest to be protected either entirely or in part from commercial exploitation.

When Roosevelt's conservation program collided with congressional representation of farmers and industrialists (who needed water power), prompting Congress to enact legislation in 1908 transferring from the president to Congress the authority to create future national forests in certain western states, Roosevelt circumvented Congress by using executive orders to implement many of his conservation initiatives. Future presidents would follow Roosevelt's example and use executive orders at times as the virtual equivalent of legislative action by Congress.

Civil Service Reform

Not surprisingly, civil service reform occupied an important place in Roosevelt's progressive program. He picked up where some of his predecessors had left off, building on the Civil Service Commission to institutionalize a merit-based system of federal appointments and significantly reducing political patronage on the federal level.

The President as World Leader

The president who elbowed aside Congress to make room for the executive office in the formulation of the nation's domestic agenda did not hesitate to expand the presidential prerogative in the area traditionally defined as the province of the chief executive, foreign policy. Whereas other presidents, including William McKinley (see Chapter 13), took the lead in foreign policy, then sought the support of Congress, Roosevelt assumed virtually the entire authority and responsibility of foreign affairs with a minimum of legislative consultation.

Defining the United States as a World Power

Roosevelt claimed the Spanish-American War had permanently elevated the United States to the status of world power. As he presented the case to Congress in his first annual address on December 3, 1901, the United States now had "international duties no less than international rights." Thus Roosevelt first articulated the nation's global role, which would be enacted during Wilson's administration, when the United States entered the "European War"—World War I—to "make the world safe for democracy"; reprised on a grander scale in the FDR years during World War II; and would persist, for better or worse, through every presidential administration thereafter.

Roosevelt's boldest action as a self-defined world leader was the construction of the Panama Canal. After persuading Great Britain to relinquish its claim to joint control of a projected Central American canal, Roosevelt convinced Congress to ratify the Hay-Herrán Treaty with Colombia—which at the time included Panama—granting the United States the right to build a canal through a 10-mile-wide strip of land across the isthmus in return for a $10 million cash payment and an annuity. When the Colombian senate held out for more money, Roosevelt threatened to build his canal through Nicaragua instead, and when the Colombians stood firm, he made it clear that he was prepared to seize the isthmus by force. Roosevelt instead fanned into flame a flickering revolution, by which Panama became an independent republic. Ninety minutes after the new nation declared its independence, Roosevelt proclaimed U.S. recognition of it and, shortly afterward, the Panamanian government approved a canal treaty. The entire process was purely a presidential initiative. It was typical of Roosevelt's approach to foreign policy—and yet another executive precedent.

Hemispherical Leadership or Naked Imperialism?

In 1823, President James Monroe put the nations of Europe on notice that the United States would brook no interference from the Old World in the affairs of the New (see Chapter 7). In 1904, in the so-called Roosevelt Corollary to the Monroe Doctrine, the president asserted the right of the United States to intervene in the affairs of Latin American states that failed to pay their debts to European lenders and thereby invited intervention from European powers. "All that this country desires is to see the neighboring countries stable, orderly, and prosperous," Roosevelt informed Congress in his December 1904 message. "If a nation shows that it knows how to act with reasonable efficiency and decency in social and political matters, if it keeps order and pays its obligations, it need fear no interference by the United States." But if a country fails in any of these respects, "the Monroe Doctrine may force the United States, however reluctantly, ... to the exercise of an international police power." The Roosevelt Corollary has been criticized as baldly imperialist, but, criticism notwithstanding, it has repeatedly served as a precedent in a long history of U.S. intervention in the Central and South America as well as the Caribbean.

The Mystique of Office

Of the many precedents Roosevelt established, perhaps the most profound is also the most difficult to quantify or even describe. Roosevelt brought to the presidency his own romantic and visionary exuberance, endowing the office with a mystique that, despite subsequent presidential disappointments, failures, and scandals, endures.

The Least You Need to Know

♦ Roosevelt's progressive political philosophy drove him to reinvent and reinvigorate the presidency, borrowing from the examples of Hamilton, Jefferson, and Jackson to do so.

♦ Roosevelt conceived the chief duty of the president as representing the will of the people; however, he used his charisma and media savvy to influence and shape the popular will in ways he saw fit.

♦ Roosevelt was the nation's first environmentalist president, establishing the chief executive as the steward of the American land itself.

♦ Roosevelt positioned the United States as a genuinely global power.

15

Third-Party Politics

In This Chapter

- ◆ Taft narrows the concept of the presidency
- ◆ The Republican Party splinters into "Old Guards" and "progressives"
- ◆ Theodore Roosevelt repudiates Taft with his 1912 Bull Moose candidacy
- ◆ Party organization trumps charisma

The history of the American presidency is not a story of evolution in a straight upward line. Precedents are set, but not always consistently followed. The most significant executives, including Theodore Roosevelt, create new potential for the office, which predecessors variously follow, modify, expand, reject, or ignore. The theory of the presidency always advances, but the practice of the presidency moves forward as well as in retreat.

The presidency of Theodore Roosevelt was marked by many real and measurable achievements, but its potential, the legacy it enabled and inspired, proved far less certain, at least in the near term.

In Washington's Footsteps

After nearly two terms—he served three-and-a-half years of McKinley's unfinished second term—Theodore Roosevelt was a very popular president. Most Americans would enthusiastically have elected T. R. to another term, but he followed the two-term tradition established by Washington. A powerful presidency was a desirable legacy, but three terms (or nearly three) of a single powerful president risked creating a cult of personality inimical to democracy.

 Tally _____

> Taft received 7,679,006 popular votes (52 percent) and 321 electoral votes. His challenger, perennial Democratic candidate William Jennings Bryan, polled 6,409,106 votes (43 percent) and received 162 electoral votes. Socialist Party candidate Eugene V. Debs polled 420,858 votes (3 percent).

The Mission of William Howard Taft

T. R. was willing to leave the White House, but he was not willing to scrap the legacy created by his progressive presidency. Much as Andrew Jackson had handpicked his first-term secretary of state and second-term vice president, Martin Van Buren, to succeed him (see Chapter 9), Roosevelt anointed his secretary of war and trusted adviser, William Howard Taft.

Taft believed in Roosevelt's progressive reforms. What he did not believe in was the legitimacy of the power of the presidency to sustain those reforms without the full participation and cooperation of Congress. He saw his mission, therefore, as securing the enactment by Congress—in the form of enduring laws—of what the president had often left only in the form of executive orders.

What They Said _____

> Don't sit up nights thinking about making me President for that will never come and I have no ambition in that direction. Any party which would nominate me would make a great mistake.
>
> —William Howard Taft to Republican Party leaders, 1903

The Problem with Projection

Roosevelt had rejoiced in finding fellow progressive in William Howard Taft, but if you look at people and see only a reflection of yourself, you never truly see anyone. Much as Jackson had mistakenly assumed that Van Buren shared his force of personality as well as his political ideas, so Roosevelt made the error of assuming that Taft had picked up his philosophy of executive supremacy along with his progressivism.

Taft's Retreat

Roosevelt was brawny and broad, the physically vigorous product of the "strenuous life" he advocated. Taft stood 6-foot-2 and weighed 332 pounds, the combination of flaccid girth and florid handlebar mustache summoning to mind the image of a walrus. If Roosevelt was the physical incarnation of the progressive spirit, Taft was the "fat cat" of America's Gilded Age incarnate. His engagement with the progressive program was tempered by his innate political conservatism and a personal tendency to complacency.

Taft lacked Roosevelt's energy and empathy. He had no sense of the temper of the people, let alone a desire to engage that temper and manipulate it through speeches or the press. Roosevelt had built the executive into a bully pulpit; Taft never ascended it.

Taft's reticence was not entirely a matter of personal inclination. His political mission of translating the reforms Roosevelt made as president into laws enacted by Congress revealed the vast gulf that lay between Roosevelt's conception of the presidency and his own. For Roosevelt, personal presidential leadership combined with executive orders was sufficient to govern, but Taft could not accept as permanent T. R.'s enlargement of the presidency. Whereas Roosevelt, like Alexander Hamilton, believed that the president could do anything that was not explicitly forbidden by the Constitution, Taft wrote, in his 1916 *Our Chief Magistrate and His Powers*, that "the President can exercise no power which cannot be reasonably or fairly traced to some specific grant of power or justly implied [power] … either in the Constitution or in an act of Congress …." As if this view were not sufficiently opposed to Roosevelt's, Taft made the contrast even more absolute: "There is no undefined residuum of power which he can exercise because it seems to be in the public interest." T. R. had rested virtually all of the power he had claimed for the presidency, including the executive's supremacy over Congress, on what he saw as the presidential duty to represent and promote the public interest. Taft summarily rejected this. He believed in Roosevelt's progressive program, but he denied, under the Constitution, the sufficiency of the presidency alone to implement that program.

My judgment is that the view of ... Mr. Roosevelt, ascribing an undefined residuum of power to the president is an unsafe doctrine, and that it might lead under emergencies to results of an arbitrary character, doing irremediable injustice to private rights.

—William Howard Taft, 1916

A Civil War in the GOP

Taft prepared for congressional action a slate of legislation intended to enshrine in law the chief Roosevelt reforms. To the credit of the legislators, some of the progressive program was enacted. But Taft refused to ride herd on Congress when it balked. He was even less inclined to follow Roosevelt's example of appealing to the people to pressure Congress. He confined himself to proposing legislation, presenting an argument in favor of it, and then leaving the rest to Congress. This passivity was consistent with Taft's personality, but, more than that, it was the product of a concept of the presidency as narrow as Roosevelt's had been broad.

When Party Discipline Breaks Down

Taft's contraction of executive power and his deference to Congress might have resulted in a satisfactory government if Congress had been sufficiently united to take up the responsibilities Taft had conceded to it. But such was far from the case from 1909 to 1912.

Not only did congressional Democrats differ sharply with their Republican colleagues, the post-Roosevelt Republican Party was itself badly splintered into "Old Guard" conservatives on the one side and progressives on the other. Because party leadership within Congress had declined during the Roosevelt years—the president had assumed full leadership of the party—there was no standout Republican senator or representative to enforce party discipline. This presented a golden opportunity for a strong chief executive to take up the leadership mantle, but Taft was not that executive. Taft was a jurist by inclination and an administrator by profession. He was not a politician. Indeed, the presidency was the very first elective office he had held.

What They Said _____

It was as though a sharp sword had been succeeded by a roll of paper, legal size.

—Gifford Pinchot, former first chief of the U.S. Forest Service, on the contrast between Theodore Roosevelt and William Howard Taft

The turmoil in the Republican-controlled Congress came to a full-blown crisis in March 1910, when disgruntled Republican progressives joined forces with House Democrats to strip the Old Guard Republican speaker, Rep. Joseph Cannon, of much of his power.

Back to the People

The chaos in Congress had two immediate effects. One was to yield to the presidency governing power that this particular president really did not want. The other was to stir up discontent among the American people.

Theodore Roosevelt, like Andrew Jackson long before him, had told the people that they reigned supreme in the American government. Under Taft and a dysfunctional Congress, however, the government seemed utterly unresponsive to the people, and so, recalling their experience with T. R., they demanded that the president provide leadership of both Congress and his own party. Taft was just not up to it.

What They Said

Taft, who is such an admirable fellow, has shown himself such an utterly commonplace leader, good-natured, feebly well-meaning, but with plenty of small motive; and totally unable to grasp or put into execution any great policy.
—Theodore Roosevelt, 1911

The Bull Moose Charges

The American electorate registered its disgust with the divided and therefore, paralyzed Republican-dominated Congress by sweeping in a Democratic majority with the midterm elections of 1910. This rebuke only deepened the division between the right and left wings of the Republican Party, prompting Sen. Robert LaFollette of Wisconsin to create the National Progressive Republican League, which was virtually a splinter third party.

It was clear that the Republican Party needed a dynamic presidential candidate if it were to hold on to the White House in 1912. With the electorate crying out for a strong executive in the mold of Theodore Roosevelt, none other than Theodore Roosevelt would have been the obvious Republican nominee. But Taft, a reluctant speaker and an even more reticent campaigner, now felt himself moved to action, and embarked on a national stumping campaign in 1911, which succeeded in preempting the nomination before T. R.—still hesitant about a third-term presidency—even announced himself as a candidate.

Roosevelt Throws His Hat in the Ring

By the time Roosevelt broke both with the Old Guard, which backed Taft, and the progressives, who backed LaFollette, and announced himself as a candidate for the Republican nomination, Taft had already sewn it up. LaFollette, however, suffered a nervous collapse early in his campaign and was forced to withdraw. This gave Roosevelt the support of LaFollette's followers, and he embarked on a vigorous campaign.

> ### What They Said
>
> "My hat's in the ring. The fight is on, and I'm stripped to the buff."
> —Theodore Roosevelt, declaring his candidacy in 1912
>
> Roosevelt is credited with originating the expression *to throw one's hat in the ring*. He took it from the tradition of one fighter challenging another to a match by throwing his hat in the boxing ring.

The Emergence of the Primary

In 1910, Oregon became the first state to establish a *primary election*, in which voters, not the party leadership, chose presidential nominees. By 1912, a dozen states had adopted the primaries, and the election that year became the first real use of the primary system.

> **def•i•ni•tion**
>
> A **primary election** is an election for the purpose of choosing candidates for the next general election. The primary, which is not provided for in the Constitution, was a twentieth-century innovation.

Roosevelt won 9 of the 12 state primaries, the ailing LaFollette won 2, and Taft, the Republican incumbent, took just 1. Despite this demonstration of overwhelming popular support for Roosevelt, the Old Guard, which still dominated the Republican Party, chose Taft in those states that still nominated the presidential candidate through conventions and closed caucuses.

A Party Is Born

At the Republican National Convention in Chicago, the struggle between supporters of Taft and those of Roosevelt became deadlocked. Reasoning that the party was too deeply divided to give him the support he needed to win the general election, Roosevelt boldly called on his delegates to leave the convention hall and reconvene in nearby Auditorium Theatre. There, Roosevelt and his allies proclaimed the creation of the Progressive Party, which was soon popularly christened the Bull Moose Party, after T. R., responding to a reporter's query concerning the state of his health, bellowed "I'm as fit as a bull moose."

Thus, almost literally overnight and in the midst of a major party's national convention, the man who had radically transformed the presidency now attempted to do the same for the American political party process.

 Executive Event _____

On October 14, 1912, while Roosevelt was campaigning in Milwaukee, Wisconsin, John Schrank, a saloonkeeper, shot him at close range just as the candidate was about to enter an auditorium to give a speech. The bullet hit T. R.'s steel eyeglass case in the inner pocket of his frock coat, penetrating it, then burrowing into the 50-page manuscript of the evening's speech, also folded (thus doubling its thickness) in his coat pocket. Greatly slowed, the round lodged in Roosevelt's chest.

As an avid hunter, Roosevelt deemed himself an expert on gunshot wounds. Aware that he had no difficulty breathing and was not coughing up blood, he concluded that the wound was superficial. He therefore refused entreaties to rush to a hospital and instead delivered his speech, with blood vividly visible seeping through his shirt.

"Ladies and gentlemen," he began, "I don't know whether you fully understand that I have just been shot; but it takes more than a bullet to kill a Bull Moose." He then spoke for an hour and a half.

In the hospital, x-rays revealed that the bullet had passed through 3 inches of the former president's formidable chest, burying itself in the chest muscle. Physicians decided to leave the bullet in place rather than risk an operation to remove it. Roosevelt carried it for the rest of his life.

Third Party or Third Rail?

Theodore Roosevelt's concept of the presidency proved too big for the well-meaning but conservative Taft, yet apparently it was just the right size for a majority of the American electorate. Had the Republican Party recognized this and nominated Roosevelt in 1912, he would almost certainly have been elected. Instead, the party's Old Guard prevailed, and nominated the incumbent.

In the end, not even the Roosevelt charisma could overcome the power of the two long-established major political parties. T. R.'s third-party candidacy divided the Republican vote between Taft and himself, thereby giving the election to the Democrat, Woodrow Wilson.

Wilson was very different from Roosevelt. Whereas T. R. had the broad and brawny body of a scrapper, Wilson's 5-foot-11-inch frame gave him, at a modest 175 pounds, the appearance of a slight man. If Roosevelt was dynamic in appearance and movement, Wilson was studious, even aloof. If Roosevelt engaged the world with sleeves rolled, Wilson was clearly the quiet thinker, an idealist.

Tally _____

Roosevelt's bullet wound took him off the campaign trail for a week while he was hospitalized. In a spirit of fair play, both Taft and Democrat Woodrow Wilson suspended their campaigns while T. R. was in the hospital. It is impossible to know what effect, if any, the suspension of campaigning had on the outcome of the race. Roosevelt drew 27 percent of the popular vote, 4,126,020 ballots, to Woodrow Wilson's 6,286,820 (42 percent). The Republican incumbent, Taft, came in behind the two with 3,483,922 votes (23 percent). Socialist candidate Eugene V. Debs polled 901,255 votes (6 percent). Roosevelt took 88 electoral votes; Wilson, 435; and Taft, only 8.

And yet the American people correctly saw that this Democrat offered them far more of what they had gotten from Roosevelt than they would ever get from the Republican Taft. Without the support of a major party, the electorate could not bring itself to vote for Roosevelt himself, but they did send to the White House another progressive, who brought the return of an executive strong enough to challenge the traditional and the constitutional boundaries of the presidency.

The Least You Need to Know

- Declining to run for what he considered a third term, Theodore Roosevelt handpicked William Howard Taft to carry on his legacy of progressive reform.

- The innately conservative Taft retreated from Roosevelt's greatly expanded concept of presidential responsibility and power.

- Taft repeatedly deferred to the Republican-dominated Congress, which, however, was so deeply divided between the party's Old Guard and progressive wings that it proved unresponsive to the demands of an electorate accustomed to Roosevelt's dynamism.

- In 1912, Theodore Roosevelt split with the Republican Party, taking the progressive wing with him to form the Progressive (or Bull Moose) Party, which came in second to Democrat Woodrow Wilson in the year's general election for president, leaving Republican Taft in third place.

16

Wilson's World

In This Chapter

◆ The president as teacher to the nation and the world

◆ The New Freedom

◆ World War I and the postwar peace process

◆ Rejection of Wilson's internationalism

The splintering of the Republican Party in 1912 presented the Democrats with a great opportunity. The question was, *what would they do with it?*

Progressivism cut across party lines, and the same forces that split the Republicans also tore at the Democrats. Although the populist wing of that party had spoken up the loudest in recent years, especially through perennial presidential candidate William Jennings Bryan, the Democrats also had an influential conservative faction answerable to business interests. The members of this wing were quick to point out the grave risk of offering the presidential nomination yet again to Bryan, who had been defeated in 1896, 1900, and 1908, or any other populist. Their objections created what looked to be a hopeless deadlock in the party's national convention of 1912. Would the Democrats, mired in discord, throw away almost certain victory?

Enter the Professor

The party found a most unlikely answer. At the convention, conservatives backed Alabama representative Oscar W. Underwood, and the party progressives divided their support between House speaker Champ Clark of Missouri and Woodrow Wilson, Ph.D., a political science professor who had, as president of Princeton from 1902 to 1910, revitalized that institution. This achievement attracted the attention of New Jersey Democrats, who backed Wilson for governor. Progressives believed they had one of their own, whereas party bosses banked on having a pliable political naïf to manipulate. Wilson won—and stunned the bosses by declaring war on them in a program of statewide progressive reform that became the marvel of the nation.

Convention delegates cast 45 nondecisive ballots before William Jennings Bryan reasserted himself into the party's destiny by throwing his formidably enthusiastic support behind the East Coast progressive Wilson rather than fellow Midwestern populist Clark. Wilson was nominated on the forty-sixth ballot.

A Presidency of Radical Reform

As explained at the close of Chapter 15, where the 1912 election tally is given, Wilson won a plurality victory in the general election, defeating fellow progressive Theodore Roosevelt and leaving the "mainstream" Republican candidate, incumbent William Howard Taft, in the dust, a distant third.

Checks and Balances: Breaking Down the Walls

Wilson wrote a distinguished series of books on American history and politics, some intended for a popular readership, others for an academic audience. It is a sure bet that few Democratic Party leaders read his more serious works. If they had, they might not have been so eager to put him in office.

In 1879, while still an undergrad, Wilson published an academic article calling for the enhancement of congressional power by tearing down the wall separating the presidency from Congress. In emulation of the British *cabinet government*, Wilson proposed amending the Constitution to give the members of the president's cabinet seats in Congress, so that they could initiate and shape legislation. This, Wilson argued, would shift the center of government to the legislature, redefining them as the symbolic and legal, but not the political, head of state.

Next, in 1885, while earning his doctorate at Johns Hopkins, he wrote *Congressional Government*, again calling for refashioning the American system on the pattern of the British cabinet government, injecting the executive branch into the legislative. Now however, Wilson also condemned what he deemed congressional domination of the executive branch. By the early 1900s, his political thought completed its academic development when he frankly argued for strong national leadership vested in a powerful president who initiated and championed legislation, using, if necessary, a direct appeal to the people.

def•i•ni•tion

In a **cabinet government**, the executive and legislative branches come together in the prime minister's cabinet, the members of which hold seats in Parliament and, like the prime minister himself, are subject to questioning from and debate with other members.

Where Taft Failed, Wilson Triumphed

Sometimes American presidential politics takes more ironic twists than a best-selling novel. Theodore Roosevelt passed the torch of executive dominance to William Howard Taft, who promptly extinguished it by his nearly abject deference to Congress. In 1912, Roosevelt repudiated Taft and ran as a Bull Moose, promising to reprise his own pre-Taft presidency. This was precisely what a majority of the voters wanted; however, instead of electing Roosevelt to reinstate the Roosevelt-style presidency, they chose Woodrow Wilson—to reinstate the Roosevelt-style presidency.

Wilson intended not merely to emulate Roosevelt, but to achieve what Taft had unsuccessfully set out to do. He intended to rationalize in theory and in practice the Roosevelt-style executive, carving out a presidency in which dynamic leadership through a direct relation with the people became the rule rather than the exception. He meant to institutionalize the expanded presidency permanently.

❝❞ What They Said

Whatever else we may think or say of Theodore Roosevelt, we must admit he was an aggressive leader. He led Congress—he was not driven by Congress. We may not approve of his methods but we must concede that he made Congress follow him.

—Woodrow Wilson, 1909

The Brain of the Nation

As Wilson saw it, the president was not just a steward of the people's welfare, but the brain of the nation. His job was to think through problems and opportunities; formulate policy; educate the people to that policy, thereby gaining their understanding and support; then, backed by the people, work through Congress to implement the policy.

Unitizing Government

For this model of the presidential government to work, Wilson understood that he would have to act on his earlier theory of borrowing from the British cabinet system. He approached this not by amending the Constitution, but by offering himself to Congress as its partner.

In his very first address to a joint session of Congress, he announced that he would approach the legislators as "a human being trying to cooperate with other human beings in a common service." Wilson regularly met with legislators on important bills, and he made it a point to visit *them* in their Capitol offices rather than summon them to the Oval Office. It was a precedent many chief executives have followed since.

Executive Event

Wilson's leadership of the Congress proved remarkably productive. During his first term, Wilson led the legislature in enacting a comprehensive program of progressive reform, including introduction of a federal income tax with ratification of the Sixteenth Amendment; the lowering of tariffs; passage of the Federal Reserve Act of 1913; sweeping currency banking reform; new anti-trust legislation in passage of the Federal Trade Commission Act and the Clayton Anti-Trust Act; and labor reform with the Adamson Act, giving railway workers an 8-hour day, and the Child Labor Act, which curtailed children's working hours.

Party Reform

In addition to the innovative concept of legislative partnership, Wilson also reasserted the president's role as leader of his party. Like Thomas Jefferson (see Chapter 6), Wilson used party discipline to aid in the passage of key legislation. Whenever innovative human-to-human cooperation might fail, old-fashioned party loyalty could fill the breach.

To get the party under presidential control, Wilson sought to weaken the old Democratic machine by promoting the spread of the primary system (see Chapter 15), which would put the choice of a party's nominee in the hands of the electorate and remove it from those of the party bosses. This would ensure that the president had a direct relationship with the people, undiminished by the party machine or by Congress.

The Ideological Presidency

Not since John Adams and Thomas Jefferson had the nation seen a presidency so thoroughly grounded in political ideology. Wilson's ideas were expressed in two arenas, the domestic and the international.

The New Freedom

Wilson supplanted Roosevelt's Square Deal and New Nationalism with a new domestic program, which he called the New Freedom.

The Square Deal/New Nationalism program had sought to protect the rights of consumers and labor by regulating big business. Although Roosevelt had earned the nickname "Trust Buster" by his vigorous application of the Sherman Anti-Trust Act of 1890 against such egregious *vertical monopolies* as Standard Oil, he accepted as a fact of life that big business would naturally and inevitably tend to create trusts (monopolies) and that strong laws were required to control them.

def•i•ni•tion

In a **vertical monopoly**, a business not only dominates and controls its own industry to the exclusion of competition, it controls all industries related to it.

Wilson's New Freedom took a different approach to eliminating the trusts. Instead of regulating them by means of the central authority of the government, the New Freedom sought to create an economic environment in which business would no longer have the capacity to create trusts. This required a coordinated package of sweeping economic legislation, including tariff reform (the Underwood Tariff Act of 1913), the creation of a Federal Reserve system to regulate and stabilize currency (generally freeing up credit for all businesses, regardless of size), and new anti-trust legislation (the Clayton Anti-Trust Act and the Federal Trade Commission Act, both of 1914) that did not "bust" trusts so much as prevent the unfair business competition that made them possible. Competition would itself curb monopolistic practices, provided that competition was protected by law.

The New Spoils System

The New Freedom required a whole new set of federal administrative appointees. Wilson's inclination was to make the appointments on a nonpartisan merit basis, but it soon became clear to him that, to keep the party firmly in his control, he needed to partially reinstate the old spoils system (see Chapter 8), distributing at least some federal appointments as rewards for party loyalty. This alienated congressional Republicans.

A New Level of World Leadership

Wilson readily embraced Roosevelt's expansion of the role of the United States in the world and the role of the president as a world leader. Whereas Roosevelt had taken a pragmatic approach to foreign policy, acting in ways he believed would be of direct and immediate benefit to the United States, Wilson was more the idealist and the internationalist. He believed that the president of the United States could influence other leaders to conduct their governments in an enlightened manner that would contribute to the stability, prosperity, and peace of the world.

In practice, Wilson's idealism did not necessarily produce disinterested and beneficent results. Wishing to stabilize the turbulent government of the nation's neighbor to the south, Mexico, Wilson withheld recognition and aid to the government under President Victoriano Huerta until it had met the test of what he called "constitutional legitimacy"—that is, had demonstrated adherence to its own constitution. Wilson was outspoken about his intention to "teach" the leaders of Latin America how to govern.

Wilson's high-handed meddling—call it ideological imperialism—even moved him to order the military occupation of Veracruz in 1914 and almost certainly contributed in 1916 to cross-border raids by the popular Mexican revolutionary leader Pancho Villa, which resulted in the deaths of 14 U.S. soldiers and 10 civilian residents of Columbus, New Mexico.

The Presidency in a World War

The culmination of Wilson's presidency as a world leader came in 1917, when he brought the United States into the "Great War" (World War I). Wilson who maintained U.S. neutrality during his first term, then campaigned for reelection on the slogan, "He Kept Us Out of War." Inaugurated for the second time in March 1917, he asked Congress for a declaration of war the very next month.

Although there were economically compelling reasons for America's entry into the conflict—U.S. financial and industrial firms were heavily invested in the Allies (principally Britain and France) and were eager to protect their investments by assuring an Allied victory—Wilson's appeal to Congress and the American people was idealistic. Germany, he argued, was a threat to democracy and to future world peace, and the United States had a duty to join the fight to "make the world safe for democracy."

What They Said

He thinks he is another Jesus Christ come upon earth to reform men.
—French president Georges Clemenceau, of Wilson at the Paris Peace Conference, 1919

Emergency Powers

William McKinley (see Chapter 13) was the first president as commander in chief during a foreign war, but the foreign war Wilson now administered was unlike any that had come before. World War I was vast, and it required the conscription, training, equipping, and transportation of an army of unprecedented size. All of the nation's resources had to be directed toward raising, preparing, and maintaining a vast military machine, which meant that the industrial economy had to be put under federal control. Through a combination of executive orders and congressional legislation, Wilson acquired a broad range of presidential powers, including (through the Lever Food and Fuel Control Act of 1917) total control of the importation, manufacturing, warehousing and stockpiling, mining, and distribution of practically everything, from commodities to food to manufactured goods.

For the most part, the nation and the Congress embraced Wilson's idealistic and internationalist motives for war, giving him all that he asked for. But when the Senate attempted to tack onto the Lever Act an amendment giving it authority to create a committee to oversee the conduct of the war—the very thing that a joint congressional committee had done during the Civil War—Wilson stood firm against what he called "an assumption on the part of the legislative body of the executive work of the administration." Such was his stubbornness, as well as the power of his popular image as *the* commander in chief, that the Senate backed down without a fight, and the amendment was withdrawn.

The wartime powers Wilson amassed for the presidency dwarfed those Lincoln had claimed during the Civil War (see Chapter 11), created a model for the office during the *second* world war (see Chapter 19), and have remained influential ever since. It is now largely accepted that, during a major war, the president may assume virtually dictatorial powers.

A "War to End All Wars"

For the United States, which was not menaced by Germany, World War I was a war of choice rather than necessity. Woodrow Wilson saw U.S. entry into the charnel house of European combat as the price of a seat at the table around which the post-war future of the world would be decided. He wanted the United States to play a leading role in those decisions. In fact, *he* wanted to make them.

America's entry into the war, at a low point in Allies' fortunes, turned the tide against Germany, and after that country surrendered, agreeing to an armistice on November 11, 1918, Wilson personally headed the U.S. delegation to the Paris Peace Conference. Instead of punishing Germany and its allies, Wilson wanted to create a magnanimous peace that would make the Great War the "war to end all wars."

Wilson's intense idealism blinded him to the political realities at home. He made no attempt to generate bipartisan support for his treaty plans or its centerpiece, the League of Nations, a forum for the peaceful resolution of international conflict. Wilson excluded Republicans from the peace delegation he led, and unduly politi-cized the League of Nations by appealing to voters to reelect a Democratic Congress in 1918 pledged to support the league. That the 1918 midterm elections gave the Republicans majorities in both houses failed to signal to Wilson that he was out of touch with the sentiments of his own countrymen.

Defeat

Wilson spent six months in Paris working on the treaty and the league. During that time, the new Republican Congress steered the nation sharply away from involve-ment in world affairs, substituting isolationism for the policies of Wilson as well as Theodore Roosevelt.

Wilson's failure to consult the Congress in the peace process prompted Sen. Henry Cabot Lodge to lead Republican opposition to the League of Nations. Wilson refused to negotiate with Lodge and the others, resolving instead to bring popular pressure on the Senate by taking his case directly to the people with a grueling 9,500-mile transcontinental whistle-stop speaking tour.

On September 25, 1919, exhausted by war and by peace, Wilson collapsed following a speech in Pueblo, Colorado. He was rushed back to Washington, where, a week later, he suffered a stroke, which left him partially paralyzed and significantly debilitated. In the depths of illness, Wilson instructed his followers and advisers to accept no compromise on the League of Nations, and, in this climate, the Senate rejected the Treaty of Versailles and the league.

Wilson served out the rest of his term as a shadow of a president. His wife, Edith Bolling Wilson, quietly carried out much of the government's day-to-day business. The nation no longer much cared. The American people, on whom Wilson had staked everything, voted into the White House in 1920 an affably pliable man who made but a single campaign pledge—a national "return to normalcy."

The Least You Need to Know

- ◆ Woodrow Wilson saw the chief executive's role as "teaching" Americans—and all nations—how to govern themselves to promote stability, prosperity, and peace.

- ◆ Wilson was a progressive who sought to make presidential leadership of the legislative branch a permanent feature of American government.

- ◆ Wilson's stubborn idealism sometimes alienated political allies and opponents alike.

- ◆ Wilson led the United States into World War I to "make the world safe for democracy," but by spurning the Republican majority in Congress, ensured that the Senate would reject the postwar League of Nations.

Part 5

From "Normalcy" to the Personal Presidency

Warren G. Harding had no aspirations to personal or national greatness but promised instead a "return to normalcy." Under Harding, the presidency bowed to the legislature, and the office itself became an instrument of the party rather than a headquarters of government. The corruption that dogged the Harding White House was largely swept away by his successor, Calvin Coolidge, who nevertheless made no move to restore the presidency to the power it had had under Roosevelt and Wilson. It was a passive presidency that Herbert Hoover inherited, and it proved tragically inadequate to cope with the onset of the Great Depression. It took another reformer, Franklin Delano Roosevelt, to rebuild the executive branch, once again putting it at the heart of government. Even more than Jackson and Lincoln, FDR made the presidency personal, a legacy that reached a high point with John F. Kennedy.

17

The Smoke-Filled Room

In This Chapter

- ◆ America rejects the Wilsonian presidency
- ◆ Politics of the "smoke-filled room"
- ◆ Harding offers "normalcy" and "party government"
- ◆ Legacy of scandal

Woodrow Wilson was not a candidate in 1920, but the election was nevertheless a mandate on his presidency. The Democratic challenger to Republican Warren G. Harding was James M. Cox, who, as governor, brought to Ohio even more progressive reforms than Governor Wilson had brought to New Jersey. He pledged to continue Wilson's progressive program and to see to it that the Senate approved League of Nations membership.

The election of 1920 was the first in which women voted, and it was widely assumed that they would turn out in large numbers for the liberal, progressive Cox. In fact, the women, like the men, delivered the White House to Harding in a landslide. Cox presented himself as the heir to the Wilson presidency, and was rejected resoundingly.

Wilsonian Sunset

The American people were wrung out and worn out by war. Like the stricken, semi-paralyzed Wilson, they craved bed rest, preferably with the covers pulled up.

Wilson had demanded thought and sacrifice. Warren G. Harding offered a "return to normalcy," by which he meant the right of the American people to be left alone.

What They Said

America's present need is not heroics, but healing; not nostrums, but normalcy; not revolution, but restoration; not agitation, but adjustment; not surgery, but serenity; not the dramatic, but the dispassionate; not experiment, but equipoise; not submergence in internationality, but sustainment in triumphant nationality.

—Warren G. Harding, campaign speech, May 14, 1920

An End to Internationalism

President Wilson had staked his legacy on the League of Nations. For him it encompassed all that he stood for in his effort to put the United States at the center of world affairs. And the American people, who understood this very well, voted for Harding, whose campaign was focused relentlessly on rejection of the league. "A world super-government," Harding declared in his March 4, 1921, inaugural address, "is contrary to everything we cherish and can have no sanction by our Republic." Whereas Wilson had defined world leadership as the very essence of American democracy, Harding condemned it as un-American. And whereas Wilson had sought to inspire the people to sacrifice in the cause of world democracy, Harding wanted nothing more than to make them feel good about forsaking such sacrifice.

Lame Duck Defiance

Harding wanted to retreat from what he and his fellow Republicans called "executive autocracy" and to return the balance of governing power to the legislature.

To drive home this message, Congress, in the late spring of 1920, passed an act to repeal the array of the wartime laws that had given the president extraordinary emergency powers. Now that the war was over, repeal made good sense. President Wilson, however, chose to interpret it as a personal rebuke as well as an assault on the presidency. Because the bill had been passed just before Congress adjourned for the summer, the president declined to sign it, thereby issuing a pocket veto.

It was a symbolic gesture, which Wilson knew would not stick. As the public saw it, the president's pocket-veto contempt for the overwhelming will of Congress smacked of petty tyranny.

The Rise of the Party Hack

Both the Democratic and Republican parties had retreated from the reforms that had begun with the election of 1912, especially the proliferation of primary elections, and instead chose their nominees through a process of closed-door meetings, designed to deliver a nominee the delegates would rubber-stamp. Despite thickly populated fields, neither party had a standout candidate.

No fewer than 17 potential nominees offered themselves at the Republican National Convention in Chicago. On the first ballot, Warren G. Harding ran sixth, and, over the next eight ballots, the convention was deadlocked between the two front-runners, U.S. Army general Leonard Wood and Illinois governor Frank O. Lowden. The trouble was that neither of these men was a party loyalist, pliable to the will of the party leaders, who cast about for a reliable party man who also possessed sufficient appeal to draw votes. Ideas, a political program, a philosophy of government—these were not only unnecessary in a candidate, they were deemed serious liabilities.

Getting In

Harry M. Daugherty played a new role in American presidential politics, that of political strategist and manager—in short, the candidate's "handler." It was he who massaged the bosses to ease his candidate, dark horse Warren G. Harding, into the nomination. The deadlock between the front-runners gave him a perfect opportunity, and by the ninth ballot, Harding had pulled ahead of the pack—though he still needed an absolute majority to win. That came on the tenth ballot. For his efforts on behalf of Harding, Daugherty was appointed U.S. attorney general.

What They Said _____

I don't expect Senator Harding to be nominated on the first, second, or third ballots, but I think we can afford to take chances that about 11 minutes after two, Friday morning of the convention, when 15 or 12 weary men are sitting around a table, someone will say: "Who will we nominate?" At that decisive time, the friends of Harding will suggest him and we can well afford to abide by the result.

—Harry M. Daugherty, shortly before the 1920 Republican National Convention

Warren G. Harding was the candidate as party man, not the people's choice, but the product of a "smoke-filled room," a phrase coined in 1920 by an Associated Press reporter who described the secretive process by which Harding was effectively nominated in a meeting of cigar-smoking party power brokers held in a private room at Chicago's Blackstone Hotel. Since then, in American politics a "smoke-filled room" has meant a meeting of a party's inner circle to choose a political candidate without regard to the will of the people.

An Ordinary Man

Although the people had not chosen him as their candidate, Harding was nevertheless the embodiment of the self-satisfied American Midwestern middle class. An affable newspaper publisher from Marion, Ohio, he was so eager to please that (as the president himself recounted in a speech to the National Press Club in 1922) his father, with a shake of his head, remarked to him one day, "Warren, it's a good thing you wasn't born a gal. … Because you'd be in the family way all the time. You can't say no."

Harding was an avid golfer and poker player, who served as an Ohio state senator (1899–1903), lieutenant governor of Ohio (1903–1905), and U.S. senator (1915–1921). If his prepresidential political career was undistinguished, it was also blameless, and because he had no political enemies, consistently voted the party line, had no significant agenda of his own, was likeable, good looking in a middle-aged way, and hailed from a key electoral state, he made an ideal party candidate.

Tally

Harding landslided his Democratic opponent by taking 61 percent of the popular vote, 16,152,200, and 404 electoral votes. Governor Cox polled 9,147,353 votes (35 percent), and Socialist Eugene Debs, 915,490 (3 percent).

After the larger-than-life vision of T. R. and the formidable intellect of Wilson, Harding came across as the president not for Jackson's common man, but for the ordinary man—and, in this first election open to women, the ordinary woman as well.

Party Government

Harding spoke of restoring "party government," which, to modern ears, sounds negative if not downright reprehensible; but Harding understood the concept as a laudable alternative to the "personal government" of Woodrow Wilson, which, Harding implied, had verged on dictatorship. Party government described the presidential practice of cooperating with Congress in all matters of government, legislative as well as administrative, marshaling party discipline to promote a desired political program. "In contrast, personal government was dominated by the president over the legislature.

Party government implied a president's working closely with the party's congressional leadership; in practice, however, Harding did not so much collaborate with the Republican majority in Congress as he consistently deferred to it. The problem with this retreat from presidential leadership was that, ever since the administration of Theodore Roosevelt, the power of Congress had been contracting and, with it, the authority of the House speaker. Gone was the powerful speaker Henry Clay had created (see Chapter 7). Thus, although Harding ceded authority back to Congress, the congressional leadership failed to regain its former potency. Harding and the speaker, therefore, could not enforce sufficient party discipline to carry out a coherent political program.

Executive Event

The first real assault on party discipline—by which party leaders could count on members of Congress to vote on strict party lines—came in 1913, with ratification of the Seventeenth Amendment, which introduced direct popular election of senators instead of selection by state legislatures. This meant that senators were no longer simply the choice of the parties; they were the choice of the people—and answerable to them.

A strong executive, such as Roosevelt or Wilson, enforced party discipline directly through the presidency, but Harding was hardly a strong executive. On the domestic front, his passivity and the absence of leadership in Congress led to a combination of executive and legislative inaction. The results in the arena of foreign affairs were more startling. Congress increasingly usurped the formulation and conduct of foreign policy, traditional preserve of the president.

Isolationist Republicans passed legislation to shrink the U.S. military establishment, especially the navy. This, they believed, would force the president to convene an international disarmament conference in Washington, thereby further reducing the need for an expensive military.

For his part, Harding was not opposed to the conference, but he believed that the United States should deal from a position of power. He had run on a platform opposed to the League of Nations, but, in the absence of an effective league, he believed that the United States should build up, not diminish, its fleet for protection from foreign aggression. It was a prudent position, but the president was unwilling to back it up by taking a stand against Congress. As usual, he behaved like the "gal who couldn't say no." Moreover, instead of attending the disarmament conference personally, he assigned his secretary of state, Charles Evans Hughes, to head the U.S. delegation, which was rounded out by two senators, Henry Cabot Lodge and Oscar W. Underwood. Such a concession of executive authority to the legislature would have been unthinkable to Woodrow Wilson, especially in the international arena.

Scandalous!

Despite making at least two highly distinguished cabinet appointments—Hughes as secretary of state and Andrew Mellon as secretary of the treasury—the Harding administration, like that of Ulysses S. Grant (see Chapter 12), was overrun with party hacks, opportunists, and outright criminals.

The spoils system had returned with a vengeance, and the result was an avalanche of scandals, the most infamous of which was Teapot Dome. As part of an effort to undo many of the conservation measures Theodore Roosevelt had initiated (and both Taft and Wilson had supported), Albert B. Fall, Harding's secretary of the interior, made many changes in the disposition of public lands. Among these was a decision to lease to private petroleum companies oil fields at Teapot Dome in Wyoming and Elk Hill in California, which had been reserved to ensure a supply of fuel oil for the U.S. Navy. This may have been questionable policy from a national security standpoint, but it was not in itself illegal. The crime was that Fall accepted loans and other gifts in return for granting the leases to the oil companies of Edward L. Doheny and Harry F. Sinclair.

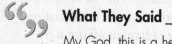

Like Grant, Harding probably did not profit from any of the felonies that dogged his administration. Like Grant, he was so passive an executive that he simply lost touch with his own executive departments. Nevertheless, even without the other scandals, Teapot Dome alone would likely have triggered the impeachment of Warren Harding had he not fallen ill during a combination cross-country speaking tour and vacation (including a fishing trip to Alaska, which made Harding the first U.S. president to visit that territory purchased from Russia in 1867). He succumbed to the effects of food poisoning, pneumonia, and a pulmonary embolism on August 2, 1923.

The scandals of fraud and graft were further colored by lurid rumors of Harding's two adulterous affairs, one with Carrie Phillips, the wife of his close friend James Phillips, which Harding kept quiet with hush-money payments that ended only with the president's death; the other (sometimes carried on simultaneously with the Phillips affair) with Nan Britton, 30 years Harding's junior, with whom he conceived a daughter on his Senate office sofa in 1919. Harding secretly paid Britton child support money, hand-carried to her by Secret Service agents.

Sex scandals were not new to the presidency. During Grover Cleveland's first campaign in 1884, the *Buffalo Evening Telegraph* exposed the candidate's affair with Maria C. Halpin, which produced in 1874 an illegitimate son. Instead of acting to deny or otherwise cover up the affair, Cleveland instructed his campaign staff to tell the truth. They did, and Cleveland was elected. In contrast, the Harding sex scandals remained rumors, confirmed only long after his death, and served to blacken his name all the more.

To be sure, Harding did not set the precedent for presidential infidelity, but the rumors, combined with the other scandals, prepared the public to view the presidency itself with a permanently jaundiced eye. The American people genuinely mourned the death of Warren Harding, but they were also somewhat relieved by his passing. His feckless passivity, total absence of vision, and all those scandals left the office of the chief executive in a depressingly diminished state, which added to the prevailing national cynicism of the Roaring Twenties.

The Least You Need to Know

- The candidacy of Warren G. Harding, an affable political nonentity, was the product of a "smoke-filled room" in which political bosses met to choose a president who would benefit the party first and the country second.

- Harding dramatically contracted the scope of the presidency, retreating from the activism of Theodore Roosevelt and Woodrow Wilson.

- Harding promised a "return to normalcy" and to "party government," in which the executive is voluntarily subordinated to the direction of the majority party in Congress.

- Dogged by political and sexual scandal, the Harding years cast an aura of disrepute on the presidency.

Chapter 18

The Politics of Silence

In This Chapter

♦ Coolidge continues Harding's passive presidency

♦ Coolidge's popularity and PR savvy

♦ Hoover introduces the moral presidency

♦ The Great Depression tests the hands-off executive

Most Americans were outraged by the scandals of the Harding era, but not by the Harding presidency. After a brief economic recession immediately following World War I, the Harding years had seen a sustained spike in prosperity, and the people were pleased that Vice President Calvin Coolidge, who succeeded Harding, clearly intended to continue his hands-off, minimal-intervention approach to government.

It was almost as if it didn't much matter whether the president were dead or alive. Affable, passive, pliant, Harding had ushered in a new era of reticent government. Under Calvin Coolidge, the silence would be nearly deafening.

Silent Cal: The Inactive Executive

In the case of Warren G. Harding, passivity of leadership, which was really no leadership at all, was a personal trait, the product of a genetic predisposition. In Coolidge, however, it was more a self-conscious, practiced skill.

As president, Coolidge would become legendary for his determined inactivity, but, in contrast to Harding, there were thresholds—isolated and extreme, that, once crossed, prompted intervention. When Harding's death thrust Coolidge into the Oval Office, his first step was to clean house.

But a quick and thorough purge of the tainted remnants of the Harding administration was the absolute limit to Coolidge's reforms. It was much like his response to the news of President Harding's death conveyed to him in the wee hours of the morning of August 3, 1923. The vice president was vacationing at his father's home in Plymouth Notch, Vermont, when his stenographer drove up, woke the senior Coolidge, and told him what had happened. Father in turn woke son, and the two knelt briefly in prayer. At 2:47 A.M., the senior Coolidge, who happened to be the local justice of the peace, administered the oath of office. This done, Calvin Coolidge, president of the United States, went back to sleep.

After tidying up the mess Harding had left behind, President Coolidge took his hands off government, then settled in for the political equivalent of a nice long nap. As for the American people, come 1924, they voiced their approval of this executive somnolence by voting "Silent Cal" to a term in his own right.

His campaign slogan? "Keep Cool with Coolidge."

 Tally _____

> Coolidge polled 15,725,016 popular votes (54 percent) and 382 electoral votes. His Democratic challenger, Rep. John Davis of West Virginia, received 8,385,586 votes, just 29 percent of the popular vote, which garnered 139 electoral votes. Seventeen percent of the vote that might have gone to Davis went instead to Progressive Party candidate Robert M. LaFollette, who polled 4,822,856 popular votes and 13 electoral votes.

Personality and PR

Will Rogers, beloved Oklahoma-born political humorist of the 1920s and 1930s, remarked of "Silent Cal" Coolidge, "He don't say much, but when he does say somethin', he don't say much." More recently, presidential historians Sidney M. Milkis and Michael Nelson observed, "Coolidge raised inactivity to an art." After his retirement, the former president himself wrote that he never felt it was his "duty to attempt to coerce Senators or Representatives .... The people sent them to Washington." He went on to observe that he had "avoided almost entirely a personal opposition" to Congress, "which I think was of more value to the country than the attempt to prevail through arousing personal fear."

The curious thing about Coolidge's philosophy of government was that he apparently saw the relationship between the executive and legislative branches as naturally adversarial, which was emotionally upsetting to the nation. This being the case, and because the people were satisfied with the status quo, the best course was to keep quiet and let the legislature go its own way.

It would be both obvious and easy to assume that the near dormancy of Silent Cal must have removed him both from the public eye in his own time and barred the possibility of his having any lasting influence on the presidency.

Both assumptions would be wrong.

Slight in build, average in height (5 feet, 9 inches), lips tightly pursed, eyes small and deep set, complexion ghostly pale with delicate features, and possessed of a speaking voice (when he did speak) marked by a nasal New England twang, Coolidge was not physically cut out to be a magnetic public figure. And yet he was one of the most popular of American presidents. In part this was due to the good fortune of his serving in a prosperous time, but it was also the case that Coolidge worked hard at developing cordial relations with the press. Tight lipped he might have been, yet he held more press conferences than any other president before or since (up through the administration of George W. Bush), establishing the White House press conference not merely as a precedent but as a veritable institution.

Although history would remember Franklin Roosevelt's "fireside chats" (see Chapter 19) as the first masterful use of radio by a chief executive, it was actually Coolidge who was the very first to exploit the brand-new medium (the first commercial station in the United States, Pittsburgh's KDKA, having debuted in 1920). He understood that his unimposing physical presence, combined with his reticent and rather whiny New England twang, made him less than impressive as an orator. Radio, however, was an intimate medium to which he was quite well suited. His 1923 State of the Union address was the first ever broadcast, and it was so well received by the listening public that Coolidge insisted on another first—a radio broadcast from the 1924 Republican National Convention, which gave the American electorate a front-row seat in a process traditionally reserved for delegates only.

If the popularity of the Coolidge presidential personality is surprising, so is the effect of his legacy. From his example, future presidents learned that people respond to their president as a human being, and they also learned that, just as people did not demand bigger-than-life personalities in their personal friends, so they could establish a bond with a quiet and reserved president. Public appeal did not have to be based on the bold strokes of a hypercharismatic presence.

The more profound aspect of the Coolidge legacy, however, was the studied inactivity of his presidency. "You hare a lot of jokes every once in a while about 'Silent Cal' Coolidge," President Ronald Reagan remarked in 1981. "The joke is on the people who make the jokes. Look at his record. He cut the taxes four times. We had probably the greatest growth and prosperity that we've ever known. I have taken heed of that because if he did that by doing nothing, maybe that's the answer." Coolidge was the patron saint of small government and a minimalist presidency.

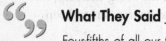

> **What They Said**
>
> Four-fifths of all our troubles in this life would disappear if we would only sit down and keep still.
>
> —Calvin Coolidge, 1920s

Handing Off to the "Great Engineer"

On August 2, 1927, Calvin Coolidge made the single shocking announcement of his entire presidency. It was delivered in a single sentence: "I do not choose to run for President in 1928."

He certainly could have. Coolidge had served out only the last few months of Harding's term, and he was so popular during the term to which he had been elected that he almost surely would have been elected to another.

Characteristically, he declined to elaborate on his surprise announcement. Some believe that his delicate health and that of his wife made him feel that, quiet as his presidency was, it was time to retire. Others have pointed out that the sudden death of his second son, Calvin Coolidge Jr., in 1924 at age 16—of the trivial infection of a blistered toe, the result of playing tennis in sneakers without socks—had taken (in the president's own words) "the power and the glory" from the office.

Exit Coolidge

"We had probably the greatest growth and prosperity that we've ever known," President Reagan observed of the Coolidge years. But others believe that Coolidge chose to decline a second full term because he saw that growth and prosperity were coming to an end. If Coolidge had the savvy to foresee the coming crash, he must also have possessed the insight to recognize that his concept of the presidency would prevent him from doing little else but stand by and watch the economy collapse. He could not have conceived of intervening—much less of how to intervene—to prevent, ameliorate, or even cope with the crisis. So he left the problem to the next president.

Enter Hoover

Herbert Hoover was not a politician. Like William Howard Taft (see Chapter 15), he had held no elective office before accepting the Republican presidential nomination in 1928. But he had an impressive resumé of public service nonetheless.

Orphaned at 9, Hoover received a catch-as-catch-can education in rural Iowa, but gained entrance to Stanford University, was trained as a geologist, and went on to make a fortune as a mining and oil engineer. During World War I, he headed the American Relief Committee and the Commission for the Relief of Belgium, bringing humanitarian aid to a ravaged Europe; he also served Woodrow Wilson as wartime food administrator, then as postwar director of the American Relief Administration and as economic adviser to President Wilson during the Paris Peace Conference. He next served as secretary of commerce in the cabinets of Harding and Coolidge.

Tally _____
Hoover polled 21,392,190 popular votes (58 percent) to Democrat Al Smith's 15,016,443 (41 percent), taking 444 electoral votes to 87 for Smith.

Presented to the American electorate in 1928 as the "Great Engineer," Herbert Hoover was widely regarded as possessing the unique administrative competence to preside over and ever-so-lightly manage the prosperity Coolidge's laissez-faire presidency had bequeathed to the nation. This popular perception more than compensated for his lack of political experience, skill, or aptitude.

Shy, mildly phobic amid crowds, and thin-skinned when it came to fielding criticism, Hoover made a stark contrast to his Democratic opponent, ebullient four-term New York governor Al Smith, dubbed by Franklin D. Roosevelt in his 1928 nomination speech "the Happy Warrior of the political battlefield." Hoover landslided him.

The Presidency of Moral Values

The "Great Engineer" examined the prosperity that had been left to him and was quick to identify the structural flaws within it. First of all, the nation's farmers were almost entirely left out of the good times. The production of wealth was largely due to financial speculation fueled by loose lending and monetary policies; it was not flowing from the farming or manufacturing sectors—and, as even Coolidge had acknowledged, manufacturers were overproducing in proportion to steadily weakening consumption.

While Hoover, therefore, was hardly oblivious to what ailed the American economy, he saw the cure not in bold, prompt, and innovative legislative or administrative intervention, but in the platform the presidency offered for what he called "moral leadership."

What They Said

By his position, [the president] must, within his capacities, give leadership to the development of moral, social, and economic forces outside of government which make for the betterment of our country.

—Herbert Hoover, speech to Gridiron Club, December 14, 1929

He attempted to encourage businesses, financial, and commercial organizations to adopt greater discipline in lending, spending, and production, and to promote the more equitable distribution of wealth through a reduction of profits to corporate owners and investors and a proportionate increase in wages to labor—which, Hoover argued, would stimulate consumption and thereby directly benefit business, including owners and investors.

The Inadequacy of the Moral Presidency

Hoover's campaign to reform business and financial practices was strictly an exercise in moral suasion and was not backed up by any legislative or administrative program. Had he been a grandly inspiring figure or a gifted orator—a Theodore Roosevelt, perhaps, or a Woodrow Wilson—that might have been sufficient to soften the blow that came on October 29, 1929, when stocks on the New York exchange began to tumble, touching off an 89 percent decline in the Dow, which would bottom out at 40.56 points in July 1932, having fallen from a September 1929 high of well over 300.

But Hoover was neither an inspiring leader nor a gifted speaker. His concept of the presidency, defined by the conservative Republican boundaries of Harding and Coolidge, did not permit him to do more than suggest to Congress certain types of legislation in the broad areas of taxation, tariffs, and conservation. He neither urged nor formulated any specific bills, let alone a full legislative program. To those who began to clamor for more aggressive presidential leadership, he responded (as he later recalled in his memoirs) that the president should never "undermine the independence of the legislative and judicial branches" by urging specific legislation or judicial reforms. Such presidential interference would serve only to "discredit" the other branches. The constitutional separation of powers Hoover deemed "the bastion of our liberties" and not "a battleground to display the prowess of presidents."

Executive Event

Herbert Hoover deserves blame for failing to act vigorously during the early phases of the Great Depression, but much of the American public went beyond this, laying the causes of the Depression itself at the president's doorstep. This surely goes too far, but it is nevertheless true that Hoover, after asking Congress to lower tariffs, failed to veto or even protest the Smoot-Hawley Tariff Act, which he signed into law on June 17, 1930. The work of Sen. Reed Smoot, Republican from Utah, and Rep. Willis C. Hawley, Republican from Oregon, the act not only *raised* U.S. tariffs on more than 20,000 imported goods, but raised them to record-high levels. The tariff was intended to stimulate domestic consumption of American-made goods, but an army of U.S. economists 1,028 strong signed a petition against the tariff bill, warning that it would bring catastrophic retaliation from abroad, which would ultimately make weak sales even weaker.

The economists proved right, and, under Smoot-Hawley, U.S. export sales were cut by half, creating one more factor that contributed to the deepening of the Great Depression.

The Enemy: Big Government

Even faced with economic collapse, Hoover responded by denying the adequacy of either the presidency or the legislature to do much of anything about it. "We could no more legislate ourselves out of a worldwide depression," he declared, than we could "exorcise a Caribbean hurricane by statutory law."

Hoover did call for the private sector and the states to initiate relief programs, ignoring the fact that neither the private sector nor state governments had the funds to finance anything of the kind. Only when he felt that his back was finally to the wall did Hoover agree to support the creation of a federal Reconstruction Finance Corporation (RFC) to provide loans to big businesses, including banks, railroads, and agricultural organizations, but not to small businesses or to individuals, who were out of work, on the streets, and going hungry.

What They Said

Prosperity is just around the corner.

—Herbert Hoover, catchphrase, early 1930s

The RFC was widely perceived as too little too late, but, even worse, also as proof that Hoover was willing to compromise his opposition to big government when it came to aiding big business, but not when the individual worker asked for a hand. Nor were the jobless and the homeless mollified by Hoover's sincere lectures on how federally funded welfare programs would irreversibly undermine the "rugged individualism" on which the American democracy had been founded.

A Marked Man, a Bankrupt Philosophy

When he ran for reelection in 1932, Herbert Hoover was a marked man, on whom Democrat Franklin Delano Roosevelt, promising the people all the presidential leadership and federal intervention the Republican had denied them, drew a clean bead.

The incumbent proved a soft target. FDR won 57 percent to 40 percent, becoming the first Democratic president to be elected in 16 years.

During the succeeding decade of the Roosevelt New Deal, a decade of big government on a scale never before imagined, it became easy to assume that the concepts of a limited executive and a small government were quite literally a bankrupt philosophy and that the presidential legacy of Harding, Coolidge, and Hoover was at an end. And indeed that assumption was correct—though only for a time.

The Least You Need to Know

- Vice President Calvin Coolidge succeeded Warren G. Harding and, after purging the late president's administration of its rampant corruption, took up the passive, hands-off presidency precisely where his predecessor had left it.

- Thanks to the president's surprising skill in managing the press and public relations, Coolidge was one of the most popular chief executives in American history, his noninterventionist approach to government serving as a model for Ronald Reagan in his crusade to "get big government off our backs."

- Herbert Hoover did not believe the president had the constitutional authority to intervene in private enterprise or the legislature's passage of financial laws; he therefore confined himself to "moral leadership."

- The onset and deepening of the Great Depression during the Hoover presidency dramatically revealed the inadequacy of the passive executive.

The Roosevelt Era

In This Chapter

- ◆ The president as the government—and vice versa
- ◆ The New Deal
- ◆ War powers
- ◆ Breaking the two-term limit

No doubt about it, Herbert Hoover was a very unpopular man, the first four years of economic depression coinciding almost exactly with the four years of his presidency. Probably any Democrat would have defeated him. But the margin of the Roosevelt electoral victory—472 to 59—suggested something more. Franklin Roosevelt had a mandate.

The Mandate Presidency

Franklin Roosevelt was the first president to be ushered into office with a *mandate* to do virtually whatever he thought necessary to rescue the country from the crisis of the Great Depression. On this basis, Roosevelt built an extraordinary presidency, assuming a range of powers unheard of in peacetime.

def•i•ni•tion

In presidential politics, a **mandate** is a command or authorization by voters to make good on a campaign pledge; the presence of a mandate is defined by a decisive margin of victory at the polls.

Redefining the Role of Government

Although Roosevelt intended to take steps toward eventual economic recovery, the program he presented to voters emphasized immediate rescue and relief rather than abstract financial policy. To establish the popular basis for a mandate, FDR set about redefining the very scope of the nation's founding documents, the Declaration of Independence and the Constitution. He persuaded a majority of the electorate that it was the job of modern government to defend economic welfare as an "unalienable right" on a par with life, liberty, and the pursuit of happiness.

Redefining Americanism

Herbert Hoover had invoked the universally accepted American tradition of self-reliance as a reason for refraining from using federal resources to directly assist individuals. This was an example of the moral leadership Hoover believed was one of the president's most important duties.

Roosevelt also exercised moral leadership, but argued that self-reliance had to be reevaluated in the light of a crisis in which individualism had to give way to working for the common good. Yes, people would have to make sacrifices as individuals, but the government would be there to provide direct help and direct support. In addition, the government would provide a means of sustaining the individual by weaving a social and economic safety net to prevent people from falling into the worst poverty, and that would keep the free market from total collapse. In short, Roosevelt intended to create a *welfare state*.

def•i•ni•tion

A **welfare state** is a nation in which the government assumes primary responsibility for the health care, social security, education, and general economic well-being of its citizens.

Redefining the Presidency

Roosevelt's formidable task was to acquire and wield the executive power necessary to create and administer this novel and distasteful role for American government.

The American president would have to be both a powerful administrator, taking on a legislative role, as well as a highly persuasive popular leader. To achieve this, FDR harked back to his fifth cousin, Theodore Roosevelt, and the presidential theory he had espoused, that the chief duty of a president was to be the steward of the public welfare. Like T. R., FDR defined himself as the direct representative of the people, the principal agent of democratic government over and above both the legislative and judicial branches and, even more important, over and above the party.

Crisis and Power

Americans saw in Italy, Germany, and elsewhere the meteoric rise of strongman dictators, and many began to doubt the capacity of democratic capitalism to survive let alone overcome the Great Depression. Perhaps it was best to sacrifice freedom and put the national destiny in the hands of a single empowered leader.

Franklin Roosevelt was prepared to exploit the economic crisis as well as the international milieu to acquire unprecedented power. To be sure, FDR was no Hitler or Mussolini, but if these avatars of dictatorial leadership had not existed, it would have been more difficult for the new president to take charge as he did.

Like the dictators, Roosevelt created about himself—albeit to a limited degree—a cult of personality. Wilson's approach to Congress as a "human being" rather than as a "department" of government (see Chapter 16) was a bold step toward a personal presidency—and one from which Harding, Coolidge, and Hoover retreated. FDR embraced the concept of personal government. He wanted the people to see him as their leader, a human being in whom they could place their full confidence.

The New Deal: Institutionalizing the Extraordinary

Roosevelt understood that popular confidence was only a means to an end, a way to alter the national mood in order to win acceptance of a powerful presidency. To legalize that presidency, he knew that he would have to move more than the people. He needed to move the government itself.

Government by Executive Order

He did this by issuing a cascade of executive orders. In an emergency, FDR reasoned, legislation was too slow and too diffuse in fixing responsibility for government.

Orders issued directly from the White House, however, were immediate and concentrated the action in the hands of a single leader. The president became not only the most powerful officer of government, but the one on whose shoulders the people were invited to place their burdens.

Speed was essential—not just to limit economic damage (as in the Bank Holiday, proclaimed during FDR's second day in office and intended to halt the rash of runs that were causing banks to fail nationwide), but also to show the people that democratic government was neither impotent nor unresponsive.

The Hundred Days

The problem with speed is that it is easily perceived as panic. Roosevelt packaged speed in a unique program on which he and his advisers unabashedly affixed a brand name: the "Hundred Days."

Bundling everything under the Hundred Days rubric would create its own momentum. FDR's executive orders were quickly augmented by congressional legislation, which, swept along by the tide of presidential action, also proceeded at a remarkable pace.

Creating Belief

The greatest presidents were always creators of belief. For FDR and his inner circle, the New Deal was no mere set of executive orders and laws, but a secular religion that would bring salvation to the nation. True believers were christened "New Dealers," and adhering to the precepts of the program was considered an act of another form of secular religion, patriotism.

In an age dominated by compelling symbols—it can be reasonably argued that the Nazi swastika was the most universally recognized symbol since the Christian cross— New Deal culture was rife with them. Businesses of every kind showed their support of the National Recovery Administration (NRA) by displaying a stylized black eagle NRA decal or placard prominently in their shops and offices and imprinting it on stationery and advertisements. Every public office—federal, state, and local—and many private offices and homes proudly hung portraits of President Roosevelt himself on the wall. In school classrooms, his image jockeyed for space with those of Washington and Lincoln.

The Image Presidency

Image has long played an important, if sporadic, role in the American presidency. For example, Andrew Jackson was "Old Hickory" the frontiersman, and William Henry Harrison and Abraham Lincoln were both "log cabin" presidents (see Chapters 8, 9, and 11, respectively). In FDR, however, the image presidency was raised to a new height.

Not only were portraits of the president ubiquitous, newspaper coverage displayed his buoyant smile, with his trademark cigarette holder clamped between his teeth at a jaunty, upturned angle. He exuded an optimism, which was amplified in his speaking style—always straight talking, never turning away from harsh reality, yet invariably affirmative.

In 1921, Roosevelt was stricken by a paralytic disease long assumed to have been polio but recently rediagnosed as Guillain-Barré syndrome, another disorder that attacks the central nervous system. The disease left Roosevelt a paraplegic, yet throughout his post-1921 career, both as New York governor and as president, FDR was careful to avoid being photographed in a wheelchair, even though he used one extensively in private. In public, he stood and even walked short distances with the aid of massive steel braces concealed under his trouser legs. Not only did he believe that neither the American people nor other world leaders would accept a wheelchair-bound chief executive, his ability to stand on his own two feet conveyed a positive message, implying that if the paralyzed president could overcome his disability, so could a nation stricken by economic paralysis.

The Speech as an Event

President Roosevelt was an eloquent speaker, who wrote his own speeches and also employed distinguished professional speechwriters, including the playwright and poet Archibald MacLeish (who served as librarian of Congress in the Roosevelt administration) and four-time Pulitzer Prize–winning Broadway playwright Robert Sherwood. FDR combined a fresh, personal style, often laced with down-to-earth figures of speech, with a trace of the genuinely poetic to create public messages of great persuasive and inspirational power.

> 66 99 **What They Said**
>
> The only thing we have to fear is fear itself.
>
> —Franklin D. Roosevelt, first inaugural address, March 4, 1933

The Fireside Chat

Counterpointed to the sheer velocity of executive orders and the formal eloquence of public speeches was the most celebrated of the FDR innovations in presidential communication, the fireside chat. As New York governor, Roosevelt had used the radio to make informal talks directly to the public. At the end of his first week as president of the United States, on Sunday, March 12, 1933, he delivered his first radio talk from the Diplomatic Reception Room of the White House. He would make 26 more in the course of his presidency. It was CBS executive Harry C. Butcher, at the time of the second broadcast (May 7, 1933), who coined the term "fireside chat."

> **What They Said** _____
>
> I see one-third of a nation ill-housed, ill-clad, ill-nourished.
>
> —Franklin D. Roosevelt, second inaugural address, January 20, 1937

FDR understood that radio was an intimate medium that literally brought personalities into the family parlor and therefore, provided a unique opportunity to create a direct relationship between the president and the people—or rather, between the president and *each person* who heard the broadcast. Roosevelt used the fireside chat format to speak on a single issue of pressing importance for 15 to 30 minutes. The fireside chat addressed each person individually, but reached a huge radio audience.

The First Lady

Most of the first ladies who had preceded Eleanor Roosevelt had either been largely invisible or had functioned primarily as the lady of the White House, the nation's "first hostess." Before she entered the White House with her husband in 1933, Eleanor Roosevelt had already built a reputation as a social activist and reformer. She used her position as first lady to broaden this work, often in coordination with the New Deal and other FDR Depression-era relief programs. She was also an advocate of social and political progressivism, including the cause of racial equality. As much as FDR transformed the presidency, Eleanor Roosevelt transformed the role of first lady, elevating it to a position of quasi-official responsibility. Some, though not all, subsequent first ladies followed the precedent she had created—though none has yet achieved the remarkable scope of her activities and impact.

Pushing the Constitutional Envelope

The social programs of the New Deal that transformed American government and life were so closely associated with Roosevelt that Americans became accustomed to thinking of the president as the government, and vice versa. This perception made it easier for the people to accept the very serious challenges the FDR social agenda posed to the Constitution. Roosevelt claimed that he, as president, functioned only as "the agency" through which "certain of the purposes of Congress" were carried out. Many others, however, believed that his radical use of the executive office usurped the proper role of Congress and was nothing less than an assault on the balance of powers.

Among these skeptics was a majority of the Supreme Court, which ruled unconstitutional a number of New Deal laws. Fearful that the centerpiece of the New Deal, the Social Security Act, would fall, Roosevelt attempted to bring the judicial branch under the control of the executive by sending to Congress early in 1937 his so-called "court-packing bill," which obliged the president to appoint a new Supreme Court justice for every sitting justice who did not retire by age 70. Because six of the nine sitting justices were 70 or older, FDR would be empowered to increase membership on the court to 15, populating it with justices amenable to Social Security and other items of New Deal legislation.

Congress voted down the "court-packing bill," but the president's boldness in even having proposed it may have had the desired effect after all. The Supreme Court never again struck down another New Deal law.

Foreign Affairs: New Vistas from the White House

Roosevelt's first two terms were mostly taken up with the domestic economic crisis. By the end of the second term, foreign affairs became an increasingly critical concern as war clouds darkened Europe and Asia.

It was one thing to convert the American people, suffering under a failing economy, to the idea of creating a welfare state administered chiefly by the president, but it was quite another to move these same people away from the isolationism of three Republican presidencies. With the rise of Mussolini and Hitler in Europe and the outbreak of the Sino-Japanese War in 1937, President Roosevelt began educating the public to the dangers of the world situation in an effort to persuade them that, in the next world war, the United States could not remain isolated, even if it wanted to.

The president's early efforts to move the nation toward engagement with the rest of the world met with considerable resistance from Congress. In response to this, Roosevelt increasingly assumed unilateral control over foreign policy. Whereas even Woodrow Wilson had taken care to build a congressional consensus before edging

America into war, Roosevelt took it entirely upon himself to choose sides, beginning with the implementation of embargos to halt the export of U.S.-made weapons to nations he deemed dangerous. When a 1936 embargo was challenged in the Supreme Court, the justices ruled in favor of the president, in effect ratifying what some earlier presidents had merely asserted: that the chief executive is the supreme authority in the conduct of foreign policy.

After the outbreak of World War II in Europe in September 1939, Roosevelt used his court-bolstered authority to gradually align the United States with the Allied powers—especially Great Britain—who struggled to stem the tide of Nazi invasion. On September 2, 1940, the administration concluded a destroyers-for-bases deal with Britain's prime minister, Winston Churchill, whereby the U.S. Navy would "lend" 50 obsolescent World War I–vintage destroyers—which the Royal Navy desperately needed as convoy escorts—in return for leases on British naval bases in the Caribbean. This program, carried out entirely by executive order, paved the way for the far more dramatic Lend Lease Act (March 11, 1941), which required congressional legislation to appropriate necessary funds. Through lend lease, Congress authorized the president to furnish material to any nation whose security he deemed essential to that of the United States and to supply these items on any basis the president saw fit, whether for cash payment, on credit, on exchange, or simply as a grant or loan.

Personal Diplomacy

In the unique relationship he forged with Winston Churchill, Franklin Roosevelt inaugurated an unprecedented era of personal diplomacy. Never before had an American president entered into an intimate partnership with another world leader. After the Japanese attack on Pearl Harbor, December 7, 1941, thrust America into the war, Roosevelt and Churchill (and, to a much lesser extent, Soviet premier Joseph Stalin) closely collaborated on strategy and war policy.

Never again would an American president work so intimately with other world leaders; however, the Roosevelt-Churchill example has served as both precedent and model for subsequent person-to-person diplomacy at a presidential level. Facilitated by modern communications technology and speedy international travel, every president since Roosevelt has assumed a great deal of direct responsibility for international negotiations and agreements, even as the direct role of ambassadors and the secretary of state has diminished.

White House Diplomacy

As President Roosevelt transformed diplomacy into a matter of personal partnership, so he tended to bring all aspects of foreign policy into the White House itself. Functions traditionally performed by the Department of State and overseen by the secretary of state were increasingly assumed by non-cabinet-level presidential advisers, such as former social worker and New Deal administrator Harry Hopkins and other more-or-less informal confidants who passed in and out of the president's inner circle. The consolidation of foreign affairs in the White House would become a common feature of all the postwar presidencies.

War Powers

Ever since Abraham Lincoln, American presidents have assumed extraordinary powers in war. Like President Wilson before him, FDR extended executive authority over wartime domestic economic and social affairs, including matters of war production, allocation of resources, and rationing, and the institution of special regulations to prevent espionage and sabotage, including the establishment of secret military tribunals.

The most egregious domestic war power FDR exercised was the removal of some 100,000 U.S. citizens of Japanese descent from their homes and businesses along the West Coast to "relocation camps" located inland. This mass dispossession and internment was instituted on February 8, 1942, by executive order, without congressional action (although members of Congress overwhelmingly approved of the action). When challenged in the Supreme Court, the legality of this unprecedented affront to the Fifth Amendment was upheld on the grounds of "military necessity."

President Roosevelt did not confine his hands-on conduct of the war to managing domestic policy. To a degree not seen since Lincoln and the Civil War, FDR assumed the role of commander in chief, taking ultimate responsibility for formulating broad U.S. military strategy and priorities, albeit always in consultation with Churchill and (to a lesser degree) Stalin.

Roosevelt frequently met with his top military advisers as well as with high-level operational commanders. Although he usually deferred to them, he took pains to demonstrate to the American people and the rest of the world that he was the ultimate war leader of the United States—just as Churchill and Stalin were the war leaders of their countries, and, for that matter, much as Hitler, Mussolini, and Tojo were the commanders in chief of German, Italian, and Japanese forces.

Tally _____

In the 1932 election, Roosevelt received 22,821,857 popular votes (57 percent) to Herbert Hoover's 15,761,841 (40 percent). The electoral tally was 472 to 59. In 1936, the landslide was even greater, Roosevelt polling 27,751,597 votes (61 percent) to Alf Landon's 16,679,583 (37 percent). The electoral victory was 523 to 8. The Roosevelt third-term victory in 1940 was narrower, but still substantial: 27,243,466 (55 percent) to Wendell Wilkie's 22,304,755 (45 percent). The electoral vote was 449 to 82. Roosevelt won a fourth term by an even narrower margin, but, again, still a solid majority, polling 25,602,505 (53 percent) votes to the 22,006,278 (46 percent) of Thomas E. Dewey. Roosevelt earned 432 electoral votes to Dewey's 99.

Breaking the Two-Term Tradition

As breathtaking as Roosevelt's expansion of the presidency was in the areas of financial and social policy and foreign affairs, nothing was more precedent shattering than his decision to break the hitherto sacrosanct tradition of the two-term presidency by running for a third _and_ a fourth term. That FDR was elected four times is a testament both to his popular success as a president and to the gravity of the emergencies that confronted the nation—a catastrophic depression followed by a cataclysmic world war. But not only did the example of FDR fail to permanently undo the two-term limit, it prompted Congress to enshrine that tradition in a constitutional amendment, the Twenty-Second, ratified in 1951. The American people were grateful to Franklin D. Roosevelt, whom most historians rank as the greatest president of the twentieth century, but they did not want to leave open the possibility that some future president would transform himself into what the Democratic-Republicans had most feared back in the days of Washington and Adams: a republican monarch.

The Least You Need to Know

♦ The first mandate president, Roosevelt enduringly identified the president as _the_ government—and vice versa.

♦ Roosevelt saw the president not as a caretaker of government, but as an agent of necessary change, which was embodied in a bold package of social and economic legislation.

♦ Like Lincoln and Wilson before him, President Roosevelt amassed for the presidency a wide range of war powers.

20

Where the Buck Stops

In This Chapter

♦ Truman's Fair Deal

♦ The battle with Congress

♦ Creation of a national security presidency

♦ The two-term limit becomes law

Harry S. Truman loved the Congress from which Franklin Roosevelt had plucked him to stand as his fourth-term running mate in 1944. Even after he had taken office as vice president, Truman regularly returned to the Capitol office of Speaker of the House Sam Rayburn for a taste of the old legislative fellowship served up with bourbon and branch. He had just arrived late in the afternoon of April 12, 1945, when he was handed the telephone. On the line was presidential press secretary Steve Early, who summoned Truman to the White House.

He knew it would not be good news. When he arrived, Eleanor Roosevelt rose, placed a gentle arm around his shoulders, and quietly said, "Harry, the president is dead."

"Is there anything I can do for you?" Truman replied, as one customarily replies to the news of the death of a loved one.

"Is there anything we can do for *you?*" Mrs. Roosevelt countered. "For you're the one in trouble now."

Riding the Tiger

The last vice president to face so daunting a transition was Andrew Johnson upon the assassination of Abraham Lincoln (see Chapter 11), and Harry S. Truman, an avid student of history, was well aware of how badly that turned out.

What They Said

The Buck Stops Here
—sign on Truman's Oval
Office desk

The United States was still heavily engaged in World War II; the struggle in Europe was clearly coming to a close, but the war against Japan showed no signs of ending soon. Looking ahead, Truman was well aware that, when the war finally ended, Stalin and the Soviet Union, staunch allies at the moment, were bound to challenge American democratic power.

As grave as these historical circumstances were, even more daunting was the reality of succeeding the president—revered and beloved as none since Lincoln—who had led the nation for the past 12 years.

Crisis of Confidence

How could anyone get out from under the shadow cast by such a giant? The nation was swept by grief, and few believed that Truman was capable of picking up where Roosevelt had left off. Many despaired over the fate of the nation.

Beyond the Cult of Personality

Where FDR had been charismatic, Truman was merely blunt. Where FDR had been a gifted speaker, Truman was plainspoken and inelegant. Where FDR had used personal charm to shamelessly manipulate others, Truman found anything other than absolute sincerity anathema. And where FDR had played the press like a virtuoso seated before a Steinway, Truman was incurably awkward in the presence of reporters and cameras.

He knew that he had to get beyond the presidency of personality that Roosevelt had created. To do this, he seized upon the content of the FDR presidency—in which he believed wholeheartedly—but made no attempt to emulate the style. With hard work and a degree of sheer intelligence that surprised many who instinctively under-rated him, Truman followed Roosevelt's path, yet without remaining in his shadow. The legacy of the New Deal, the conduct of the war with the objective of the enemy's unconditional surrender, and Roosevelt's intention to promote the successful creation of a United Nations to replace the failed League of Nations—all of these he intended to see through to their realization.

For Truman, the presidency (he famously remarked) was like "riding a tiger. You have to keep on riding or be swallowed." He did not view the office as a glamorous and prestigious exercise in national and global leadership, but as first and last a job, which required relentlessly hard work in the service of the people. He rolled up his sleeves.

From New Deal to Fair Deal

Given Truman's origins as a Missouri Democrat, most political pundits predicted that he would retreat from the liberal program of the Roosevelt New Deal. Although he did no such thing, neither did Truman simply adopt the New Deal. On September 6, 1945, with World War II just ended, he addressed Congress to present what he called the "Fair Deal."

The Presidency and the Economy

The Fair Deal was intended to make permanent many of the New Deal provisions that had been implemented during an economic emergency that no longer existed. Truman explained that his intention was to fulfill his late predecessor's vision for a postwar economy, in which the federal government would be responsible for promulgating what FDR called a "Second Bill of Rights," guaranteeing the opportunity to enjoy adequate employment, good medical care, decent housing, and a good education. The Fair Deal called for extending Social Security to more workers, increasing the federal minimum wage, instituting a "full employment" program, funding urban development, and providing national health insurance.

> **What They Said** _____
>
> If I think it is right, I am going to do it.
>
> —Harry S. Truman, quoted in Richard S. Kirkendall, ed., *The Harry S. Truman Encyclopedia* (1989)

By institutionalizing the welfare state Roosevelt had gone a long way toward creating, Truman also sought to institutionalize the economic role FDR had staked out for the presidency, permanently putting the president in the lead when it came to formulating national economic policy.

The Presidency and Civil Rights

In presenting his concept of a "Second Bill of Rights" in his final State of the Union Address in 1944, President Roosevelt had noted that the new rights would be guaranteed "regardless of station, race, or creed." President Truman stunned practically everyone by interpreting this phrase as a mandate to promote civil rights, including racial equality and racial integration.

Truman's native Missouri was very much a southern state, in which segregation was a way of life. The president did not depart from his upbringing for ideological reasons or, for that matter, out of respect for FDR's intentions. To him, civil rights were a simple matter of justice. African Americans had fought and died in World War II. It was just plain wrong to welcome them back from war as second-class citizens.

As a personal sense of justice had prompted Truman's decision to promote civil rights, so he decided that it would be futile to rely on Congress for legislative action on racial equality and integration. Most Republicans would not be won over to this form of liberalism, and southern Democrats were certain to resist it. Therefore, Truman became the first president since Abraham Lincoln to use the presidency itself as a means of implementing measures to ensure civil rights. He created the President's Committee on Civil Rights in 1946, which produced the landmark report *To Secure These Rights* in 1947, and he issued Executive Order 9981 in 1948, ordering the integration of the U.S. armed forces.

The "Worst-Ever" Congress

The midterm elections of 1946 brought Republican majorities to both houses of Congress, with the result that few of Truman's Fair Deal measures were passed and those that gained passage were enacted in highly diluted form. Nevertheless, the example of the Fair Deal would serve as a model for John F. Kennedy (see Chapter 21) and, even more, for Johnson in formulating their own social reform agendas.

"Dewey Defeats Truman!"

Truman was nominated in 1948 to run for the office in his own right. No one expected him to win—and with good reason. The Democratic Party was badly splintered. On the one hand, the extreme left wing favored former Secretary of Agriculture Henry A. Wallace, and, on the other, Truman's civil rights positions had driven many southerners to walk out of the Democratic National Convention and create the breakaway "Dixiecrat" party, which nominated segregationist South Carolina governor Strom Thurmond. Moreover, the Republican candidate, Thomas E. Dewey, was so strong that every pollster called the election for him more than two weeks before America went to the polls. Most notoriously, the *Chicago Tribune* hit the streets early in the morning after the election with a headline blaring "Dewey Defeats Truman!"

But Truman, who had campaigned with a spectacular cross-country whistle-stop tour—much as Wilson had done in his failed effort to promote the League of Nations—effectively brought his quasi-populist message to the people, exhorting them not to give up to Republican-backed big business interests everything they had gained under FDR. In the end, he managed to cajole a 49 percent plurality victory.

 Tally

Truman captured 24,105,812 votes (49 percent), taking 303 electoral votes. His Republican opponent, Thomas E. Dewey, almost universally predicted to win, polled 21,970,065 votes (45 percent), for 189 electoral votes. Strom Thurmond, running on the Democratic breakaway States' Rights ("Dixiecrat") ticket, polled 1,169,063 votes (2 percent), drawing 39 electoral votes. Left-leaning Henry A. Wallace ran on the Progressive Party ticket and took 1,157,172 votes (2 percent), but received no electoral votes.

"Give 'Em Hell, Harry"

Elected in his own right in 1948, Truman still had to face what he called the "worst-ever Eightieth Congress." On the campaign trail, the slogan "Give 'em hell, Harry" had more or less spontaneously developed from the cheers of supporters, and it came to characterize the combative approach Truman adopted.

It was not simply a case of a Republican Congress fighting a Democratic president, but of a Republican Congress systematically attempting to undo the New Deal, which Truman's Fair Deal was designed to perpetuate. The president fought Congress at every turn, exercising veto after veto in an effort to preserve liberal policies on labor and taxes. Some of his vetoes stuck, but others were overridden by a coalition between the Republican majority and conservative Democrats—mostly the Dixiecrats. Yet these battles, disheartening as they may have been for Truman, were not fought in vain. The president's unflagging defiance entrenched the presidency as the source of policy and the political agenda. These might or might not prevail in Congress, but, prevail or not, they were the products of the executive, not the legislative branch. Even in defeat, the Truman presidency emerged as dominant in legislative affairs.

The Nuclear Presidency and the Cold War

In August 1945, Harry S. Truman became the only U.S. president—and only world leader—to authorize the use of nuclear weapons against an enemy. Two atomic bombs, products of the epic Manhattan Project, were dropped on Japan, devastating Hiroshima on August 6, 1945, and Nagasaki on August 9. Within days, Japan surrendered, and World War II ended.

Truman was the first commander in chief to bear the responsibility of nuclear warfare. As America's nuclear arsenal grew, he understood that he held the keys to Armageddon—and he held these keys even as the Soviet Union, soon joined by the newly emergent People's Republic of China, contested for dominance of the very planet. Truman found himself in the excruciating position of having to resist the aggressive spread of communism without going so far as to trigger World War III.

Containment

In 1823, James Monroe promulgated the Monroe Doctrine, warning European powers that the United States would act to block any new attempts to colonize the Americas (see Chapter 7). In 1947, Truman presented what the press dubbed the "Truman Doctrine," warning the Soviet Union, which supported a threatened communist takeover of Greece and Turkey, that the United States would act to halt the spread of communism wherever in the world it menaced democracy. The Truman Doctrine was based on a proposal by State Department official George F. Kennan, who held that the most effective way of combating communism without touching off a new world war was to "contain" it by confronting the Soviet Union—using economic and political measures rather than military force, if at all possible—whenever and wherever it sought to expand its influence.

Thanks to U.S. financial and military aid, both Greece and Turkey successfully defeated communist threats after World War II, and in 1948, after the Soviet Union began detaining troop trains and other surface transport bound for West Berlin—a democratic enclave in Soviet-controlled eastern Germany—Truman led the other western powers, Britain and France, in declaring, on June 7, 1948, their intention to create the separate, permanent capitalist state of West Germany. Two weeks after the announcement, the Soviet Union blockaded West Berlin.

If Truman backed down, containment would fail. If he acted aggressively, a new world war might be the result. Instead of taking armed action against the Soviets, he ordered the Berlin Airlift, which kept West Berlin supplied for more than 321 days, ultimately forcing the Soviet Union to lift the blockade.

The success of the Berlin Airlift vindicated the policy of containment as well as the president's preeminent role in waging the limited warfare—combining military action, economic aid, and diplomacy—required to keep the Soviets and communist Chinese at bay.

Common Cause with Congress

The demands of the Cold War concentrated foreign policy power in the hands of the president, but also promoted the kind of bipartisan consensus between the president and Congress that eluded Truman in the arena of domestic policy. Leadership came from the president, but in such Cold War measures as the creation of the North Atlantic Treaty Organization (NATO) and the Marshall Plan—an unprecedented package of aid to war-ravaged Europe—Congress proved compliant as Truman navigated a moderate, non-partisan course in foreign affairs.

The National Security Presidency

One of the most consequential pieces of legislation Truman persuaded Congress to pass was the National Security Act of 1947. This omnibus bill reorganized the War Department into the Department of Defense (under which the armed forces were unified), created the U.S. Air Force as an independent military arm, and established the Central Intelligence Agency (CIA), which had as its mission covert intelligence gathering. The objective was to tightly coordinate all branches of the military with an intelligence apparatus, which would thereby enable the president to use the military judiciously and effectively in the difficult and delicate situations the Cold War era frequently presented.

The National Security Act in effect created a national security presidency, bringing into the office of the executive every military function and prerogative, making the combined intelligence and military communities direct extensions of the presidency. The consolidation of foreign policy within the White House, which had begun under Roosevelt, was intensified during the Truman administration and would continue to do so throughout the modern presidency.

The Limits of Containment

The Korean War, which broke out on June 25, 1950, when the Soviet-backed forces of communist North Korea invaded U.S.-supported South Korea, was the first major shooting war of the Cold War era. Although President Truman characterized it as a "police action," military intervention to defend the sovereignty of South Korea, it was a major war, involving 480,000 Americans and ultimately resulting in 36,516 U.S. military personnel killed and 92,134 wounded. Although President Truman secured the approval and cooperation of Congress in the conduct of the war, operations were controlled chiefly by the president as commander in chief and also through executive orders.

President Truman had a sound political reason for avoiding a declaration of war. First, he believed that a formal declaration would recognize North Korea as a sovereign nation, a degree of legitimacy the United States did not want to give it. Second, Truman feared that a formal declaration would force the Soviets and perhaps even the Chinese to declare war as well, escalating the Korean "conflict" into a new world war. However, Truman inadvertently established a precedent for war by executive action, which has made it relatively easy for presidents to commit the nation to major armed conflict with a minimum of congressional input.

The Korean War revealed the limits of the containment policy. The war was at once large and costly, yet also limited in that it did not trigger World War III but also failed to achieve a decisive victory. Communism was contained above the Thirty-Eighth Parallel in Korea, but the nation was not unified under a democratic regime friendly to the United States. Many came away from the armistice that ended the fighting on July 27, 1953 (during the first year of the Eisenhower administration), feeling that America had suffered military defeat for the first time in its history.

Executive Event

Already unpopular for his conduct of limited warfare in Korea, President Truman courted outright political suicide when, on April 11, 1951, he relieved the widely revered five-star general Douglas MacArthur, hero of the Pacific campaign in World War II, as supreme commander of U.S./United Nations forces in Korea. This action came in response to MacArthur's defiance of the constitutionally mandated authority of the president as commander in chief by publicly disagreeing with Truman's policy of limiting the Korean war to avoid a larger war with China. Determined to enforce the principle that military commanders are subordinate to the civilian commander in chief and to prevent a general from usurping a president's authority to make foreign policy, Truman fired MacArthur. Although the members of the Joint Chiefs of Staff concurred with the president's decision, it ignited a popular firestorm, including calls for Truman's impeachment.

Amendment Twenty-Two

The presidency of Franklin Roosevelt firmly established the president as the source of U.S. foreign policy in wartime, and the Truman administration translated this role into the difficult "peace" that followed World War II. Since Truman, no Congress has ever seriously challenged the principle of presidential initiative in the arena of foreign affairs. This, in combination with the creation of the national security presidency, constitutes the most profound legacy Truman bequeathed to the office of the chief executive.

Truman did not support the Twenty-Second Amendment, which was passed by Congress in 1947 and ratified by the states in 1951, imposing a constitutional two-term limit on the presidency. He did endorse the *tradition* of the two-term limit, but he believed that the option for more than two terms should not be arbitrarily denied. Nevertheless, because the amendment was passed and ratified during his administration, the constitutional term limit on the presidency is considered an enduring aspect of the Truman legacy to the office.

The Least You Need to Know

◆ In the Fair Deal, Truman presented a comprehensive program of economic and social legislation intended to carry FDR's New Deal into postwar America.

◆ Truman was often in battle with the Republican-controlled Eightieth Congress, and although he was often defeated, his unwavering defiance of congressional opposition reaffirmed the presidency as the principal source of the U.S. legislative agenda.

- ◆ Through his response to the Cold War, Truman created the national security presidency.

- ◆ Despite Truman's opposition, the Twenty-Second Amendment was ratified, transforming the presidential tradition of the two-term limit into law.

Chapter 21

From Ike to Camelot

In This Chapter

- ◆ Eisenhower's attempt to restore balance between Congress and the presidency
- ◆ Ike's behind-the-scenes presidency
- ◆ Kennedy: the charismatic presidency
- ◆ Creation of the covert presidency

"Ulysses Simpson Grant's period in office seems to prove the theory that we can coast along for eight years without a president," Harry S. Truman wrote from his postpresidential retirement in Independence, Missouri. "Well, of course, we've also recently done it with Eisenhower." Truman thought Ike had been a fine general in World War II, but (in his words) a "dumb son of a bitch when he took his uniform off." His chief complaint was that Ike was lazy, content to defer to Congress while serving as little more than a smiling caretaker.

Although Eisenhower sailed into the White House with 55 percent of the vote over Democrat Adlai Stevenson's 45 percent and proved a highly popular two-term president, Truman was hardly alone in his assessment. Washington reporter Joseph C. Harsch believed the view of Eisenhower as a do-nothing was partly an "illusion" produced by the contrast with FDR, who made Ike look by comparison like "a man who slipped into the White House by the back door ... and hasn't yet found his way to the President's desk."

Roosevelt in Reverse

As supreme commander of Allied armies in Europe during World War II, Dwight D. Eisenhower had proven himself an adept politician, forging and holding together by a combination of goodwill, restraint, and firmness a contentious alliance among U.S., British, and Free French forces. As a general among generals, his idea of leadership was less a matter of issuing orders than of creating and guiding consensus among subordinates who were expected to do their jobs without having to be goaded.

What They Said _____

Humility must always be the portion of any man who receives acclaim earned in blood of his followers and sacrifices of his friends.
—Dwight D. Eisenhower, Guildhall Address, London, June 12, 1945

Surrendering to Duty

In place of a thirst for glory, "Ike" had a determination to do his duty, and, like many other career military officers in the U.S. Army, he believed that one of his duties was to abstain from civilian politics. He did not even vote, and he declared allegiance to neither the Republican nor the Democratic Party. So while Eisenhower the military commander was politically skilled, he was precisely the opposite of either Roosevelt or Truman, both of whom were intensely political animals.

"I Like Ike"

In a climate of popular discontent created by the frustrations of the Korean War, an unprecedented "Draft Eisenhower" movement developed within the Republican Party, and a majority of the American people saw in this general, who had brought victory in Europe, an opportunity for a return to national well-being. The public perception of Eisenhower was neatly summed up in the leading slogan of his 1952 campaign: "I Like Ike."

Tally _____

In 1952, Eisenhower defeated Democrat Adlai Stevenson, 33,936,234 (55 percent) to 27,314,992 (44 percent), taking 442 electoral votes to just 89 for his opponent. The two men were rematched in 1956, with Ike scoring an even bigger victory: 35,590,472 popular votes (57 percent) to 26,032,322 for Stevenson (42 percent). The electoral tally was 457 to 73.

In his influential 1960 study, *Presidential Power and the Modern Presidents,* Richard E. Neustadt put it this way: Eisenhower was "a sort of Roosevelt in reverse." Whereas FDR "was a politician seeking personal power," Eisenhower "came to crown a reputation not make one." In effect, he intended his presidency to reprise his role as supreme Allied commander: "He wanted to be arbiter, not master. His love was not for power but for duty."

Executive and Legislative: Restoring the Balance

Eisenhower's experience as supreme Allied commander had been as much about ceding as assuming authority. He was never a partisan Republican, let alone a Republican ideologue; however, the Republican notion that the Roosevelt and Truman presidencies had trespassed on the domain of Congress, usurping the legislature's prerogative, appealed to his own conception of "supreme" leadership, which included letting everyone do the job assigned to them. *General* Eisenhower would not presume to lead a corps, division, or regiment—there were other generals assigned to do that— no more than *President* Eisenhower would presume to usurp the legislative duties of Congress. What former president Truman criticized as laziness, Eisenhower regarded as restoring the proper constitutional balance between the presidency and the legislature. He went so far as to avoid submitting to Congress any executive legislative program when he took office in 1953.

The President's "Hidden Hand"

From a strict constitutionalist perspective, Eisenhower's concept of the presidency in relation to the other two branches of government could not be faulted. Yet many Americans had come to expect their presidents to do more than "go by the book."

The truth was that Eisenhower did not simply abdicate responsibility for policy. Instead, he created what Professor Fred I. Greenstein used as the title of his 1982 study of the Eisenhower administration: *The Hidden-Hand Presidency.* Instead of overtly claiming power, boldly appealing to the people, and forcing on Congress a legislative agenda, Eisenhower quietly used the authority of his office behind the scenes to persuade legislators to make the policy he favored.

But why should a president be so reluctant to appear onstage? Why should this *public* leader go out of his way to work *behind* the scenes?

Even after becoming the Republican president, Eisenhower could not shake off his soldierly ideal of avoiding partisan politics. Whereas both FDR and Truman had defined themselves as Democratic leaders against a Republican opposition, Eisenhower sought to return the presidency to a nonpartisan status as the office of the U.S. head of state, not the leader of one party or the other. It was a long step backward, to the nonpartisan presidency as conceived by George Washington (see Chapter 4).

The Nonpartisan Presidency

After Eisenhower, most (not all) presidents have claimed "bipartisan" intentions for their administrations. Objectively evaluated, none ever truly delivered on the bipartisan claim (although, as of this writing, we have yet to see what the latest claimant to bipartisanship, Barack Obama, will achieve). Moreover, for most Democrats, Eisenhower remained a distinctly Republican president, socially conservative and resolutely pro-business stance, and those fellow Republicans who criticized Eisenhower called him insufficiently Republican—that is, too moderate. Thus it can be argued that not only was the nonpartisan presidency a failed legacy, it never really came to realization even during Eisenhower's own two terms.

It can be argued thus. Evaluated more objectively, however, the Eisenhower presidency emerges as one of the least ideologically partisan of the twentieth century.

Eisenhower steadfastly defied calls from the right wing of his party to radically roll back the New Deal, especially Social Security. It was not that he considered Social Security a desirable policy, but that he judged it to be an established institution of American government. As such, he claimed that defending Social Security and other programs born of the New Deal was genuinely conservative in that it defended the status quo.

The same held true for the internationalist foreign policy established by FDR and continued by Truman. Conservative Republicans preached a return to a more iso-lationist posture, whereas Eisenhower responded that there was, in the post-war world, no turning back from internationalism.

In both domestic and foreign affairs, Eisenhower did what he had done as supreme Allied commander. He created consensus. Most remarkably, he created con-sensus mainly by winning a high degree of acceptance *among Republicans* of the lib-eral legacy of FDR and Truman in domestic affairs and their internationalist orientation in foreign affairs.

> **What They Said**
>
> There is—in world affairs—a steady course to be fol-lowed between an assertion of strength that is truculent and a confession of helplessness that is cowardly.
>
> —Dwight D. Eisenhower, State of the Union Address, February 2, 1953

Civil Rights: Ambivalence and Ambiguity

The hidden-hand presidency did have its limitations, and nowhere were these more apparent than in the area of civil rights. The landmark school desegregation case, *Brown* v. *Board of Education of Topeka*, was introduced during the Truman admin-istration. The Truman Justice Department submitted materials supporting the plaintiffs—that is, supporting an end to racial segregation in public education—thereby uniting the executive with the judicial branch to bring pressure to bear upon a reluctant and resistant legislative branch.

The Supreme Court did not hand down its decision, in favor of the plaintiffs, until 1954, during the Eisenhower presidency. Had the president voiced approval of the high court's position, he would have reaf-firmed the status of the presidency as a source of social justice and civil rights. Instead, Eisenhower remained silent. The judicial branch had done its job, and it was not the place of the executive branch to approve or disapprove.

> **What They Said**
>
> In the councils of gov-ernment, we must guard against the acquisition of unwar-ranted influence, whether sought or unsought, by the military-industrial complex.
>
> —Dwight D. Eisenhower, Broadcast Farewell Address, January 17, 1961

Ultimately, in 1957, Eisenhower was forced to send federal troops to Little Rock, Arkansas, to enforce the racial integration of Central High School there. This might not have been necessary if he had taken a stand in 1954.

The Torch Is Passed

The razor-thin victory of Democrat John F. Kennedy over Eisenhower's vice president, Richard M. Nixon, testifies to the American people's ambivalence concerning the status quo presidency of Dwight Eisenhower. President Kennedy chose, however, to treat his election as an outright mandate for change, as his inaugural address boldly conveyed:

> Let the word go forth from this time and place, to friend and foe alike, that the torch has been passed to a new generation of Americans—born in this century, tempered by war, disciplined by a hard and bitter peace, proud of our ancient heritage—and unwilling to witness or permit the slow undoing of those human rights to which this Nation has always been committed, and to which we are committed today at home and around the world.

> Let every nation know, whether it wishes us well or ill, that we shall pay any price, bear any burden, meet any hardship, support any friend, oppose any foe, in order to assure the survival and the success of liberty.

Charisma Resurgent

The contrasts between Eisenhower and Kennedy could not have been more dramatic. Eisenhower was grandfatherly, balding, and at the end of his career. Kennedy was young, virile, and at the outset not merely of a career, but a great adventure he wanted to share with the nation. Where Ike had represented contentment with the status quo, Kennedy embodied a youthful, restless desire for change.

Tally _____

Kennedy won 34,227,096 popular votes (49.7 percent) to Nixon's 34,108,546 (49.5 percent). Kennedy took 303 electoral votes, Nixon 219.

The Kennedy presidency was a return to the presidency of charisma. But whereas the last charismatic president, Franklin Roosevelt, had used his personality to inspire hope for economic recovery and victory in desperate war through the subordination of selfish wants and aspirations to the greater common good, the Kennedy charisma exhorted Americans to do their personal best in order to realize a new vision of national greatness.

There had been presidencies of moral leadership and political leadership, but Kennedy's was the first presidency that deliberately set out to lead the nation toward greatness. Theodore Roosevelt had had his Square Deal, Franklin Roosevelt his New Deal, Truman his Fair Deal. Kennedy proposed the New Frontier, a phrase that simultaneously summoned up the mythology of America's pioneering past and looked far into an American future.

> **What They Said**
>
> And so, my fellow Americans: ask not what your country can do for you—ask what you can do for your country.
>
> —John F. Kennedy, Inaugural Address, January 20, 1961

Executive Event

On September 26, 1960, seventy million Americans tuned in to the first-ever televised presidential debate. After the debate—it was the first of four—the majority of those who had heard the debate on radio judged Richard M. Nixon the winner. But a majority of those who viewed the same debate on TV said that John F. Kennedy had won. It was a profound lesson in the power of television to shape popular political perception. Kennedy was younger, better looking, and sexier than Nixon, who was pale and thin, having just emerged from hospitalization for a severe knee injury. Worse, Nixon declined the offer of make-up to touch up his pallor, hide his five o clock shadow, and dry the perspiration that adorned his upper lip. Beyond this, something else was obvious. Kennedy was a natural in front of the TV camera, whereas Nixon was acutely uncomfortable. Kennedy was ideally suited to the age of television. Nixon had a lot of catching up to do.

Family Affair

The inspiration, glamour, and enchantment of the Kennedy presidency came not just from his speeches but also from the image of the handsome young president and his beautiful family, who made the White House a lively, exciting place. The image extended beyond the White House to the entire Kennedy clan, a grand social, financial, cultural, and political dynasty that was the closest thing the United States had to a royal family.

JFK was a highly partisan president, but his rhetoric and image, together with the image of his family, elevated the presidency in the public imagination far above politics. More than any other president of the twentieth century, Kennedy emerged as an American head of state.

The End of Extraordinary Isolation

For all his ability to inspire, Woodrow Wilson (see Chapter 16) was a distant, even aloof man, who cherished what he called the extraordinary isolation of the presidency because it made the chief executive appear more august and therefore, more capable of impressing and persuading the public. What Kennedy understood was that extraordinary isolation was no longer a realistic possibility for the presidency. Television now routinely brought two things into America's living rooms: celebrities and the whole world. The new president used the medium to present himself as a celebrity, fully engaged with the whole world. He televised all of his press conferences—the first president to do so—creating a precedent each of his successors would follow.

Reaching Out ...

As a result of his campaign debates with Richard Nixon, Kennedy discovered that he was a natural for TV. This probably came as no surprise to him, because he was a natural when it came to reaching out to people, and television was just a medium that extended his reach. Whereas Nixon had risen through the traditional Republican Party organization, Kennedy captured the Democratic nomination not by clawing his way up the Democratic Party organization, but by inspiring a grassroots organization outside of the traditional party structure.

... But How Far?

When Kennedy attempted to apply the lessons of his nomination and candidacy to his presidency, he met with very limited success.

There was no doubt that Kennedy inspired millions, but his efforts to govern by working outside of traditional party and legislative channels by making a direct appeal to the people repeatedly failed to produce significant change. Substantial Democratic majorities populated both the House and the Senate during the Kennedy years, yet most of the president's legislative initiatives addressing civil rights and other social issues failed to become law.

We can never know whether, given another term, Kennedy would have succeeded in gaining passage of his legislative program; therefore, we cannot finally assess the legislative limits of Kennedy's presidency of personal appeal.

The White House: Policy HQ

If Woodrow Wilson had been aloof *but* inspiring, John Kennedy came across as both open *and* inspiring. The openness, however, was more the product of a consciously crafted image than of the actual conduct of his presidency.

We now know, for example, that hidden behind the public image of Kennedy the wholesome family man was Kennedy the serial womanizer, whose liaisons both inside and outside of the White House ranged from paid call girls to celebrities, including (according to many sources) Marilyn Monroe. But more significant than the president's hidden sex life was the closed manner in which some of his most important foreign policy decisions were formulated.

From Cabinet to Staff

The president's closest political confidant was his own brother, Attorney General Robert F. Kennedy, with whom he assembled an inner circle of advisers. Like Franklin Roosevelt and Harry S. Truman, this in-house staff usurped much of the role traditionally assigned to the Department of State. Kennedy took this further than either Roosevelt or Truman, so that the influence of staff advisers often trumped that of the cabinet.

The Covert Presidency

The transfer of executive decision making from cabinet to staff made possible the creation and implementation of covert policy and encouraged the development of what might be termed the covert presidency, the most controversial and disturbing aspect of the Kennedy legacy.

Covert decision making in the Kennedy White House sometimes cut both the cabinet and Congress out of the loop, and certainly pushed the limits of constitutionality. America's early involvement in the ongoing war between North and South Vietnam had its origin in both the Truman and Eisenhower administrations, but the first substantial escalation of involvement was the result of covert planning and policy decisions made in the Kennedy White House.

The Mythology of an Unfinished Journey

John F. Kennedy was an unfaithful husband and, when it came to certain foreign policy issues, a covert schemer. His relations with Congress were poor, and his effectiveness in promoting his legislative agenda to that body even poorer. Yet most people, historians included, classify his presidency as great or near great, and Kennedy himself is remembered with affection and even reverence by those old enough to have lived through his presidency. In the years following his assassination, thousands of streets, highways, parks, schools, and public buildings have been named for him. No one has ever suggested removing those names.

Much of our enduring veneration for the memory of the John F. Kennedy comes from the brevity of his presidential journey. Cut down in his prime, he remains forever young, and his presidency forever unfinished. It consists, perhaps, more of potential than achievement; yet that potential is limited only by our own imagination of it. Whatever his flaws and failures, Kennedy infused the presidency with the possibility of greatness.

The Least You Need to Know

♦ Dwight Eisenhower's efforts to restore what he considered the constitutional balance between Congress and the presidency appeared to some as a diminishment of the chief executive's office.

♦ Eisenhower developed a behind-the-scenes approach to wielding presidential power.

♦ John F. Kennedy ushered in a new era of the charismatic presidency, even as he consolidated much of the government's policy-making apparatus within the White House itself.

♦ Cut down by assassin Lee Harvey Oswald, Kennedy left a legacy built more on the potential of greatness than on great things achieved.

Part 6

The Imperial Presidency

In very different ways, Lyndon Johnson and Richard Nixon remodeled the personal presidency into what has been widely called the "imperial presidency," transforming the White House into a headquarters in which the vision of chief executive was formulated and from which it was executed—often in defiance of the other two branches of government and sometimes even the president's own cabinet. When Nixon pressed the imperial presidency too far beyond constitutional limits, he became the only chief executive to resign office. He was succeeded by the only nonelected president in American history, Gerald Ford, who was followed by a little-known Georgia governor, Jimmy Carter. Establishing an "outsider presidency," Carter sought to tear down the vestiges of presidential imperialism, but ultimately governed with disappointing results.

22

From the Great Society to the Tonkin Gulf

In This Chapter

♦ Significance of the Twenty-Fifth Amendment

♦ A legislator enters the White House

♦ The Great Society creates presidential government

♦ The presidential credibility gap

A month before the 2008 election, Republican vice presidential candidate Sarah Palin participated in the "Questions from the Third Grade" segment of a local Denver TV news program. To the question "What does the vice president do?" Palin answered that, in addition to being the president's "teammate," the VP was "also … in charge of the United States Senate." This was not only more authority than Dick Cheney, the most powerful and presumptuous vice president in U.S. history, claimed (see Chapter 3), it was also, quite simply, wrong. The vice president's principal function is to step into the presidency when the president is removed from office by death or some other cause.

Yet perhaps Palin can be excused for this gap in her knowledge of civics. After all, suitability for the presidency has not always been uppermost among a party's criteria for selecting presidential running mates. Certainly this had been the case in 1960, when the Democratic Party nominated Lyndon Baines Johnson to run with John F. Kennedy.

Ticket Balancing and the Twenty-Fifth Amendment

The choice of the populist Texan, the politician's politician who served as majority leader of the Senate, was a throwback to the old-fashioned party practice of geographical ticket balancing (see Chapter 3). Kennedy of Massachusetts, who spoke with a thick Brookline accent, was perceived as more liberal than he actually was; party leaders tapped the drawling Johnson to campaign in the South, especially his native Texas and neighboring Louisiana.

A Transition Heartbreaking, Heroic, and Humble

Kennedy and Johnson had not been close Senate colleagues. They weren't friends. They didn't even particularly like each other. In terms of style, looks, and personality, they could not have been more different. And the shock and heartbreak of that November afternoon in Dallas were made all the more bitter for most Americans when they realized that the dashing, vigorous youth they had elected had been replaced by a Texas politician educated, as far as anyone could tell, in the old southern school.

What few among the heartbroken public stopped to consider was the simple heroism the vice president showed in assuming office immediately upon the death of the president—JFK was pronounced dead at 1 P.M. (CST), and LBJ was sworn in aboard Air Force One by a local federal judge about two hours later, a blood-stained Jacqueline Kennedy by his side. Many within the government, including those closest to both Kennedy and Johnson, believed that the assassination was part of a larger Soviet decapitation attack against the government in advance of a preemptive nuclear war and advised Johnson to take refuge in a secret location rather than return directly to Washington. Johnson insisted on immediately flying to Washington to ensure a continuity of government that would avert widespread panic and avoid sending any signal of weakness to the Soviets.

> **What They Said**
>
> He hasn't got the depth of mind nor the breadth of vision to carry great responsibility. ... Johnson is superficial and opportunistic.
>
> —President Dwight D. Eisenhower, 1960

Upon landing at Andrews Air Force Base, the newly sworn-in president made a brief broadcast from the side of the aircraft, which bore the body of the slain president. "I will do my best," he promised. "That is all I can do. I ask only for your help and God's."

Codifying Succession

It was only in the aftermath of the Kennedy assassination that the American people and their lawmakers began to give serious thought to the vice president as a presidential understudy. Ticket balancing would still be practiced in subsequent presidential races, but the credibility of the running mate as a potential president assumed increasing importance.

Executive Event _____

In the post-Kennedy assassination era, voters have been at least twice disturbed by vice presidential picks precisely because of questions concerning their suitability to serve in the Oval Office. In 1988, many voters expressed concern when Republican George H. W. Bush chose Indiana senator Dan Quayle—widely perceived, fairly or not, as an intellectual featherweight—to be his running mate. Even those who voted for Bush joked that Quayle was his "assassination insurance," meaning that no one would kill President Bush knowing that Quayle would become president. Similar concerns surfaced in 2008 over Republican candidate John McCain's choice of the obscure governor of Alaska, Sarah Palin, as his running mate. While her presence on the ticket energized the conservative Republican base, she ultimately diminished McCain's chances for victory.

More immediately, the Kennedy assassination and its aftermath motivated the proposal in Congress of the Twenty-Fifth Amendment and its ratification two years later.

The first section of the amendment dispelled the inherent ambiguity of Article II, Section I, of the Constitution, which stipulated only that in case the president was unable "to discharge the Powers and Duties" of his office, "the Same shall devolve on the Vice President." This wording did not specify whether the vice president merely acted as president or actually became president, nor did it stipulate whether or not he would serve out the elected president's full unexpired term. The amendment made clear that if the president died, was removed, or resigned, "the Vice President shall become President" and serve to the end of his term.

Section II of the amendment required the president to fill by appointment any vacancy in the office of the vice president, and sections III and IV defined presidential "disability" and under what circumstances disability warranted takeover by the vice president, as well as under what circumstances a president might resume his office.

From Legislative Insider to President of the United States

Johnson had grown up in a poor part of Texas and taught in a rural school south of San Antonio. He identified with the disadvantaged and in 1935 was appointed head of the Texas National Youth Administration, administering educational and vocational programs. He became an ardent New Dealer, taking this passion into the House of Representatives and then into the Senate, where he served from 1949 until his inauguration as vice president in 1961.

Johnson was the consummate insider politician, with an uncanny ability to cajole and coerce party discipline in the Senate, where he served as majority whip from 1951 to 1953 and Democratic leader from 1953 until his vice presidency.

Pulling the "Levers of Presidential Influence"

Johnson came to the presidency having earned many friends in Congress, and he combined his abilities as a legislative insider with an appeal to the incomplete legacy of the "martyred" JFK to do what Kennedy himself had been unable to do: persuade Congress to pass the entire New Frontier social agenda. To a small circle of intimates, he confessed his ambition to be a great president in his own right by doing for the current generation what Franklin Roosevelt had done for his.

His approach was to pull what he called the "levers of presidential influence," by which he meant exercising the same intense degree of personal inside politicking that had made him so effective in the Senate. He stroked, scolded, and leaned on key legislators to obtain each of the House and Senate votes he needed. He also reached out to governors, mayors, cabinet heads, and members of his own staff. A heady compound of rational discourse and pure salesmanship, insiders called Johnson's persuasive approach "The Treatment."

Yet as effectively as he pulled the levers, Johnson fell far short of Franklin D. Roosevelt when it came to turning from the inside of government to the outside. He was neither an eloquent nor effective orator, and, for all his skill at communicating with his colleagues, he was neither passionate nor persuasive when it came to addressing the American people. Whereas Theodore Roosevelt, Woodrow Wilson, FDR, and Kennedy himself had all forged bonds directly with the public, Johnson barely tried, preferring always to work from the inside. Through these means, he achieved a great deal, but, in the end, it was not enough.

The 1964 Landslide

Johnson repackaged the social and civil rights initiatives Kennedy had proposed, synthesizing the New Frontier with the New Deal to produce something bigger than either. LBJ called it the Great Society.

Under this banner, Johnson ran against Arizona Republican senator Barry Goldwater in 1964, whose conservatism was to the Great Society what Herbert Hoover had been to the New Deal in 1932: its antithesis. Promising to bring "abundance and liberty for all" through the programs of the Great Society, Johnson landslided his opponent.

Tally

Johnson polled 43,126,506 popular votes (61 percent) to Republican Barry Goldwater's 27,176,799 (39 percent). Johnson captured 486 electoral votes, Goldwater just 52.

Johnson took his 1964 electoral victory as a mandate for the Great Society—and the fact was that many voters supported it, as their parents had the New Deal; but the Johnson campaign had also exploited Goldwater's reputation as a *hawk*, painting him as a potential commander in chief ready and willing to nuke Russia, Red China, and North Vietnam. Many of those who voted for Johnson did so because they feared Barry Goldwater.

def•i•ni•tion

A **hawk** is a politician who favors an aggressive military policy, in contrast to a dove, who favors peace. The Vietnam War sharply divided U.S. lawmakers into hawks and doves.

The Great Society: the Presidency at the Center of the Political Process

Johnson claimed a popular mandate for the Great Society, but it was his work with the legislature, not the people, that gained implementation of the program. Johnson believed that the keystone to the entire Great Society was civil rights, and to win passage of the landmark Civil Rights Act of 1964, Johnson knew that he would have to do more than manage Democratic Party discipline. Because of southern resistance within his own party, he enlisted the support of moderate Republicans by forging an extraordinary alliance with Senate Republican leader Everett McKinley Dirksen, whose endorsement of the bill turned the tide in its favor.

The act desegregated such public accommodations as restaurants, hotels, and theaters, and banned job discrimination on the basis of race. It was followed in 1965 by the Voting Rights Act, squarely aimed at knocking down southern state impediments to full African American enfranchisement. In 1968, another civil rights act outlawed housing discrimination.

In addition to the civil rights agenda, the Great Society included Medicare (passed in 1965), which aided all Americans over the age of 65, regardless of need, in paying for medical treatment. This was expanded the following year by Medicaid, which covered all welfare recipients. Great Society education initiatives included the 1965 Elementary and Secondary Education Act, which provided federal funds to poor school districts across the country, and the Higher Education Act of 1965, furnishing tuition assistance to college and university students.

The Great Society enlarged the executive branch by creating two cabinet-level departments—the Department of Housing and Urban Development, and the Department of Transportation—and two important cultural agencies, the National Endowments for the Humanities and the Arts, and the Corporation for Public Broadcasting. The Department of the Interior was given responsibility for administering a National Wilderness Preservation System, the National Trails System, and the National Wild and Scenic Rivers System, as well as the provisions of the Land and Water Conservation Act of 1964.

Perhaps the most dramatic items of Great Society legislation were laws enacted under the aegis of what Johnson called the "War on Poverty." The 1964 Economic Opportunity Act created the Office of Economic Opportunity, an executive agency that oversaw such community programs as the Job Corps, Volunteers in Service to

America (VISTA), the Model Cities Program, Upward Bound, the Food Stamps Program, and Project Head Start.

Like the New Deal before it, the Great Society created and empowered a vast federal bureaucracy within the executive branch, putting the presidency at the center of enormous legislative power. Moreover, even as the Great Society legislation co-opted many congressional prerogatives, it also created a strong link between the presidency and the judiciary, since enforcing the civil rights and labor aspects of the program often required the assistance of the courts.

Guns and Butter, Decline and Fall

Not since the New Deal had so much of the day-to-day administration of the government as well as its long-range strategic planning been concentrated in the presidency. A profusion of programs, task forces, and presidential commissions created a *presidential government* administered directly by the White House.

Ultimately, the intensity and degree of this form of insider government removed much of the Great Society from both the legislature and the people. The more this was perceived to be happening, the less popular understanding and support the Great Society received. More than anything else, however, the growing involvement of the nation and the Johnson administration in the Vietnam War severely hobbled the president's social agenda.

def•i•ni•tion

Presidential government is government administered directly from and by the White House, from the president and through his immediate staff, with minimal participation by either the cabinet or the legislature.

Tonkin Gulf

The United States had been involved in the Vietnam War since the Truman administration, and President Johnson, with Secretary of Defense Robert McNamara, expanded that involvement—cautiously at first, but with tragic velocity after the so-called Tonkin Gulf Incident.

On August 2, 1964, the destroyer USS *Maddox*, on a reconnaissance mission in the Tonkin Gulf off the coast of North Vietnam, reported itself in international waters and under attack by five North Vietnamese patrol boats. The USS *Maddox* withdrew to South Vietnamese territorial waters, where it was joined by the destroyer USS *C. Turner Joy*. Damage was nothing more than a single ding made by a .50-caliber machine gun bullet. Two days later, however, a U.S. patrol craft detected what its crew interpreted as signals indicating another attack. In response, *Maddox* and *C. Turner Joy* fired their guns against what were believed to be hostile radar contacts—although no enemy vessels were actually sighted.

In response to the reported attacks, President Johnson set caution aside and ordered immediate retaliatory strikes against North Vietnam. On the evening of August 4, he made a television address describing the attacks and the retaliation. In the meantime, Secretary McNamara testified to Congress that the North Vietnamese attacks had been unprovoked—although he knew that the mission of *Maddox* had been to provide intelligence to support South Vietnamese strikes against the North. He also testified to "unequivocal proof" of the "unprovoked" August 4 attack, about which there was actually considerable doubt.

After Senate debate and in response to a message to Congress Johnson delivered on August 5, the Tonkin Gulf Resolution was passed by both houses. It authorized the president "to take all necessary steps, including the use of armed force, to assist any member or protocol state of the Southeast Asia Collective Defense Treaty requesting assistance in defense of its freedom."

In effect, the resolution abrogated much of the legislature's war-making authority, giving the president a blank check to conduct the Vietnam War without seeking congressional approval.

The Waste of War

The president many Americans had voted for because they feared Barry Goldwater would vastly expand the Vietnam War sent more than a half-million young men to Vietnam in 1968 alone, and there was no end in sight. The Johnson presidency was increasingly identified with the catastrophe of Vietnam rather than the triumph of the Great Society—which itself became a casualty of war, its funding drained by the cost of combat.

President Johnson desperately hoped to fund both guns and butter. In the end, the guns won.

Credibility Gap

Like the Great Society, the Vietnam War was, first and last, the business of the president. LBJ immersed himself painfully in the role of commander in chief, participating in every strategic decision and almost every tactical decision, down to personally approving bombing targets.

The downside of presidential government is that the president must bear responsibility for that government. Increasingly, the public turned against a war that seemed both misguided and unwinnable. Congress, which had given LBJ a blank check in 1964, progressively divorce itself from the war, even as many representatives and senators began directly opposing it. Vietnam became Johnson's war, and the president who had sought to unite the nation in a Great Society became the single most divisive figure in that nation. Worse, the more the president tried to justify the war, the more he attempted to claim progress toward victory, the less he was believed. The press routinely touted a credibility gap between what the president said and what the people believed.

What They Said

The battle against Communism must be joined in Southeast Asia … or the United States, inevitably, must surrender the Pacific and take up our defenses on our own shores.

—Vice President Lyndon Johnson, memo to President Kennedy, 1961

The presidency had survived scandals and corruption in the past, but its essential credibility had never before been subject to question, let alone doubt. A war-weary nation assumed that Johnson routinely lied. By 1968, Americans began to assume that *all* presidents routinely lie. After Vietnam, the presidency was never a quite trustworthy institution. After Johnson, presidents had to prove themselves truthful. They were no longer popularly accorded the presumption of honesty.

A Party in Disarray

On March 31, 1968, Lyndon Johnson made two surprise television announcements. He declared that he would restrict bombing most of the North Vietnamese homeland in an effort to bring the communists to the peace table, and he announced that he would not seek another term as president. Johnson recognized that his total identification with the war was contributing to the division within America.

Cease-fire negotiations did begin in May, but soon stalled. In August 1968, a badly splintered Democratic Party held its convention in Chicago. The most charismatic and promising anti-war candidate, Robert F. Kennedy, brother of the slain president, had himself fallen to an assassin's bullet on June 6, 1968, just after winning the California primary. Eugene McCarthy, another anti-war hopeful, garnered little support at the convention, which favored Johnson's vice president, Hubert H. Humphrey, who did not embrace an anti-war platform.

Outside the convention hall, a few miles to the north, anti-war activists occupied the city's lakefront Grant Park. Anti-Humphrey demonstrations—"Dump the Hump"— erupted, which the overzealous Chicago police escalated into what eyewitnesses universally described as a police riot. Amid the acrid scent of tear gas, Humphrey received the nomination.

In November 1968, just before the election, President Johnson agreed to Hanoi's onerous negotiating conditions, and ceasefire talks recommenced, giving Humphrey's sagging presidential campaign a much-needed boost. But it was too little too late. Republican nominee Richard M. Nixon, whose hawkish party was not divided over the war, ran on a platform that included a vague promise of a "plan to end the war." Running against Democratic chaos and rage, Nixon narrowly defeated Hubert Humphrey to become the thirty-seventh president of a deeply discontented United States.

The Least You Need to Know

♦ Ratified in 1967, the Twenty-Fifth Amendment explicitly defined the vice president's assumption of the presidency and defined his role in the event of presidential disability.

♦ Johnson appealed to his former congressional colleagues instead of establishing an effective bond with the American people.

♦ A synthesis of FDR's New Deal and JFK's New Frontier, LBJ's Great Society created a presidential government.

♦ Johnson led an ever-expanding American role in the Vietnam War, creating a crisis that finally devoured his presidency and all but destroyed the Great Society.

Chapter 23

Power

In This Chapter

- ♦ Nixon's efforts to rebuild and expand the presidency
- ♦ The New Federalism
- ♦ Nixon consolidates power within the White House
- ♦ White House or palace?
- ♦ Watergate downfall

No Democrat had been enthusiastic about Hubert Humphrey, the candidate of a broken party. Yet Nixon's margin of victory over him was hardly decisive: 43.4 percent of the popular vote to Humphrey's 42.7 percent. And, even worse, like Humphrey's candidacy, the office Nixon had won was damaged. It was not just that the American people were disgusted with Lyndon Johnson, they were disappointed in and disheartened by the presidency itself.

Paradoxical Shadows

But the United States presidency was never simply or entirely about popular opinion. Johnson had not left the office so much in a state of disarray as in a state of paradox. While the presidency was at low ebb—George E.

Reedy, LBJ's press secretary from 1964 to 1965 and special assistant in 1968, believed America was "witnessing the first lengthening shadows" foreboding the "twilight of the presidency"—Johnson had expanded presidential government so boldly that the next occupant of the office found himself armed with an arsenal of legal precedents for increasing executive power. Although the office was held in low esteem and therefore, suffered a decline in political influence, it had been enhanced in terms of sheer legal authority.

Tally _____

In 1968, Nixon polled 31,785,480 popular votes (43.4 percent) to Democrat Hubert Humphrey's 31,275,166 (42.7 percent). George Wallace, running on the segregationist American Independent ticket, polled 9,906,473 votes (13.5 percent). Nixon won 301 electoral votes; Humphrey, 191; and Wallace, 46.

Reclaiming the Presidency

Nixon faced daunting challenges. The presidency was tarnished, and the nation was deeply divided. Voters in unprecedented numbers had split their tickets, electing a Republican president, but giving control of both houses of Congress to the Democrats.

Nor was this the limit of national and political division. Most of the federal bureaucracy, expanded by Johnson's Great Society, was staffed by Democratic liberals, most of whom were civil servants, who could not simply be dismissed by the new president.

Executive Event _____

The bitter and even violent Democratic National Convention of 1968 fielded a candidate who was decidedly not the people's choice, but a product of the party leadership. The results of the subsequent election were so disappointing that the Democratic Party made a sweeping revision of its rules in 1971 in an all-out effort to reconnect the Democratic Party with Democrats themselves. The changes prompted most states to adopt direct, binding primaries—for Republicans as well as Democrats. The 1968 Democratic convention completed the transition that had begun in 1912, from the smoked-filled room to the fresh air of the direct primary.

War on the Bureaucracy

President Nixon declared war on the bureaucracy he had inherited, urging his cabinet officers to shake up their departments, stripping them of whatever Kennedy- and Johnson-era appointees they could within the constraints of civil service regulations.

The Johnson social initiatives had created such a large and complex organization that, far from shaking up the bureaucracy, Nixon's newly installed department heads more often than not found themselves carried along by its seemingly irresistible momentum. The massive administrative apparatus created by presidential government transformed the executive branch into a giant battleship—formidable in appearance and potential, but very slow to respond to the hand on the helm.

Expanding the Presidency

Unable to quickly co-opt the executive bureaucracy, Nixon prepared to seize the political initiative from the legislative branch.

Dwight Eisenhower, the president under whom Nixon had served as vice president, entered office with the intention of restoring what he considered the appropriate balance between executive and legislative authority. Nixon, in contrast, wanted to expand the powers of the presidency, even beyond what LBJ had established.

On the face of it, this approach made common sense. Republican Eisenhower had faced a Republican Congress, whereas Nixon was confronted by a Democratic congressional majority. If he intended to press a socially conservative agenda—to roll back the Great Society—he had no choice but to stand up to the legislative liberals.

But the Nixon approach also signaled a more profound revision of the concept of presidential power. Theodore Roosevelt, Woodrow Wilson, Franklin Roosevelt, and Lyndon Johnson had all used the presidency to introduce varying degrees of liberal reform. Indeed, throughout U.S. history, social reform was by definition liberal. But President Nixon resolved to use presidential power to introduce conservative reform.

> **" "** **What They Said**
>
> Richard Nixon is a no-good lying bastard. He can lie out of both sides of his mouth at the same time, and if he ever caught himself telling the truth, he'd lie just to keep his hand in.
>
> —Harry S. Truman

A Question of Motive

Yet, on closer examination, the social agenda of the Nixon administration does not appear very conservative at all. Much as Eisenhower had maintained the major features of the New Deal, so Nixon made no attempt to radically dismantle the welfare state. His approach to civil rights was very much in line with that of Johnson, including his advocacy of the most controversial aspect of the LBJ civil rights agenda: affirmative action, the policy requiring government contractors to demonstrate their efforts to hire minority workers. Nixon created an Office of Federal Contract Compliance to administer affirmative action and, through his labor secretary, promulgated the Philadelphia Plan, by which federal contractors were obliged to formulate goals and timetables for the acquisition of minority employees.

That Nixon did not wield power to make bold conservative reforms suggests that he expanded the presidency not to promote a particular ideology, but for the sake of presiding over an expanded presidency. For Richard Nixon, presidential power was an end in itself.

The New Federalism

As a number of prior presidents provided a label for the leading themes of their administrations—the Square Deal, New Freedom, New Deal, Fair Deal, New Frontier, and Great Society—so Nixon offered the New Federalism to describe his purportedly conservative redefinition of the roles of the presidency and the federal government.

In practice, the New Federalism was less ideological than organizational, an attempt to sort state from federal responsibilities. Insofar as the New Federalism contained a genuinely conservative Republican message, it was that the federal government could not be expected to do everything for everyone.

The Shift from Legislative to Administrative Action

Although Nixon's New Federalism was less sweeping than its name implies, the Democratic Congress reflexively declined to enact many of the president's legislative initiatives designed to reapportion federal and state responsibilities. After about two years of frustration with the legislature, Nixon took a new tack, which, unlike the New Federalism, was genuinely radical.

EOP

The president decided that most government action in the sphere of domestic policy was operational, administrative, and regulatory, rather than legislative. The implication of this, as Nixon saw it, was that much of the government could be run directly by the executive. Of course, the administrative presidency or presidential government was a trend that can be traced to Wilson, was intensified by Franklin Roosevelt, and expanded even further by Lyndon Johnson. Nixon upped the ante nearly twofold, as measured by the population of the staff of the Executive Office of the President (EOP), which had been created by FDR. Johnson had brought the EOP staff to a record 292 members; Nixon broke that record with 583 staffers by the end of his first term.

Nixon's EOP consisted of proven Nixon loyalists (this addressed his problem with a Democrat-heavy civil service bureaucracy), who not only formulated policy, as in the Johnson White House, but also went a long way toward implementing policy, thereby upstaging both legislative and cabinet-level roles.

A Council, a Bureau, and an Office

In addition to empowering the EOP, Nixon created a Domestic Council, chaired by White House counsel and domestic affairs assistant John Ehrlichman, which directed the making of domestic policy.

Nixon initially expanded the Bureau of the Budget, which had been established in 1921 by President Warren G. Harding; then, by an executive order of on July 1, 1970, he replaced it altogether with the Office of Management and Budget (OMB). The OMB not only took over the presidentially directed budgeting role, it introduced a layer of management on top of the senior civil servants who had been carried over from the Bureau of the Budget. By this restructuring, another move to neutralize the power of Kennedy- and Johnson-era civil servants, the OMB became directly answerable to the president.

From Cabinet to Super Cabinet

To consolidate his administrative presidency further, Nixon diminished the role of the cabinet secretaries by reassigning their influence and power to an inner circle of advisers, who did not have the constitutional standing of cabinet officers and who reported only to the president.

Even more boldly, in 1973, the president designated four senior loyalist cabinet members and others as what were officially called "White House consultants." They were better known by their unofficial title: the "Super Cabinet." The elevated cabinet personnel included the secretaries of the treasury (George P. Schultz), Health, Education, and Welfare (Caspar Weinberger), Agriculture (Earl L. Butz), and Housing and Urban Development (James T. Lynn); OMB director Roy L. Ash; National Security Adviser Henry Kissinger (later officially appointed as secretary of state); John Ehrlichman; and White House Chief of Staff H. R. (Bob) Haldeman. The Super Cabinet formulated policy on economic affairs, human resources, natural resources, community development, and foreign affairs, not only excluding the rest of the conventionally constituted cabinet from the president's policymaking circle, but bypassing both legislative input and oversight.

By the end of Nixon's first term, many had the impression that the White House was coming more closely to resemble a palace than what President Truman had often called it, the "people's house."

Nixon's War

The paradox of the Nixon administration was the decentralization of federal governing authority via the New Federalism and the simultaneous aggrandizement of presidential power. If anything, this aggrandizement was even greater in the area of foreign affairs than it was in the domestic sphere.

The Rise of the National Security Adviser

The first national security adviser was appointed by Dwight Eisenhower in 1953, and the role became even more important during the Kennedy and Johnson administrations. Nixon's national security adviser, former Harvard political scientist Henry A. Kissinger, emerged as the president's full partner in the formulation and conduct of foreign affairs, thoroughly marginalizing the Department of State through the creation of a foreign policy staff answerable only to Kissinger and the president.

def•i•ni•tion

Détente is the easing of tensions between rival nations through increased diplomatic, cultural, and commercial interaction.

The Nixon-Kissinger duo created and managed the two great foreign policy initiatives of the Nixon presidency, *détente* with the Soviet Union, and the opening and normalization of relations with the People's Republic of China. Both of these initiatives were designed to hasten the end to the Cold War, but, in the nearer term, they were also intended to cut loose North Vietnam from Soviet and Chinese support, thereby motivating the North Vietnamese leadership to negotiate not only an end to the Vietnam War, but to do so in a way that would bring what Nixon had promised the American people, "peace with honor."

The Fate of "Peace with Honor"

There can be no doubt that, having inherited Vietnam from Lyndon Johnson, Richard Nixon wanted to end the war quickly—but to do so honorably, which, for Nixon, meant not simply surrendering to the communists. This dual requirement drove Nixon to bring the war into the White House even more thoroughly than LBJ had, so that Johnson's war soon became Nixon's war, and—much to the president's consternation—the vituperative anti-war demonstrations that had targeted Johnson personally were now aimed at him, and were more numerous and intense.

Nixon took a devious new approach to the conduct of the war. To placate anti-war interests, he steadily reduced the number of U.S. ground troops in Vietnam through a program of "Vietnamization," the training and equipping of South Vietnamese forces to take over combat from U.S. personnel. Yet, even as he de-escalated U.S. ground involvement, he dramatically escalated the U.S. air war through stepped-up bombing campaigns and the secret bombing of North Vietnamese encampments and supply and infiltration routes in Cambodia, Vietnam's neutral neighbor. When this covert action failed to stem the flow of communist troops and equipment into South Vietnam, the president announced on April 30, 1970, a ground invasion of Cambodia.

The announcement touched off massive anti-war demonstrations across the nation, especially on college campuses. It also goaded Congress, which had long felt abused by Nixon, to a level of hostility commensurate with the prevailing mood of a growing majority of the American people.

Executive Event

On May 4, 1970, the governor of Ohio called in 900 National Guardsmen to quell a major anti-war protest at Kent State University, triggered by the U.S. invasion of Cambodia. In the heat of a confrontation between 28 young Guardsmen and students, the troops "overreacted" (a word much used during this period) with horrific results. They fired into a crowd of unarmed protesters, killing four students and wounding nine. A haunting photograph of a bewildered, grief-stricken young woman kneeling beside the body of a slain student was soon published in *Life* magazine and became an instant icon of the senseless nature of a war few believed in any longer. The message seemed all too clear: President Nixon had literally brought the war home.

Before the Cambodian invasion, the greatest obstacle to peace with honor had been the implacable will of the North Vietnamese leadership and people. After these events, it was, increasingly, the will of the American people and Congress that presented the greater obstacle.

Pragmatic or Imperial?

Even many of those who despised Nixon conceded that, misguided as he was, the president believed he was doing what was best for the country. These critics believed that Nixon had fallen into the Machiavellian trap of believing that laudable ends justify questionable means.

An increasing number of Americans, both in Congress and in the public, were no longer willing to accept Richard Nixon as a well-meaning if misguided pragmatist. They believed he had deliberately set out to create an imperial presidency, in which the executive trumps the other two branches of government, making a mockery of the constitutional balance of powers, not to mention the popular will.

"It Was a Greek Tragedy"

The Watergate scandal would seem to vindicate the position of those who believed Nixon was an imperialist with an insatiable appetite for power. Henry Kissinger said of the affair that destroyed the Nixon presidency, "It was a Greek tragedy. Nixon was fulfilling his own nature. Once it started it could not end otherwise."

The Plumbers: Nixon's Palace Guard

Kissinger, who deeply admired his chief, understandably tried to put as noble a face as he could on Watergate, but his assessment—that "Nixon was fulfilling his own nature"—rings with truth.

As the 1972 elections approached, no one—except, apparently, Nixon—doubted that the incumbent would be reelected, especially against a Democratic Party still in disarray and offering in George McGovern a well-meaning but lackluster candidate. Nevertheless, the president directed his campaign organization, the Committee to Re-elect the President (CREEP), to sabotage the Democratic Party with a combination of illegal espionage and so-called dirty tricks aimed at smearing any challengers.

On June 17, 1972, five burglars were arrested in the headquarters of the Democratic National Committee at the Watergate office building in Washington, D.C. It was soon revealed that these were no ordinary second-story men, but members of a White House covert action team dubbed by White House insiders "the Plumbers," because they had been created—secretly and illegally—to plug any leaks (security breaches) that might embarrass the White House. This counterespionage role was soon expanded, so that the Plumbers became a kind of palace guard, assigned to missions outside of the chief executive's constitutional mandate and even outside of the law. The Watergate burglary, which involved bugging (planting electronic listening devices) Democratic headquarters, was such a mission.

Tally _____

In 1972, Nixon was reelected over Democrat George McGovern by a landslide, winning 47,165,234 popular votes (61 percent) to McGovern's 29,168,110 (38 percent). Nixon swept the Electoral College, 520 to 17.

The Conspiracy Unravels

Thanks to a combination of the Plumbers' amateurish incompetence, the limits of loyalty among the members of Nixon's inner circle, the dogged journalistic brilliance of *Washington Post* reporters Bob Woodward and Carl Bernstein, and the eagerness of a hostile Congress to "nail" Nixon once and for all, the Watergate conspiracy unraveled during the president's second term, finally destroying the thirty-seventh presidency of the United States.

The congressional Watergate Hearings riveted Americans to their television sets. After each shocking disclosure, President Nixon would announce the resignation of a key White House insider, including Ehrlichman and Haldeman, among others.

White House crimes uncovered by the congressional investigation included the fact that former Nixon attorney general John Mitchell, in his capacity as Nixon's reelection campaign manager, had controlled secret monies used to finance "dirty tricks" intended to sabotage the Democratic party; that major corporations had made millions of dollars in illegal campaign contributions; that Nixon promised the Plumbers clemency and even bribes in return for their silence; that L. Patrick Gray, Nixon's nominee to replace the recently deceased J. Edgar Hoover as FBI director, had illegally turned over FBI records on Watergate to White House counsel John Dean; that Mitchell and CREEP finance chairman Maurice Stans took bribes; that the White House possessed illegal wiretap tapes; that Nixon directed the CIA to instruct the FBI not to investigate Watergate; and that, during 1969 and 1970, Nixon had secretly bombed Cambodia without the knowledge of Congress.

Executive Event _____

In the midst of the Watergate turmoil—though unrelated to it—Vice President Spiro
T. Agnew was indicted for federal income tax fraud and for bribes taken when he
had served as Maryland governor. After pleading no contest to charges of tax evasion
and money laundering, he resigned as vice president in October 1973. In his place,
Nixon appointed congressman Gerald Ford of Michigan.

The Limits of "Executive Privilege"

Late in the investigation, it was discovered that President Nixon had covertly taped
White House conversations—a practice that presidents Kennedy and Johnson had
also engaged in. To a congressional subpoena of the tapes, the president responded
with a claim of "executive privilege," a special right of privacy in matters relating
to presidential documents. While his lawyers fought the subpoena in court, the
president ordered Elliot L. Richardson (who had replaced John Mitchell as attorney general when Mitchell resigned that post to head up CREEP) to fire special
Watergate prosecutor Archibald Cox. On October 20, 1973, Richardson refused
and resigned in protest; his deputy, William Ruckelshaus, likewise refused and also
stepped down. The duty to discharge Cox fell to Nixon's solicitor general, Robert H.
Bork, who complied. What the press dubbed the "Saturday night massacre" served
only to suggest that Nixon had much to hide.

On July 24, 1974, the Supreme Court handed down its unanimous decision in *United
States* v. *Nixon*, holding that, while there was a "valid need for protection of communications between high Government officials
and those who advise and assist them," to "read the
Article II [constitutional] powers of the President as
providing an absolute privilege as against a subpoena
essential to enforcement of criminal statutes on no
more than a generalized claim of the public interest
in confidentiality of nonmilitary and nondiplomatic
discussions would upset the constitutional balance of
'a workable government' and gravely impair the role
of the courts under Article III."

> **What They Said** _____
>
> When the President does
> it, that means that it is not
> illegal.
>
> —Richard M. Nixon, televised
> interview with David Frost, 1977

Accordingly, Nixon released transcripts of some of the tapes. On July 27 through 30,
the House Judiciary Committee recommended that the president be impeached on
three charges: obstruction of justice, abuse of presidential powers, and attempting

to impede the impeachment process by defying committee subpoenas. Nixon then released the remaining tapes on August 5, 1974. These included the infamous "smoking gun" revelation that he had taken steps to block the FBI's inquiry into the Watergate burglary. Four days later, on August 9, 1974, Richard Milhous Nixon became the first president in U.S. history to resign from office, leaving to an already battered presidency a dark and murky legacy of imperial ambition and criminal behavior.

The Least You Need to Know

♦ Nixon inherited from Johnson a presidency that was tarnished and diminished in public and political influence, yet that also had behind it a number of legal precedents for expanded executive authority.

♦ Nixon counterpointed his New Federalism, ostensibly a reduction of federal authority, to a remarkably expansive conception of presidential power, creating what many have called an imperial presidency.

♦ As the Nixon White House assumed increasing control of all aspects of domestic policy, so Nixon and National Security Adviser (later Secretary of State) Henry Kissinger took full charge of foreign policy.

♦ The debacle of Watergate was born of a presidency that refused to be bound by ordinary law, including the Constitution.

24

Gerry and Jimmy

In This Chapter

♦ America's only nonelected chief executive

♦ The president as national healer

♦ The Ford Nixon pardon and its consequences

♦ How Watergate diminished the presidency

♦ Carter and the outsider presidency

♦ Separating the man from the office

The first of director George Lucas's *Star Wars* films was released just three years after Richard Nixon resigned the presidency, and more than one fan of the 1977 blockbuster identified the thirty-seventh president with Darth Vader, the foreboding and ruthless leader of "the Empire" who had chosen allegiance to the "dark side." The two chief executives who followed "Darth" Nixon could not have been more different in personality, image, and ethical orientation from their brooding predecessor. Their very names suggested the contrast. The first was often called Gerry, the second insisted on being called Jimmy.

The First Nonelected President

Vice President Gerald R. Ford was sworn in as president of the United States on August 9, 1974, immediately succeeding Richard Nixon, when his resignation became effective at noon of that day. Ford was not only the first U.S. vice president to succeed a president who resigned from office, he was also the first entirely nonelected president. He had not been Nixon's running mate in 1972, but was appointed to the vice presidency pursuant to the Twenty-Fifth Amendment (see Chapters 3 and 22) on October 12, 1973 (and confirmed by the Senate on November 27) when Vice President Spiro T. Agnew resigned after pleading no contest to income tax evasion and money laundering (he was charged with having taken $29,500 in bribes while governor of Maryland).

Much of popular reaction against Nixon had developed from his having isolated the White House and the presidency itself not only from the rest of the government, but from the people. Now Gerald Ford, in whose appointment the people had had no voice whatsoever, was expected to rehabilitate the office.

Executive Event

Gerald Ford entered office not only under unique and uniquely unhappy circumstances, at a moment of low moral ebb for the presidency, he inherited the worst U.S. economy since the Great Depression. To combat depleted gold deposits in the U.S. Treasury, Nixon had taken the United States off the gold standard, thereby preventing foreign countries from depleting the reserves further by claiming gold in exchange for the dollars they held. This action, however, seriously weakened the exchange rate of the dollar against other currencies, which touched off runaway inflation. By the time Ford took office, the inflation had combined with the kind of economic stagnation characteristic of recessions, prompting economists to invent a new word to describe the state of the American economy: stagflation.

The President as National Healer

Remarkably, Ford found that a majority of the American people and the media were friendly and receptive to him. To all appearances, a naturally gentle, affable man, the long-serving Michigan congressman (1949–1973 and House minority leader from 1965) was as open as Nixon had been emotionally closed and officially secretive. Where Nixon had been dark, Ford was sunny. Where Nixon had been remote, Ford was genially avuncular.

To flatly declare that Gerald Ford believed that his role as president at his moment in history was to be the national uncle would oversimplify and trivialize his approach to the office. Yet there is truth in this assessment.

Ford saw his mission as one of national healing in an effort to restore confidence in the institution of the presidency and, by extension, the government itself. After taking the oath of office, he sought immediately to soothe. "My fellow Americans," he said in a televised speech, "our long national nightmare is over." He went on, seeking to preempt any assumption that the government had become dysfunctional: "Our Constitution works; our great Republic is a government of laws and not of men." He then seemed to echo Abraham Lincoln's Second Inaugural Address by offering a message of forgiveness, reconciliation, and healing:

> Here the people rule. But there is a higher Power, by whatever name we honor Him, who ordains not only righteousness but love, not only justice but mercy.

> As we bind up the internal wounds of Watergate, more painful and more poisonous than those of foreign wars, let us restore the golden rule to our political process, and let brotherly love purge our hearts of suspicion and of hate.

The Pardon Controversy

Most Americans believed that Ford had struck just the right note—until, on September 8, 1974, he put his sentiments into the form of a legally binding "full, free, and absolute pardon [of] Richard Nixon for all offenses against the United States which he, Richard Nixon, has committed or may have committed or taken part in during the period from July [January] 20, 1969 through August 9, 1974."

In his inaugural remarks, Ford had sought to preempt any suggestion of there having been a deal between him and Richard Nixon: "If you have not chosen me by secret ballot," Ford told the nation, "neither have I gained office by any secret promises. ... I am indebted to no man, and only to one woman—my dear wife—as I begin this very difficult job."

In his September 8 speech granting the pardon, Ford was more explicit:

> [It] is not the ultimate fate of Richard Nixon that most concerns me.... My concern is the immediate future of this great country....

> My conscience tells me clearly and certainly that I cannot prolong the bad dreams that continue to reopen a chapter that is closed. My conscience tells me that only I, as President, have the constitutional power to firmly shut and seal this book. My

conscience tells me it is my duty, not merely to proclaim domestic tranquility but to use every means that I have to insure it.

And, with this, he issued the *pardon*.

def•i•ni•tion

Article II, Section II, of the Constitution gives the president the authority to **pardon**—to release from penalty and punishment (*not* to proclaim innocent)—anyone found guilty of an "offense against the United States." The provision specifically exempts impeachment from the scope of presidential pardon, and it is silent on the validity of the preemptive exercise of the pardon, in advance of any formal indictment or verdict.

The genuine decency that seemed to emanate from Gerry Ford persuaded many to take him at his word, yet he never succeeded in fully laying to rest suspicions of a dirty deal.

Lame Duck in Chief

Ford inherited a lame duck presidency and never succeeded in transforming it into anything else. Congress was decidedly unsympathetic to his domestic policies, especially his attempts to curb inflation by urging Americans to spend less.

In foreign affairs, Ford tried in vain to coax from Congress $300 million in supplemental aid to South Vietnam in 1975. But the legislators had given up on Vietnam, and Ford absorbed the full impact of the reassertion of congressional authority over the making and unmaking of war. At the nadir of the Watergate scandal, in November 1973, Congress had delivered to the "imperial presidency" of Richard Nixon a Sunday punch in the form of the War Powers Act, which effectively voided the Tonkin Gulf Resolution, the "blank check" it had given LBJ (see Chapter 22). The War Powers Act required the president to inform Congress within 48 hours of deployment of U.S. military forces abroad and required the withdrawal of such forces within 60 days if Congress did not approve the deployment.

Ford secured the Republican nomination for the presidency in 1976, only to lose to an obscure Georgia governor named Jimmy Carter. Political pundits—and Ford himself—attributed his defeat to lingering suspicions surrounding the Nixon pardon.

Tally

Democrat Jimmy Carter polled 40,825,839 popular votes in 1976 (50 percent) to Ford's 39,147,770 (48 percent). The electoral vote count was 297 to 240.

The Watergate Legacy: An Office Diminished

Gerald Ford soothed but did not finally heal the nation. He did not (and could not) undo the legacy of Watergate.

As most Americans saw it, Nixon had claimed more power than any president before him. They had been largely willing to grant him the right to do so. Despite the unpopularity of Lyndon Johnson, the example of the likes of Lincoln, Theodore Roosevelt, Woodrow Wilson, Franklin Roosevelt, and even John F. Kennedy inclined most Americans to admire strong executives. But when Nixon pushed his claims beyond the Constitution by claiming unlimited executive privilege, in effect asserting that the president, unlike all other Americans, was above the law, the people and Congress drew the line. And *that* affected the presidency.

The office of the executive emerged from the Nixon-Ford years a diminished institution. Not only was the presidency exposed to lingering suspicion and contempt, the office was curbed by new laws. The Case Act of 1972 sought to rein in a leading Nixon modus operandi, personal presidential diplomacy, by requiring all executive agreements made with foreign powers to be reported to Congress. The War Powers Act of 1973, as mentioned, curbed the president's unilateral authority to make war. The Congressional Budget and Impoundment Control Act of 1974 barred the president from unilaterally *impounding funds*. without congressional approval. Additional legislation related to this act made the directors and deputy directors of the Office of Management and Budget (OMB) subject to Senate confirmation, thereby ensuring that budget matters would no longer be the exclusive province of the executive.

def•i•ni•tion

Impounding funds occurs when a president declines to spend the monies appropriated by Congress to implement an act of Congress, thereby circumventing the will of Congress by functionally preventing implementation of the act.

A President Named *Jimmy?*

Beginning with the very name he used, *Jimmy*, James Earl Carter Jr. appeared on the national stage with the disarming informality of a genuine political outsider. He was untainted by "Washington politics" (which Watergate had made a dirty phrase) and uncontaminated by conventional party politics. His platform was not particularly populist—indeed, as a southern Democrat, Carter was a moderate centrist, not a left-leaning liberal—but his image was decidedly so. Although he was an Annapolis graduate, trained as a nuclear engineer, Carter presented himself as a simple "peanut farmer" from Plains, Georgia.

Carter earned the 1976 Democratic nomination through victories in mostly small-state primaries rather than by climbing the party ladder, and he defeated Ford in large part by campaigning against the imperial trappings of Richard Nixon.

A Revolution in Style and Symbolism

On one of the coldest inauguration days in memory, Jimmy Carter walked hand in hand with his wife Rosalynn the entire mile from the Capitol steps, where he had been sworn, to the White House. It was an act of humility and openness intended to usher in a new presidential era that, whatever else it might become, was unmistakably the opposite of everything the Nixon presidency had been.

Carter's soft-spoken drawl and easy-going manner had played well with voters, but, strangely enough, it seemed that the electorate did not want this style to carry over after the inauguration. The press had been hard on Gerald Ford, unfairly demeaning his intellect and even mocking his purported clumsiness.

What They Said

For myself and for our nation, I want to thank my predecessor for all he has done to heal our land.

—Jimmy Carter, inaugural address, January 20, 1974

The media's real target was Ford's regular-guy informality, which, despite what people living in a democracy claimed they wanted, came off as insufficiently "presidential." Once in office, Carter became the next target—and for the same reason. The most widely lampooned lapse in presidential image was his appearing on television in a cardigan sweater rather than a suit and tie to give a talk on energy conservation in which he asked the American people to turn down their thermostats at home, as he had in the White House.

Carter was well aware of the force of the symbolic trappings surrounding the presidency, but instead of carefully modulating their use, he discarded them altogether. It was as if a judge had appeared on the bench in shirtsleeves sans judicial robes.

Even more disturbing was the idea of offering a cardigan and a lowered thermostat as the answer to problems with the economy, the state of the energy markets, and the Arabs who controlled much of the oil supply. Carter dished up the homely and practical advice one expected from one's grandparents, not from the president of the United States.

A Deficiency of Leadership, an Absence of Goodwill

In his zeal to undo the imperial presidency, Jimmy Carter came off as prosaic and even weak. Instead of succeeding in redesigning the presidency to fit this new image, Carter appeared too small for the presidency.

The popular image of Jimmy Carter poisoned his early relations with Congress. Even though the Carter-era Congress was two-thirds Democratic in both houses, the president proved unable to enforce party discipline in order to move his legislative agenda along. In part this was a dramatic symptom of the dire alienation of the legislative from the executive branch that had been created during the Nixon years and that was carried over into the 29 months of the Ford presidency. However, Carter's inability to move Congress, mainly during the first year of his administration, was also a failure of presidential leadership.

Military professionals often speak of "command presence," a nearly indefinable quality that endows an effective officer with the ability to lead. The presidency, it seems, requires a version of this. President Carter had a plainspoken gift for attracting an electoral constituency, but this did not translate into sustained popular leadership at the presidential level. Worse, his success as a political outsider persuaded Carter that he did not really need to build a constituency in Congress because he had "the people" on his side. This was precisely opposite of the error Johnson had made—he failed to appeal to the people because he was more comfortable managing Congress— yet it was an error nevertheless.

Triumph and Disappointment

Jimmy Carter's first year as president was disappointing, and no one was more disappointed by it than Carter himself. A man of great intelligence and possessed of an open mind, he learned to mend his ways with Congress and, by his second year, managed to usher through a good part of his legislative agenda, including, most momentously, ratification of the treaties by which the United States turned over control of the Panama Canal and restored sovereignty over the Panama Canal Zone to Panama. A controversial act, it went a long way toward improving chronically strained relations between the United States and Latin America.

Indeed, Carter's greatest successes were in foreign affairs, most notably his catalytic work in bringing together two apparently implacable enemies, Egyptian president Anwar el-Sadat and Israeli prime minister Menachem Begin at the Camp David presidential retreat in Maryland to hammer out the Camp David Accords, which brought an enduring peace between Egypt and Israel, greatly contributing to the stability—at least for a time—of the Middle East.

Despite improving relations with Congress and his achievements in foreign affairs, Carter never succeeded in creating a strong theme on which to build his presidency. His informality was refreshing to some, but failed to compel most. Coming across as a decent man did not convey the charisma that had become a necessary adjunct to the presidency in an era of mass media.

Blame Without Credit

Without a theme and without charisma, Carter found himself receiving little credit for his achievements yet much of the blame for anything that went wrong, even if he had no direct connection to it. The deepening energy crisis brought on by the sharp increase in oil prices imposed by OPEC (Organization of Petroleum Exporting Countries) was beyond his control, to be sure, yet Americans' anger over high gas prices and critical gasoline shortages was laid at the doorstep of the White House. Similarly, when "students" loyal to the revolutionary Islamic ruler of Iran, the Ayatollah Khomeini, stormed the U.S. embassy in Tehran and took much of the embassy staff hostage on September 4, 1979, Carter was blamed for his inability to secure their release. The president became virtually a hostage to the hostage crisis, which blighted the final 15 months of his administration and cost him any hope of reelection.

Afterlife

The electorate demonstrated their disdain for the presidency of Jimmy Carter by delivering the White House to Republican Ronald Reagan with 51 percent of the vote to Carter's 41 percent (independent John B. Anderson took 7 percent). Where Carter had called for the common-sense sacrifice symbolized by a humble cardigan, Reagan exhorted Americans to reclaim their greatness. Where Carter asked for patient cooperation with the government, Reagan promised liberation from government. Where Carter had many beliefs but presented no one great overriding theme, Reagan preached the faith that (in the words of his most effective TV campaign ad) it could be "morning again in America."

During the eight years of the Reagan presidency, many Americans decided that the four Carter years had been truly bad ones—and yet even these people conceded considerable admiration for Jimmy Carter the man.

There was indeed much to admire. No American president (save perhaps John Quincy Adams) has had a richer presidential "afterlife" than Carter, who wrote best-selling memoirs and essays; founded in Atlanta the Carter Center, a nongovernmental organization dedicated to the advancement of human rights everywhere on the planet; has served several of his White House successors as an international peace negotiator, election observer, and goodwill ambassador; has traveled on his own to advance humanitarian causes; and has been active in the United States promoting the Habitat for Humanity project. In 2002 his work was recognized with the Nobel Peace Prize, Carter becoming only the second U.S. president to earn the award. (Theodore Roosevelt received it in 1906 for his role in negotiating an end to the Russo-Japanese War of 1905.)

It has often been said that there are no second acts in American political dramas. Jimmy Carter gave the lie to this chestnut and, in so doing, endowed his presidency, long after he left the White House, with a retrospective luster.

The Least You Need to Know

- Gerald Ford, the only nonelected vice president to become president, conceived his principal role as the nation's healer in the wake of Watergate.

- Watergate diminished the presidency, both in the public perception and by prompting legislation intended to restore the balance of power between Congress and the executive.

- Jimmy Carter won the 1976 Democratic nomination without working through the traditional party apparatus and became the first outsider president since Andrew Jackson.

- Carter's informality was intended to efface the Nixon imperial presidency. Although this style played well with voters, it finally made Carter look insufficiently "presidential."

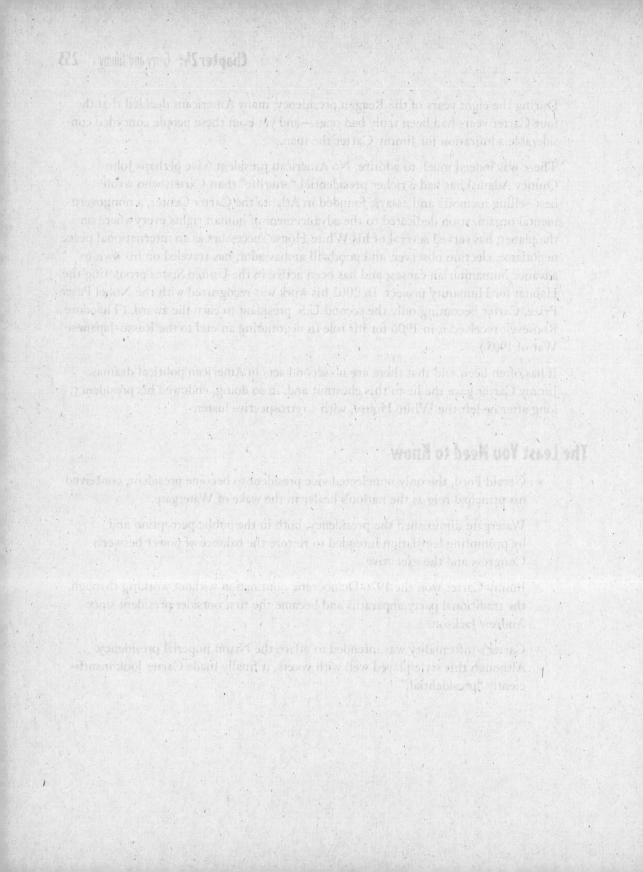

Part 7

The CEO Presidency

Ronald Reagan promised to use the presidency to "get big government off our backs." His two terms were controversial, but President Reagan himself achieved and maintained great popularity, and Republicans predicted the long reign of their party. Reagan's vice president and successor, George H. W. Bush, lacked his predecessor's vision, charisma, and outsider mystique. He was defeated for reelection by Democrat Bill Clinton, who endeavored to create a less partisan "centrist" presidency, but incited Republican resentment that produced the second impeachment in American history. Clinton was succeeded by George W. Bush, who greatly expanded executive authority, which a majority of Americans believed he used poorly. Bush used it to start an unpopular war in Iraq and a massive economic meltdown, in part associated with his deregulatory policies. Bush's unpopularity undermined Republican candidates everywhere in the 2008 election, which brought into office Democrat Barack Obama, the nation's first African American president.

25

The Reagan Revolution

In This Chapter

- ◆ Campaigning against the Carter "malaise"
- ◆ The rhetorical presidency
- ◆ Assassination attempt and the failure to invoke the Twenty-Fifth Amendment
- ◆ Impact on Congress and the judiciary
- ◆ From Reaganomics to the Iran-Contra scandal

Of the three branches of government, only the executive—not the legislative, not the judicial—has led genuine political realignment of American government.

Such realignment has been relatively rare. In the twentieth century, Theodore Roosevelt and Woodrow Wilson set a course for progressive reform, which the presidencies of Harding and Coolidge reversed in a return to laissez-faire government. Propelled by the dire emergency of the Great Depression, Franklin Roosevelt led a sweeping realignment toward a welfare state, which succeeding presidents up through Jimmy Carter either rolled back, perpetuated, or advanced—but never substantially changed. From the 1930s to 1980, the United States remained under the glow or the shadow (depending on one's political point of view) of the New Deal.

Then came Ronald Reagan, the first executive since FDR to use the presidency to radically realign American government and politics.

A Hunger for Greatness

Ronald Wilson Reagan was a highly unlikely revolutionary—so unlikely, in fact, that Democratic liberals may be forgiven, if not entirely excused, for having almost universally underestimated him.

Born above a grocery store in the central Illinois town of Tampico in 1911, Reagan worked his way through college and successively became the two things he most wanted to be, a sportscaster and a screen actor. His B-picture talent was less than spectacular, but with 53 films and, later, many TV appearances to his credit, he was a universally familiar face and never out of work.

What They Said _____

How can you take this man seriously? Perhaps even he doesn't know what he's talking about.... He is the biggest liar of all the American Presidents ... the worst terrorist in the history of mankind ... a madman, an imbecile and a bum.... His ideas are from the era of Buffalo Bill, not the nuclear age.

—President Fidel Castro, 1985

A Democrat during his on-screen years, Reagan's yen for politics earned him the presidency of the Screen Actors' Guild (SAG). He left both the acting profession—though he would always remain an actor at heart—and the Democratic Party to enter Republican politics with a strong stop-communism and end-big-government message. In 1966, Reagan handily defeated incumbent Democrat Pat Brown for the governor's office in California and served two terms, during which he made a national reputation as a ruthless tax cutter and an implacable foe of the welfare state, having vigorously endeavored to make good on his campaign pledge of sending "the welfare bums back to work."

Reagan left the California state house in 1975 and campaigned against Gerald Ford for the 1976 Republican presidential nomination. Although he lost—narrowly, picking up 1,070 delegates to Ford's 1,187—his strong anti-Soviet, anti–big government, anti-tax, and anti-welfare positions made an impact, and when Ford lost to Carter in the general election, most Republicans were more than ready to abandon Ford's moderation and embrace Reagan's conservatism.

Executive Event _____

Reagan left the profession of acting, but never stopped being an actor. No one ever questioned his patriotism or doubted his belief in the vision he had for the nation; however, many observers also had the distinct impression that, for Reagan, the presidency was yet another role. Jim Wright, Democratic House majority leader in 1980, believed that "Reagan was an entertainer, a super salesman, an enjoyable companion .... His grasp of issues, and of history, was superficial." Wright recalled in a 1996 memoir the day president-elect Reagan visited him and House speaker Tip O'Neill in O'Neill's Capitol office. "Tip sat behind a large desk which, he explained to the president[-elect], had once belonged to Grover Cleveland. 'I played him once in a movie,' Reagan said. 'No, Mr. President,' Tip gently corrected, 'you played Grover Cleveland Alexander, the baseball player.'"

Caught a Malaise? Here's the Cure

On July 15, 1979, President Carter addressed the nation concerning what he called an "erosion of our confidence in the future [that] is threatening to destroy the social and the political fabric of America." Although he never used the word in the address, media commentators pointed out that Carter had diagnosed a national "malaise" and they immediately dubbed his talk the "Malaise Speech."

It was against this sense of malaise and what many believed was Carter's feckless response to it—end the energy crisis by obeying the 55-mile-per-hour speed limit and turning down your thermostat —that Ronald Reagan directed his campaign. The answer, he told voters, was not to whine about a "malaise" or to impose limits on energy consumption, but to take bold steps to return Americans to their birthright of greatness by cutting taxes and vastly reducing the size of government ("getting government off our backs," Reagan called it). These goals would be achieved by eliminating much government regulation of the "private sector"—business of all kinds—and by radically rolling back the welfare state. The one area of government that Reagan proposed to enlarge was the military, which needed to be bigger and stronger in order to defeat, once and for all, the Soviet Cold War threat.

The "Great Communicator"

Reagan's oratorical gifts made for a dramatic contrast with Carter. Not only were his speeches well written—and, contrary to what many of his critics believed, Reagan often took a strong personal hand in writing them—they were delivered with all the dramatic polish a journeyman actor could give them. Even more important, unlike Carter, Reagan based his candidacy and his subsequent presidency on powerful themes: how strong government weakens those governed and the proposition that the Soviet Union still constituted the greatest international threat the United States faced.

It was the anti–big government message that rang most resoundingly. Reagan delivered its most concentrated distillation in his first inaugural address: "In this present crisis, government is not the solution to our problem; government is the problem." Like Woodrow Wilson and Franklin Roosevelt before him, Ronald Reagan created a rhetorical presidency. It was not simply that he gave a good speech. It was that he delivered superb lines very effectively. Wilson's "The world must be made safe for democracy," FDR's "The only thing we have to fear is fear itself," and Reagan's "Government is not the solution to our problem; government is the problem" were all cut from the same rhetorical cloth. For his ability to put his policy beliefs into the capsule form of an inspiring formula, Ronald Reagan was justly dubbed "the Great Communicator."

Grace Under Pressure

On March 31, 1981, at the end of his second full month in office, President Reagan left the Washington Hilton Hotel after delivering a speech. Six shots were fired from the crowd near the door. Secret Service agent Timothy J. McCarthy and Washington police officer James Delahanty were wounded, as was White House press secretary James S. Brady, who suffered a severe head wound from which he would never fully recover.

> **" "** **What They Said** _____
>
> I hope you're all Republicans.
> —President Ronald Reagan,
> to his surgeons, just before the
> operation to remove a bullet
> lodged in his lung, March 31, 1981

Apparently unhurt, the president was bundled into his limousine. Although it soon became apparent that he, too, had been wounded, he insisted on walking unaided into the emergency room of George Washington University Hospital, where it was discovered that a bullet had entered his lung—a .22-caliber "devastator," intended to explode on impact. Fortunately, this one failed to detonate and was removed in a 2-hour emergency operation.

Ronald Reagan was the oldest man ever elected president, and the public now saw their 70-year-old president not only survive a severe bullet wound, but joke about it—"Honey, I forgot to duck," he told wife Nancy as he was being wheeled into surgery—and then recover with apparently remarkable speed. The incident drew even more popular admiration for Reagan and support for his legislative agenda. The man who preached the conservative Republican message of self-reliance seemed hardly fazed by a bullet in his chest.

The President as Legislative Leader

Much like Jimmy Carter in 1976, Ronald Reagan ran in 1980 as an outsider, whose fresh perspective positioned him to criticize politics-as-usual Washington. Once he entered the Oval Office, however, Reagan discarded his predecessor's playbook. Where Carter had spurned Congress—at least initially—Reagan endeavored to establish a close working relationship with key members. In this, his presidency recalled Lyndon Johnson's; however, whereas Johnson habitually summoned members to the White House, Reagan reached out to them, either by telephone or with a trip to Capitol Hill.

Ronald Reagan had strong popular appeal; however, he recognized the disparity between his stunning electoral vote victory—489 to 49—and the fact that he was barely a majority president, having captured 51 percent of the popular vote (Carter lagged at 41 percent, and Independent John Anderson captured 7 percent). Accordingly, he was careful not to repeat Carter's error of bypassing Congress in a direct appeal to the people. In his view, Carter had squandered the Democratic congressional majority that existed during his presidency. Although in 1980 the Democrats still controlled the House, the Republicans won a Senate majority, and the president was determined to make the most of it.

Tally _____

Reagan polled 43,899,248 popular votes (51 percent) in 1980 to Democrat Carter's 35,481,435 (41 percent) and Independent John Anderson's 5,719,437 (7 percent). Reagan swept the Electoral College, 489 to 49, Anderson receiving no electoral votes. In 1984, Reagan's popular majority was much greater. He polled 54,281,858 votes (59 percent) to Democrat Walter Mondale's 37,457,215 (41 percent). In another Electoral College sweep, Reagan received 525 votes to Mondale's 13. It was the largest electoral total in American history.

Yet Ronald Reagan did not bow to Congress. He positioned himself unmistakably as the nation's legislative leader. Whereas Carter, like LBJ, had been on hands-on executive, whom critics accused of transforming the Oval Office into the Office of Micromanagement, Reagan was infamously averse to details. He therefore put together an Executive Office of the President (EOP) that tightly packaged his agenda and handed it to him in a form for which he could readily lobby Congress. The result was a legislative steamroller propelled by Reagan's breezily appealing confidence and steered by hard-nosed EOP bureaucratic operatives.

OMB

The president did not rely on lobbying alone to assert executive legislative leadership over Congress. The Reagan budget was the heart of the domestic policy popularly known as Reaganomics, and OMB director David Stockman became Reagan's point man for pushing his budgetary agenda through the legislature.

Reagan sent Stockman charging up Capitol Hill under the banner of supply-side economics, the theory that the economy thrives by stimulating the production of goods and services (the supply side) because (according to advocates of the theory) supply *creates* demand. To stimulate the supply side, the president called for a sharp reduction in government regulation of commerce and industry and aggressive tax cutting for wealthy investors and for businesses. This, Reagan and Stockman claimed, would free up money for investment and employment, the benefits of which would ultimately "trickle down" to the middle and working classes in the form of more and better jobs.

Deregulation and tax cutting required aggressive budget cutting—and *that* is what Stockman and Reagan had to sell to Congress.

They did not do it exclusively through lobbying. Stockman deftly used the very law Congress had passed to rein in Nixon's imperial presidency, the Budget and Impoundment Control Act of 1974 (see Chapter 23), to reclaim from the legislature control over the budget. As Sidney M. Milkis and Michael Nelson explain in *The American Presidency: Origins and Development, 1776–2007* (see Appendix C). Stockman used the "reconciliation" provision of the 1974 act, which allowed the congressional budget committees to consolidate all of a president's budgetary changes into a single bill, to create a budget package that was far easier to push through Congress than each separate authorization would have been.

Having seized the whip hand on the budget, the Reagan White House slashed both taxes and spending on social programs—going further than any president after FDR to dismantle the New Deal—while simultaneously making unprecedented increases in defense spending (tripling the national debt from just under $1 trillion in 1981 to $2.9 trillion in 1989).

Building the "Reagan Court"

President Reagan reached out to the judicial branch as well as the legislative. No president since George Washington has had a greater effect on the judiciary.

President Reagan appointed four Supreme Court justices: Sandra Day O'Connor, the first woman associate justice; William H. Rehnquist, whom Reagan later appointed chief justice; Antonin Scalia; and Anthony M. Kennedy. All were chosen for their conservative orientation, which the Reagan White House defined as a reluctance to create new constitutional rights for the individual and due deference to states' rights; however, both O'Connor and Kennedy proved more moderate than conservative on the bench.

Executive Event

Ronald Reagan's appointments profoundly skewed the federal court system to the right; however, he was not always successful in appointing the judges he wanted. Senator Ted Kennedy, Democrat from Massachusetts, led the opposition to the confirmation of Robert Bork, citing on the Senate floor a resolutely conservative record: "Robert Bork's America is a land in which women would be forced into back-alley abortions, blacks would sit at segregated lunch counters, rogue police could break down citizens' doors in midnight raids, schoolchildren could not be taught about evolution, writers and artists could be censored at the whim of the Government, and the doors of the Federal courts would be shut on the fingers of millions of citizens for whom the judiciary is—and is often the only—protector of the individual rights that are the heart of our democracy." On October 23, 1987, the Senate rejected Bork's confirmation, 58 to 42. Reagan then nominated Judge Douglas Ginsburg, who withdrew from consideration after admitting to having smoked marijuana.

Beyond the Supreme Court appointments, Reagan disseminated his conservative philosophy widely throughout the federal judiciary with life-tenured appointments to 372 federal benches, including key appeals court positions.

The President as Party Leader

Complementing Reagan's leadership of all three branches of government was his leadership of the Republican Party. The president's ambition was to ensure Republican domination of American political life for a generation or more—maybe even permanently. His motive was not simply to acquire and hold power, but to transform the nation ideologically, to move it from New Deal–based liberalism to laissez-faire conservatism. Reagan therefore sought to instill throughout the party a conservative mind-set. Whereas previous party leaders emphasized politics—locally based and relying on quid pro quo patronage to create loyalty—Reagan sold ideology. The Republican Party would henceforth be the "party of ideas," by which was meant the party of conservative ideas.

Iran-Contra and the Curse of the Second Term

Two related clichés have long dominated American political life: "There are no second acts in American politics" and "No president has a successful second term." As with most clichés, tired though they may be, there is some truth to both.

President Reagan was reelected in 1984 with 59 percent of the popular vote over Democratic challenger Walter Mondale's 41 percent; however, the Democrats retained a large majority in the House and, in 1986, took the Senate as well. There was a growing sense among the public that the Reagan presidency, from the beginning a rhetorical presidency, was little more than rhetoric. The feel-good message that had worked so well against the Carter "malaise" in 1980 began to ring hollow. Worse, the president often seemed out of touch, his edge dulled, perhaps, with age. The extraordinary machine that was his EOP began to appear too efficient, too powerful, as if the machine were running the president rather than the other way around.

A New Watergate?

In November 1986, President Reagan confirmed reports that the United States had secretly sold arms to Iran, the nation that had held the U.S. embassy staff hostage for 444 days during the Carter administration. After initially denying rumors that the arms sale had been intended to gain the release of U.S. hostages held by terrorists in Lebanon, Reagan later admitted the existence of an arms-for-hostages swap. Hard on the heels of this admission came the revelation from Attorney General Edwin Meese that a portion of the arms profits had been diverted to finance the Contra rebels fighting against the communist Sandinista government of Nicaragua. The Reagan administration favored a right-wing rebellion in Nicaragua, but Congress, hoping to avoid a Central American incarnation of the Vietnam War, specifically barred Contra aid. The diversion of the secret arms profits was therefore blatantly unconstitutional, and the affair was variously dubbed the "Iran-Contra scandal" or, more pointedly, "Iran-gate."

A congressional investigation gradually revealed how, in 1985, an Israeli group had approached National Security Adviser Robert MacFarlane with a scheme in which Iran, in exchange for arms, would use its influence to free the Lebanon hostages. Secretary of State George Schultz and Secretary of Defense Caspar Weinberger objected to the plan, but (MacFarlane testified to Congress) the president agreed to it. That is when U.S. Marine Lt. Col. Oliver (Ollie) North suggested adding the twist by which profits from the sales would be funneled to the Contras. The beauty of the scheme was downright Nixonian: Illegal arms sales produced illegal profits, which would be totally concealed from Congress because the money would be slipped to the Contras.

In what seemed an eerie replay of Watergate, the congressional investigation climbed the White House ladder, ascending through national security advisers John Poindexter and MacFarlane, through CIA Director William J. Casey (who died in May 1987), and up to Defense Secretary Caspar Weinberger. This left one question: Was President Reagan in on the scheme or was he the dupe of rightwing zealots in his administration? Either answer was bad.

The Teflon Legacy

As a result of the congressional inquiry into Iran-gate, North, Poindexter, CIA administrator Clair E. George, and Weinberger were either indicted or convicted. All of the convictions except Weinberger's were overturned on appeal, and Weinberger, like the others, was subsequently pardoned by President Reagan's successor, George H. W. Bush.

As for Ronald Reagan, Iran-gate was biggest of several second-term missteps. He had sleepily bumbled his way through a 1986 summit with Soviet premier Mikhail Gorbachev, and he had watched helplessly as the stock market, in the high times that followed deregulation, crashed precipitously in 1987.

Within a single month after the revelation of the Iran-Contra scheme, Reagan's approval rating fell from a lofty 67 percent to an earthly 46 percent. Yet there was no truly serious talk of impeachment, and people took to calling him the "Teflon president"—a chief executive against whom nothing could be made to stick.

What They Said

I was cooking breakfast this morning for my kids, and I thought, "He's just like a Teflon frying pan. Nothing sticks to him."
—Rep. Patricia Schroeder (Dem., Colorado), quoted in *Boston Globe*, October 24, 1984

There was a backlash against the Reagan presidency for a few years following the end of his second term, some historians even ranking him among the worst of American presidents. But driven in part by "Reagan Republican" acolytes, the public and academic assessment of Reagan dramatically improved with age. Even before his death in 2004 at the age of 93, government buildings, schools, roads, and Washington's in-town National Airport had been named in his honor. After his death, there were rumors that the Reagan likeness would soon appear on some coin—possibly even replacing Franklin D. Roosevelt on the dime.

Over the years, Republican presidential candidates—and even some Democrats—have scrambled to compare themselves to Ronald Reagan. As of 2008, however, that trend seems destined to diminish if not die as the nation reels from an economic meltdown caused to a significant degree by the massive deregulation of the financial sector begun during the Reagan years and accelerated during the two terms of George W. Bush. As of this writing in 2009, it remains to be seen whether the Teflon that served President Reagan in life will flake away from his posthumous legacy.

The Least You Need to Know

- ◆ Ronald Reagan successfully campaigned against incumbent Jimmy Carter by inviting Americans to throw big government off their backs in a return to greatness built on rugged individualism.

- ◆ Dubbed the "Great Communicator," Reagan brought the rhetorical presidency to a height not seen since Franklin Roosevelt.

- ◆ Reagan restored highly effective relations between the president and Congress based largely on party discipline and his own popularity.

- ◆ Ronald Reagan had an impact on the Supreme Court and federal court system greater than any other president since George Washington.

26

In Reagan's Shadow

In This Chapter

- ◆ The George H. W. Bush presidency: management without vision
- ◆ Foreign affairs vs. domestic policy
- ◆ Emergence of the signing statement
- ◆ The presidency and the new media
- ◆ The New Democrat presidency
- ◆ The Clinton impeachment and its legacy

Consider this analogy: George H. W. Bush was to Ronald Reagan what William Howard Taft was to Theodore Roosevelt: overshadowed. Both Taft and Bush lacked the dynamism, vision, and charisma of their predecessors. It is a measure of the length of the Roosevelt and Reagan coattails that Taft and Bush were so readily elected; but were it not for the fact that Taft weighed in at 332 pounds, it would be easy to say that because T. R. and Reagan seemed larger than life, Taft and Bush, by comparison, appeared rather smaller than life.

Return of the Insider

In part, the perceived "smallness" of both Taft and Bush resulted from the contrast of their insider identities with the bold outsider identities of those who had preceded them. Taft had held only low-visibility appointed offices before he became president, and Bush, although he had been a U.S. representative from 1967 to 1971, was better known for having been ambassador to the United Nations (1971–1973), liaison to China (1974–1975), and CIA director (1976–1977) before he served as vice president to Ronald Reagan.

The Vision Vacuum

George H. W. Bush always came across as what he was: supremely competent. However, as an indifferent public speaker, he was incapable of continuing Ronald Reagan's rhetorical presidency. Moreover, unlike Reagan, he was not driven by any particular vision of America. Yet a clear majority of American voters were nevertheless willing to elect competence on the assumption that Reagan had pointed the way, and all his successor had to do was follow it.

Tally

Bush defeated Democrat Michael Dukakis, 47,946,422 (54 percent) to 41,016,429 (46 percent), earning 426 electoral votes to 111 for Dukakis.

But as the Bush presidency wore on, the want of vision was increasingly felt. President Reagan had raised the bar of expectation for the presidency—or, perhaps, restored that bar to the position it had occupied during the administrations of Kennedy and Franklin Roosevelt. People expected their president to be, at least in some measure, a visionary and an inspiration.

Bush always looked and sounded awkward on television, whereas Reagan, the screen veteran, was master of the medium. Perhaps even worse, Bush projected the appearance of what he had spent much of his life being—a successful businessman and a government bureaucrat. To many Americans, this came across as elitist and "Ivy League."

But the deficiency of the Bush presidency went deeper, and the president himself recognized it. He admitted that he lacked what he termed "the vision thing": a passionate package of ideas and principles that could be conveyed both passionately and clearly. Reagan possessed this in abundance. Bush did not, and it would cost him a second term. As conservative commentator George Will remarked, Bush "does not say why he wants to be there [in the White House for another four years], so the public does not know why it should care if he gets his way."

What They Said

George is a damn good guy, but he doesn't come through well. It's a case of choking. It takes 11 hours to get George ready for an off-the-cuff remark.
—Robert Strauss, former Democratic Party chairman, 1988

Diplomacy vs. Domesticity

In foreign affairs, Bush may have lacked an inspiring vision, but he certainly knew where he wanted to steer the nation—to the place of quiet global supremacy made ready for it by the decline and fall of the Soviet Union. By inclination and profession, Bush was a diplomat, and he transformed the presidency into the nucleus of personal, methodical diplomacy.

Throughout his presidency, both the House and the Senate were controlled by the Democrats, yet Bush was able to coax Congress into authorizing financial assistance to the pro-American Contras in Nicaragua—the very group at the heart of Reagan's Iran-Contra affair—to resist the leftist Sandinista government. Simultaneously, the president worked with the nations of Europe and Latin America as well as the Soviet Union to pressure the Sandinistas into holding elections in 1990—which resulted in their replacement by a centrist government friendly to the United States.

More controversially, Bush launched military action in Panama to topple and arrest strongman dictator Manuel Noriega on charges of drug trafficking. Operation Just Cause (December 20, 1989–January 31, 1990) succeeded in capturing Noriega, bringing him to trial in the United States, and installing a new government.

Bush also managed U.S. policy through the collapse of the Soviet Union, which occurred on his watch. The president steered a delicate course between allowing events to unfold among the Soviet-dominated governments of Eastern and Central Europe and actively encouraging the leaders and people of these countries to strike out for independence. By no means did Bush "win" the Cold War, but he was sufficiently careful and skillful not to lose it. Had he been more overt in promoting the dissolution of the old Soviet bloc, the Kremlin might have taken drastic steps to suppress independence. Had he turned his back on events, the breakdown of what Ronald Reagan famously called the "evil empire" probably would have been slower and less certain.

Yet Americans were stingy with the credit they gave Bush the diplomat—precisely because his success in foreign affairs seemed to come at the expense of any interest in domestic affairs. The budget deficit created by the Reagan tax cuts and extravagant defense spending continued to pile up during the Bush administration and, with it, the economy went into recession, yet the president seemed not to care. It was an impression driven home by the notable paucity of a domestic legislative agenda during the last two years of the Bush administration.

Bush's focus on foreign affairs returned the presidency to what the earliest presidents saw as its primary role. But Americans had come to expect their presidents to lead in domestic legislation as well as foreign affairs. Bush therefore came up short.

Executive Event

Operation Just Cause is unique in American military history as an act of war directed against a single person, Manuel Antonio Noriega, the president of Panama. In 1988, he had been indicted by a U.S. federal grand jury for drug trafficking, and when economic and diplomatic sanctions failed to pressure the dictator into resigning, President Bush used the murder of an off-duty U.S. Army officer by Panamanian soldiers as the premise for approving the creation of an alternative government for Panama and launching a war to arrest Noriega.

The U.S. Army Rangers' innovative light infantry and special operations forces bore the brunt of the operation, but among the 24,000 invaders, navy SEALs, air force personnel, and Air National Guard units also participated. After house-to-house fighting in Panama City against Panama Defense Forces, Noriega was arrested at the Vatican diplomatic mission, where he had taken refuge. Returned to the United States, he was convicted on April 10, 1992, of eight counts of cocaine trafficking, racketeering, and money laundering and was sentenced to 40 years' imprisonment, later reduced to 30 years, then 17 for good behavior. His sentence ended September 9, 2007, but as of January 2009 he remains in prison pending a demand for extradition to France to face drug trafficking charges.

Operation Just Cause cost the lives of 314 PDF soldiers, 19 U.S. military personnel, and significant casualties among Panamanian civilians.

Management

Under George H. W. Bush, the presidency was neither a bully pulpit nor the legislative helm, but rather an office of management. In foreign affairs, Bush tended to deal—and to deal well—with situations, challenges, and opportunities as they rose. He *managed* them. In domestic affairs, he attempted to substitute management for the bold leadership that the faltering economy required.

War by Coalition

The high point of Bush's managerial presidency was his response to the Iraqi invasion of Kuwait in the summer of 1990. Instead of leaping to unilateral military action against Iraq's dictator Saddam Hussein, President Bush and his Department of State first persuaded the United Nations to sanction action against Iraq, then, with masterful personal diplomacy, Bush assembled an unprecedented coalition of 31 nations to oppose the invasion. The result was Operation Desert Shield, followed by Operation Desert Storm—the brief Persian Gulf War of 1990 and 1991.

Massaging Congress and Expanding the Conservative Court

President Bush managed Congress almost as effectively as he managed the Persian Gulf War coalition. He developed cordial relations with a Congress that, throughout his term, had a solid Democratic majority. Bush was able to add to the conservative population of the Reagan-era Supreme Court by successfully shepherding two nominees through contentious Senate confirmation hearings, David Souter (who, like many conservative jurists, proved relatively moderate once on the bench) and Clarence Thomas, an African American conservative who became one of the most reliably conservative members of the court.

 Tally _____

Congress overrode just one of George H. W. Bush's 47 vetoes—a 98 percent record unequaled by any president forced to deal with an opposition majority in Congress.

Emergence of the Signing Statement

Bush treated the members of Congress with great courtesy, bestowing on key leaders the ultimate honor in his gift, an invitation to a game of horseshoes, an enthusiasm for which was among the president's few obvious idiosyncrasies.

But courtesy could only go so far, and when Congress passed legislation the president found distasteful but not meriting veto, he accompanied his signature with a *signing statement*, a tactic that his son, the forty-third president, would use even more extensively.

def•i•ni•tion _____

A **signing statement** is the president's written pronouncement on a signed bill, which may modify the legislature's intentions by narrowing or skewing its provisions by executive interpretation.

Bush's signing statement to the Civil Rights Act of 1991—a law that shifted the burden of proof in anti-discrimination lawsuits from the plaintiff (employee) to the defendant (employer)—made it clear that the president intended to administer the act far more narrowly than what the legislative authors intended. Most of Bush's signing statements generated controversy that recalled the stir created by Andrew Jackson's assertion that the president's judgment on the constitutionality of a law was just as valid as that of the Supreme Court (see Chapter 8). Arguably, as a means of counteracting Congress without the showdown of a direct veto, the signing statement stands as the single most important contribution George H. W. Bush made to the institution of the presidency.

Return of the Outsider

The election of 1992 pitted against the incumbent insider two outsiders, the Democratic governor of Arkansas Bill Clinton and independent candidate H. Ross Perot. Clinton's top campaign adviser, James Carville, understood the advantages of the outsider image, but he believed the single issue that overrode everything was the economic recession, which he urged candidate Clinton to pin on the president's lack of engagement with domestic affairs.

> 66 99 **What They Said** _____
>
> It's the economy, stupid.
>
> —Phrase James Carville advised Bill Clinton to repeat to himself if he ever needed a reminder of the main issue of the 1992 presidential campaign

The Third-Party Equation

Candidate Clinton never staked everything on the outsider card because he understood that the independent in the race, maverick businessman H. Ross Perot, had a far better hand. A self-made billionaire, Perot financed his own campaign, which was built on the premise that his complete absence of political or electoral experience made him just the man the nation needed. He was beholden to no party and no one.

Perot had built his own fortune, and he could do the same for America. He had no campaign managers, no handlers, and no party agenda. What he did have was a set of simple charts and graphs and an abundance of homely metaphors—"If someone as blessed as I am is not willing to clean out the barn, who will?"—and enough money to finance a series of half-hour televised infomercials. His appeal was populist in the traditional late-nineteenth-century sense, but Perot went further than the likes of William Jennings Bryan by aiming his campaign directly at the people. In effect, he presented his candidacy as a referendum on two-party political business as usual and a plebiscite on change.

The Perot candidacy generated considerable excitement and even more curiosity, posing the most significant threat to the major parties since Theodore Roosevelt's Bull Moose run in 1912 (see Chapter 15). He played especially well in the new environment of mass media—cable television, which featured CNN and its 24-hour news cycle, as well as a profusion of political talk shows. These new outlets gave Perot generous coverage. Clinton and his advisers recognized this media sea change early in the campaign, and the Democratic candidate elbowed his way onto the same shows that featured Perot. The more traditional Bush was left far behind.

Tally

In the three-way 1992 race, Clinton earned a plurality victory, 44,908,233 (43 percent) votes to 39,102,282 (37 percent) for the incumbent Bush and 19,741,048 (19 percent) for independent H. Ross Perot. The electoral tally was 370 for Clinton, 168 for Bush, and 0 for Perot. Clinton fared better in 1996, taking 47,402,357 (49.2 percent) popular votes against 39,198,755 (40.7 percent) for Republican Bob Dole and 8,085,402 (8.4 percent) for H. Ross Perot, who ran this time as the candidate of his own Reform Party. Clinton took 379 electoral votes, Dole 159, and Perot none.

Presidential Packaging

Clinton's media-savvy campaign believed that a presidential candidate should package himself—and that the package had to promise more than the benefits of electing an outsider. Merchandising professionals have long known that no word is more powerful on a package than "new," and so Clinton was marketed as a New Democrat, one who possessed the social consciousness of an FDR-era Democrat but without the lock-step allegiance to the welfare state entitlements of the New Deal and with a more sympathetic embrace of the interests of business, a traditional constituency of the Republican Party.

The problem with the "package" was that it reflected an attempt to please all constituencies, to claim a sizeable tract of every parcel of social, economic, and political territory. As the old saying goes, "If you try to please everybody, you'll please nobody," and Clinton found himself floundering in the early months of his presidency.

The Presidency and the Press

Perhaps surprisingly, Clinton, who had used the media so well during his campaign, mishandled the press once he was installed in the Oval Office. Taking advantage of the profusion of cable TV networks and the 24-hour news cycle that CNN and its newly emerging competitors scrambled to fill, the president often appeared on television to speak directly to the people, marginalizing the traditional White House press corps by holding few press conferences. The result was corps of hostile correspondents, who drew unflattering parallels between Clinton and the other recent southern Democratic president, Jimmy Carter. Both men had tried to please everyone, the commentators said, and neither had a strong sense of direction, let alone a compelling national vision. Both the governor of Georgia and the governor of Arkansas, they said, were way out of their depth in the White House.

66 99 What They Said _____

> At the [Democratic National] convention, Clinton was like a used car salesman peddling his vehicle for change. The wax job was shiny, the hubcaps sparkled, the upholstery was spotless, the paint was new. But when you look under the hood you discover he is hawking a model from the Seventies, a Carter mobile with the axle broken and frame bent to the left.
>
> —Sen. Phil Gramm, Republican from Texas, in *The New York Times*, September 18, 1992

Partisan Poison

Adding to the popular discontent kindled by a hostile press corps was a tide of unprecedented partisan hostility. Whereas George H. W. Bush had been able to forge civil, even cordial relations with a Democratic Congress, Clinton was met with sharply focused opposition from the Republican minority during the first two years of his administration and much more of the same from the Republican majority that prevailed during its last six years.

It was more than argument and name calling. The Republican minority made relentless use of the filibuster to thwart passage of major Clinton legislative initiatives. The result was not a Republican victory, but repeated Democratic defeats—and, worst of all, a legislative gridlock that frustrated and enraged many Americans.

Victory, Pyrrhic Victory, and Defeat

Like Jimmy Carter, Bill Clinton was an extremely intelligent man open to many ideas. He strove to make the New Democrat concept more than an empty label by ushering through Congress a massive half-trillion-dollar deficit-reduction plan, which stormed into the fiscal responsibility territory the Republicans had long claimed as their exclusive preserve. The plan passed in the House by two votes and resulted in a Senate tie, which Vice President Al Gore broke.

The REGO Project

Having achieved a tangible victory with deficit reduction, President Clinton assigned Vice President Gore the task of chairing the National Performance Review (NPR), a key feature of Clinton's program to "reinvent government" (REGO) by streamlining bureaucracy in ways that would more adequately address the nation's social and economic needs. In September 1993, Gore's NPR issued proposals designed to save $108 billion over five years by eliminating more than a quarter-million federal jobs and introducing many other systemic innovations, the most stunning of which was the creation of a "customer service contract" with the American people.

To this invasion of President Reagan's old stomping grounds, the reduction of big government, Republicans (and many Democrats) responded with skepticism often bordering on sarcasm. The public, however, liked REGO, as did most civil servants, who were eager to get rid of unnecessary practices that got in the way of their doing the best possible job.

Backing Away from Foreign Policy

Despite Republican resistance and even ridicule, President Clinton laid claim to important victories on the domestic front, including deficit reduction and those aspects of REGO he was able to get through Congress. But whereas his predecessor had been absorbed in foreign affairs at the expense of domestic policy, Clinton initially devoted little attention to foreign policy, except for his promotion of the North American Free Trade Agreement (NAFTA), which created free trade with Canada and Mexico. He used television effectively to sell the controversial agreement directly to the American people, who, in turn, influenced legislators—actually more Republicans than Democrats—to approve it.

While Clinton counted NAFTA a triumph, even he had to admit disappointment over his handling of the mission of U.S. troops deployed in Somalia. President Bush had sent them on a humanitarian mission, but Clinton allowed this force to become part of a U.N. peacekeeping mission in a war-torn country that had no legitimate government. The result was a chaotic military failure and a threat from Congress that it would cut off funding for the mission if the president did not order an immediate withdrawal.

The Failure of Health-Care Reform

With NAFTA controversial and Somalia a failure, the American public went to the polls in the midterm elections of 1994 profoundly uneasy over Clinton's apparently unsteady foreign policy and frustrated by the collapse of a much-touted design for universal health care.

Whereas most other presidents formulated a leading policy or theme, Clinton took a protean and pragmatic approach. As a "New Democrat," he claimed the right to draw on whatever portion of the political spectrum he believed would provide the best approach to national challenges and opportunities. His deficit reduction plan smacked of conservative Republicanism, whereas his healthcare program, as formulated by the huge Task Force on National Health Reform, looked as if it had come straight out of Roosevelt's New Deal.

Expensive and entailing the creation of an entirely new bureaucracy, the health care plan never had a chance with Republicans and became the source of extremely bitter partisan protest.

The Comeback and the "Third Way"

The 1994 midterms came after NAFTA (which many people opposed) and Somalia (a frustrating tragedy) and in the midst of the health-care reform debacle. Even the Clinton victory with deficit reduction proved Pyrrhic, as many Americans were unhappier over cuts in *entitlements* and increases in taxes than they were happy over the reduction in the deficit. Voters showed their displeasure by sending Republican majorities to both houses of Congress.

The new Republican speaker of the House, Newt Gingrich, seized on the midterm electoral rebuff of the Democrats to promulgate a "Contract with America," which trumped Gore's customer service contract and which sought to preempt relations between the presidency and the people by interposing Republican congressional pledges to eliminate federal programs, cut taxes, and reduce regulatory "burdens."

Bill Clinton seemed destined to a one-term presidency. But he was a politician at his best with his back to the wall. Clinton redoubled his New Democrat initiatives, taking new aim at taxes, crime reduction,

> ## def•i•ni•tion
>
> **Entitlements** are government programs that provide guaranteed benefits—usually financial—to defined groups, such as ethnic minorities, people with disabilities, senior citizens, and so on.

welfare reform, and budget cutting in his boldest moves to encroach on the traditional Republican issues. Whereas Democrats had traditionally addressed the needs of the poor while Republicans tended to identify their constituency as those who were comfortable or better, Clinton redirected his presidency and his party toward the middle class.

It was to the middle class that he directly appealed to promote a balanced budget that did not require rolling back such New Deal and Great Society institutions as Medicaid, Medicare, education initiatives, and environmental protection. Clinton harked back to the days of his candidacy and embarked on promoting his agenda as if it were a brand-new political campaign. In the end, he achieved what Woodrow Wilson and Jimmy Carter had both failed to do—outmaneuver Congress in a direct appeal to the people, specifically to the middle class, who, long accustomed to being ignored by both parties, responded enthusiastically.

As his first term drew to a close, Bill Clinton had found his constituency—the middle class—and he trounced Republican challenger Bob Dole in the 1996 elections, emerging as an increasingly popular and respected president, who was effective despite the continued Republican majority in Congress.

Casualties of Impeachment

The presidency of the middle class was the elusive "third way," the alternative to traditional Democratic liberalism on the one hand and traditional Republican conservatism on the other. Clinton was riding high at last.

Gotcha Politics

On September 11, 1998, the Republican-controlled Congress published on the Internet the full text of a report written under the direction of Kenneth Starr, an independent counsel appointed to investigate allegations of possibly impeachable offenses committed by President Bill Clinton. Millions of Americans pored over detailed accounts of the president's liaison with a 21-year-old White House intern, Monica Lewinsky.

> **What They Said**
>
> I did not have sexual relations with that woman, Miss Lewinsky.
> —President Bill Clinton, televised press conference, January 26, 1998

Starr had begun investigating the involvement of the Clintons in a shady real-estate undertaking known as Whitewater (a name that coincidentally echoed "Watergate") and other possible financial improprieties, but, finding no evidence of wrongdoing in these areas, Starr hit pay dirt with the Lewinsky affair.

At issue, Starr claimed, was not extramarital sex, but the violation of the presidential oath of office by lying about the affair in a sworn deposition he had given in a sexual harassment civil lawsuit brought against him by a former Arkansas state employee, Paula Jones. Starr also alleged that the president had lied about the Lewinsky affair to a grand jury.

Although few Americans believed that the lies rose to the level of impeachable offenses, the House of Representatives voted, along party lines, to impeach Clinton. While the Republicans held a simple majority of Senate seats, removal of a president from office requires a two-thirds Senate vote. Even though achieving such a supermajority was clearly impossible, Senate Republicans pressed on with what they grimly called their "constitutional duty," but which was nothing more or less than an effort to destroy the president's rapport with the people by causing him months of humiliation. On February 12, 1999, to the surprise of no one, the Senate acquitted the president.

> **Tally**
>
> On December 21, 1998, with impeachment proceedings at full tilt, a CNN/USA Today/Gallup poll gave Clinton his highest public approval ratings ever: 73 percent.

Butcher's Bill

The president was acquitted, but any hope of bipartisan cooperation—or even rudimentary civility—was gone. For the remainder of his second term, the president, unable to get any of his legislative agenda through Congress, resorted to the extensive use of executive orders and proclamations to bypass the legislative roadblocks. It was not an ineffective presidency, but yet another modern presidency embattled.

Nor did the damage end with Clinton's presidency. Vice President Al Gore, in his 2000 contest against Republican George W. Bush, deliberately distanced himself from the president, whose personal conduct had clearly disturbed him. In this, however, he failed to acknowledge the enduring popularity of Clinton. No one liked the infidelity and the lying about it, but a majority of Americans recognized that they had fared very well during the Clinton years, for the most part years of peace and prosperity. For the first time in generations, the U.S. budget was not only balanced, but showed a surplus. Unemployment was low, and although there were some troubling signs on the horizon, economic growth had been steady and vigorous overall. The Clinton coattails were ample and there for the grabbing. But Al Gore decided not to reach out.

The Least You Need to Know

♦ George H. W. Bush followed the vision-driven presidency of Ronald Reagan with a "management presidency," which substituted competent stewardship for the dynamic leadership of his predecessor.

♦ Bush returned the presidency to its earlier role as the nation's diplomatic center, from which foreign policy was formulated and directed, but substantially neglected domestic policy, which he left largely to Congress.

♦ Bush cultivated cordial relations with a Democratic Congress, but controversially used the presidential signing statement as a tactic for interpreting many bills in ways that Congress never intended.

♦ Clinton and his advisers packaged the presidency through skilled—though some-times flawed—exploitation of the new television broadcast venues, including cable and 24-hour news channels, and by creating a New Democrat presidency, which synthesized traditional Democratic and traditional Republican issues in an appeal to the often-neglected middle class.

♦ The impeachment of Bill Clinton was a dramatic symptom of the partisan rancor that came to characterize presidential politics and the relationship of the presidency to Congress throughout most of the 1990s.

27

Pushing the Envelope

In This Chapter

♦ The problematic election of 2000

♦ Building a unitary executive

♦ Impact of 9/11 on the presidency

♦ The presidency as a permanent political campaign

♦ Iraq War and Hurricane Katrina

♦ Obama's challenge

George W. Bush was not the first candidate to lose the popular vote but win the electoral vote and become president. Yet the fact remains that, in 2000, a majority of Americans did not want as their president the man Green Party candidate Ralph Nader called "the bumbling governor of Texas." This alone would have led the 48.5 percent of the electorate who voted for Vice President Al Gore and the 2.7 percent who voted for Nader to conclude that American democracy had failed at the dawn of the twenty-first century.

But there was an even more compelling reason for loss of faith in our system. The election came down to a disputed count over a small number of votes in Florida—a state governed by candidate Bush's brother—and was "settled" by a 5-to-4 vote of an ideologically conservative, possibly partisan, United States Supreme Court.

Nor would the election be the last of the doubts surrounding the Bush presidency. For no modern president had posed greater challenges to American government than the forty-third.

The Broken Election

The 2000 contest was not the first flawed presidential election in American history. The 1824 election of John Quincy Adams (see Chapter 7) and the 1876 election of Rutherford B. Hayes (see Chapter 13) both presented deeply disturbing problems. The issues in 2000 were, however, at once uniquely trivial and profound.

Too Close to Call

The first returns gave Gore 50,996,116 votes against 50,456,169 for Bush, but the electoral vote tally all came down to Florida, governed by candidate Bush's younger brother, Jeb, where the popular vote was a dead heat. Initial counts gave Bush a lead of 1,784 votes; after a recount mandated by state law, the Bush lead narrowed to 327 votes. Dissatisfied with an automatic recount, Democrats demanded a hand recount in four counties where they believed significant numbers of Gore votes had not been counted. The basis of this assumption was the state's use of antiquated punch-card ballots, on which voters indicated their choices by pushing a stylus through a card. If a voter failed to push the stylus all the way through, the resulting hole might be blocked by a tiny rectangular fragment of cardboard—called a "chad"—which prevented the tabulating machine from registering the vote. In accordance with Florida law, election officials struggled to evaluate disputed ballots so as to "determine the intention" of the voter. This led to endless canvassing board disputes. The future of the nation—indeed, the world—depended on 327 Floridians and fragments of scrap cardboard, each smaller than a piece of confetti.

Executive Event

Chad was not the only issue in Florida. In Palm Beach County, a confusing two-page "butterfly ballot" design caused some Gore voters (mostly elderly) to mistakenly cast their ballots for Reform Party candidate Patrick J. Buchanan, whose name appeared opposite Gore's. In other Florida counties (and in Ohio, where the election results were also close), African American voters (overwhelmingly Democratic) complained that they had been subjected to intimidation and other attempts to prevent their casting ballots. Finally, in a number of states, questions were raised about voting machines manufactured by Diebold, a well-known business-machine firm whose CEO reportedly had ties to the Republican Party.

Legal Battle

The Bush and Gore camps filed a series of suits and countersuits halting and restarting the manual recounts, even as Katherine Harris, Florida's secretary of state, declared that she was prepared to certify Bush as winner on November 14, the legal deadline. The state's top election official, Harris was not only a Republican, but had served as a Bush delegate to the Republican National Convention and was one of eight co-chairs of the state Bush campaign. When the Florida Supreme Court (most of whose justices had been appointed by Democratic governors) enjoined certification until November 26, which it set as the deadline for recount results, the Bush legal team appealed to the United States Supreme Court, which, on December 12, 2000, voted 5-4 to overturn the Florida Supreme Court and barred further manual recounts. The Supreme Court having spoken, Al Gore conceded the election to George W. Bush on December 13. It was decided that Bush had carried Florida by 537 votes.

> ### What They Said
>
> [W]e may never know with complete certainty the identity of the winner of this year's Presidential election, [but] the identity of the loser is perfectly clear. It is the Nation's confidence in the judge as an impartial guardian of the rule of law.
>
> —Associate Justice Stephen Breyer, December 12, 2000, in his dissent from the majority decision ending the Florida recount of the 2000 election

The Worst of It

Those who objected to the result protested that George Bush had been elected not by the people, but by a one-vote margin in the Supreme Court. In the end, however, the breakdown in the election process, a combination of antiquated technology, partisan manipulation, and (some believed) judicial partisanship, was less disturbing than the fact that the election had been so close in the first place. In part, this reflected deep partisan divisions in the nation. But it was also the result of uninspiring campaigns in which neither major-party candidate had generated much enthusiasm. Whatever else the result may have been, it seemed indisputably arbitrary. Had a few more voters voted, had a few more votes been counted, had more voters pressed their punch cards harder, had fewer been confused by the "butterfly ballot," Gore would have been elected. Is this what the leadership of the biggest and most enduring democracy on the planet had come to?

Tally _____

In 2000, Bush polled 50,456,167 votes (48 percent) against Democrat Al Gore's 50,996,064 (48.5 percent), but Bush took 271 electoral votes to Gore's 266 and was elected. Green Party candidate Ralph Nader, deemed a "spoiler" by many Democrats, received 2,864,810 votes (2.7 percent), and Reform Party candidate Patrick Buchanan polled only 448,750 votes (0.4 percent), just ahead of Libertarian Harry Browne's 386,024 votes (0.4 percent). Bush was reelected in 2004 by a slim popular majority, 62,028,285 votes (51 percent), to Democratic challenger John Kerry's 59,028,109 (48 percent) and 406,924 (1 percent) for Ralph Nader, who, this time, ran as an independent. Bush received 286 electoral votes to Kerry's 252.

"W"

The affable if inarticulate George W. Bush—whom many voters characterized as a "guy you'd like to have a beer with" (though he was, in fact, a recovering alcoholic)—liked to be called "W" by way of distinguishing himself from his father, former President George *H. W.* Bush.

"W" was as straightforward a name as you could have, and W was a politician who strove to reduce things to their simplest form. As he would later famously remark to Joe Biden, the Democratic senator from Delaware who would be elected vice president in 2008, "Joe, I don't do nuance." Yet the campaign he conducted was by no means straightforward.

Compassionate Conservatism vs. Ideological Conservatism

Bush entered the race backed by the Republican evangelical base, which the party had first seriously cultivated during the Reagan campaign of 1980. The agenda of these voters was overwhelmingly values based; they were less concerned about specific political issues than about promoting such "Christian" values as opposition to abortion, government support for faith-based charities and schools, and an acknowledgment that the United States was founded on Christian or Judeo-Christian values. That Bush presented himself as a "born-again" Christian, a "person of faith," was particularly important to these voters.

What They Said _____

It's amazing I won. I was running against peace, prosperity, and incumbency.

—George W. Bush, press conference, June 14, 2001

Another Bush constituency comprised ideological conservatives, whose beliefs were rooted in the Reagan presidency and who believed that the best government was the least government. A subset of this Reagan-style ideological conservatism were the neoconservatives—the neocons—who embraced interventionist foreign policy intended to sow democracy wherever possible in the world on the assumption that democratic nations were, ipso facto, pro-American.

Bush had campaigned neither as a narrow "values" candidate nor as an ideological conservative. Much like his Democratic rival, he portrayed himself as a centrist and a pragmatist, hoping to transcend the partisanship that had become so bitter during the Clinton years. His father had invented a phrase for this political philosophy, "compassionate conservatism," which W adopted. The result was a blurring of distinction between Bush and Gore, who were, in reality, dramatically different.

Toward a Unitary Executive

For the most part, George W. Bush began his presidency in a highly pragmatic manner with a moderate conservatism that seemed to lack any sharp ideological edge. It was a useful approach, since the Republicans held only a very narrow majority in the House and were tied 50-50 with the Democrats in the Senate (Vice President Dick Cheney could cast tie-breaking votes, however). The president could claim no compelling mandate, ideological or otherwise, from voters.

The president told the American people that he wanted to unite the nation rather than exploit partisan divisions. Yet there was one major conservative issue on which he could not resist acting early in his administration. He ushered through Congress a monumental $1.3 trillion tax cut, which (in a throwback to "trickle-down" Reaganomics) disproportionately benefited the wealthiest Americans. The result was the defection in May 2001 of Vermont Republican James M. Jeffords to the Democratic caucus (he declared himself an Independent), thereby giving the Democrats a Senate majority that allowed them to take all Senate committee and subcommittee chairmanships from the Republicans. This development prompted Bush's former campaign manager and now chief political adviser, Karl Rove (Bush called him "the Architect," because he had designed his rise to office), to work with Republican candidates in an intensive effort to help ensure the election of the party's congressional hopefuls in the 2002 midterms.

By sidestepping the traditional Republican Party structures, Rove made the White House the source of Republican political power. This was a first step toward realizing in practice what political theorists had called the "unitary executive," a form of government in which the president reigns supreme over every aspect of the executive branch and is thereby enabled to take broad action without input or interference from Congress or the judiciary.

The World Changed

The consolidation of governing power within the White House was greatly accelerated in the aftermath of September 11, 2001, when 19 Islamic extremists hijacked four U.S. airliners and deliberately crashed two into New York's World Trade Center, one into the Pentagon, and a fourth—apparently intended for the White House or Capitol—into the Pennsylvania countryside.

After an unsteady beginning in which the president seemed uncertain of what to do or say, Bush rallied the nation to fight what he called "the first war of the twenty-first century." His approval rating shot up from 51 to more than 90 percent, and Washington partisanship instantly dissolved much as it had in the aftermath of the Japanese attack against Pearl Harbor on December 7, 1941.

Immediately, an Office of Homeland Security, based in the White House and under the direct control of the president, was created to coordinate the efforts of law enforcement and intelligence on every level, as well as certain aspects of the military. Much as Lyndon Johnson had done after the Tonkin Gulf incident in 1964 (see Chapter 22), President Bush drew from the legislature a virtual blank check to fight "terror." In a stirring address to a joint session of Congress on September 20, he struck a Churchillian tone, speaking both of defending the nation and advancing "human freedom—the great achievement of our time and great hope of every time." In the coming struggle, he pledged, "We will not tire, we will not falter, and we will not fail."

Bush rushed through Congress a flurry of laws to expand the investigative reach of U.S. law enforcement agencies, all coordinated through the White House. The most important new law was the USA PATRIOT Act, passed by the Senate on October 11, 2001, and the next day by the House. This omnibus legislation provided measures against money laundering to finance international terrorism; expanded provisions for wiretaps and surveillance; ensured immunity against prosecution for the providers of government-requested wiretaps; expanded systems of personal identification; instituted a foreign-student monitoring program; mandated improved passports to prevent forgery; allowed "Sneak-and-Peek" searches, authorized surreptitious search warrants and seizures; and authorized investigators to examine library records to determine who was reading what. At the time, few voices were raised in protest of measures that abridged constitutional guarantees in ways not seen since the emergency war measures of Franklin Roosevelt, Woodrow Wilson, and Abraham Lincoln.

The Bush White House amassed its extensive war powers by painting any incipient opposition to the "War on Terror," whether from Congress or elsewhere, as both unpatriotic and desperately dangerous. The president repeatedly claimed that "9/11 had changed everything," meaning that it was an event the framers of the Constitution could not possibly have contemplated and that, therefore, certain aspects of the Constitution had to be set aside temporarily.

The Bush presidency carried its challenge beyond the U.S. Constitution, claiming the right to fight terror with unilateral action anywhere in the world, with or without the approval of other nations, including long-standing American allies. In the immediate aftermath of the 9/11 attacks, the nations of the world rallied behind the United States. In stark contrast to his father, who had assembled a 31-nation coalition against Saddam Hussein's Iraq in 1990, George W. Bush's claims to unilateral freedom of action alienated much of the world, thereby squandering the solidarity initially produced by the attacks.

The Faith-Based Presidency

The presidential response to the 9/11 attacks not only abridged the Bill of Rights and challenged the constitutional separation of powers, it brought to the fore the concerns of the evangelical base on which the success of the Bush candidacy had been partly founded. The president was careful to avoid alienating moderate Muslims by portraying what he called the "War on Terror" as a religious war, although, after the 9/11 attacks, he himself heedlessly spoke of "This crusade, this war on terrorism," thereby offending Muslims, who understood the historical Crusades as a war of Christianity against Islam. The president's verbal misstep was evidence of just how fine a line he had to walk. Yet even as he defined the objective of the "War on Terror" as the defense and dissemination of "freedom," President Bush appealed to the Christian right for support.

A White House Department of Religion

The role of religion in the Bush presidency was not just rhetorical, but institutional. On January 29, 2001, nine days after taking office, President Bush issued an executive order creating the White House Office of Faith-Based and Community Initiatives as a department under the Office of the President of the United States. Its function was to strengthen faith-based and community organizations nationwide, expanding their capacity to provide federally funded social services. Although the faith-based organizations (FBOs) were prohibited from using government funds to support prayer, worship, religious instruction, or proselytization, constitutional rights activists challenged the office as a violation of the separation of church and state, and at least one former White House insider, David Kuo, who had been the number-two official in the Office of Faith-Based Initiatives, charged that it had sometimes been used to promote "a political agenda ... with organizations friendly to the administration often winning grants."

The "Permanent Campaign"

Critics of the Bush administration have claimed that both the "War on Terror" and the faith-based presidency were used to claim a moral high ground that no opponent of the president could successfully assail. The objective of this, the critics assert, was less to promote the successful prosecution of the war or to carry out "compassionate conservatism" through faith-based organizations than it was to acquire and preserve political power. In his 2008 *What Happened: Inside the Bush White House and Washington's Culture of Deception*, Scott McClellan, who served as President Bush's press secretary from 2003 to 2006, identified such activities as part of the administration's "permanent campaign." McClellan borrowed the term from Norman J. Ornstein and Thomas E. Mann (*The Permanent Campaign*, 2000) to describe government as an "offshoot of campaigning rather than the other way around." In the permanent campaign, the "sources of public approval" are "manipulated ... using such tools as the news media, political blogs, popular websites, paid advertising, talk radio, local organizations, and propaganda disseminated by interest groups to shape narratives to one's advantage."

Ever since George Washington lost his battle to keep political parties out of American government, all presidents have been simultaneously politicians as well as national leaders; however, Bush took this to an extreme by appointing his long-time political consultant/campaign manager Karl Rove as deputy White House chief of staff, thereby deliberately blurring the distinction between governing and campaigning.

Neocon Presidency or a New Wilsonianism?

Shortly after the 9/11 attacks, the Bush administration took the "War on Terror" to Afghanistan, where the extremist Islamic Taliban government was sheltering al-Quaeda and its chief, Osama bin Laden, who had masterminded the attacks. After the fall of the Taliban, there was much national discussion about the next step in the war. It was at this point that the Bush administration neocons, foremost among them Vice President Cheney and Secretary of Defense Donald Rumsfeld, encouraged the president to make a case for invading Iraq, even though that nation had had nothing to do with 9/11 and, in contrast to most Arab countries, was governed by a secular leader, Saddam Hussein. Nevertheless, the neocons argued that imposing democracy on Iraq would plant a seed that would take root throughout the entire region, transforming it into a set of democratic nations friendly to U.S. interests. At the time, political pundits friendly to the Bush administration compared the neoconservative doctrine to Woodrow Wilson's motive for bringing the United States into World War I to make "the world safe for democracy" (see Chapter 16).

Preemptive War

President Bush began the preparations for a war against Iraq by addressing the United Nations General Assembly on September 12, 2002, declaring that Saddam Hussein posed an imminent threat to the United States and other nations. A month later, arguing that the White House had intelligence revealing that Hussein possessed weapons of mass destruction (WMD), the president secured congressional resolutions authorizing the use of military force against Iraq. On November 8, the United Nations approved a U.S.-sponsored resolution that obliged Iraq to prove that it had divested itself of all WMDs. Although UN inspectors found no weapons, the president, citing his own White House intelligence reports, persisted in his claim that Saddam Hussein had WMDs.

On February 5, 2003, Secretary of State Colin Powell took the administration's case to the UN Security Council, but most of the international community withheld support for a war. Yet even as international and domestic debate was under way, President Bush shifted his rationale for war, issuing on March 16, 2003, a remarkable ultimatum to Saddam Hussein, demanding that he and his inner circle, including his sons, permanently leave Iraq within 48 hours. When the deadline passed, on March 19, Operation Iraqi Freedom, the Iraq War, began.

Shaping Perception, Dealing With Critics

The first phase of the war, toppling the Hussein regime, proceeded quickly, but the occupation of the country proved to be what the war's critics had warned it would be: a bloody, extravagantly costly, politically divisive quagmire. Before the war even began, Secretary of Defense Donald Rumsfeld had predicted that the conflict would last a matter of weeks, certainly no more than six months and that American troops would be greeted as liberators. Other administration neocons promised that Iraqi oil revenues would completely pay for the war. As of January 2009, as this chapter is being written, the Iraq War continues at an estimated cost of $12 billion per month and with the loss of more than 4,200 U.S. military personnel killed and some 31,000 wounded.

Throughout the war, the administration devoted a great deal of effort to "spinning" reports of progress in an effort to shape public perception. Those who criticized the conduct of the war were dealt with decisively, as U.S. Army Chief of Staff General Eric Shinseki discovered after he had testified to the U.S. Senate Armed Services in February 2003 that "something in the order of several hundred thousand soldiers" would be required to effectively occupy postwar Iraq. Defense Secretary Donald Rumsfeld, who had budgeted a far smaller force, rejected the estimate with contempt, and Shinseki suddenly found that he no longer enjoyed any influence on the Joint Chiefs of Staff. He retired later in the year.

Executive Event

The most notorious suppression of criticism was the so-called "Plame affair." On July 14, 2003, conservative columnist Robert Novak disclosed the identity of Valerie Plame Wilson, a covert CIA operative. Her husband, former Ambassador Joseph C. Wilson, had published in *The New York Times* just eight days earlier an op-ed piece reporting on his mission to Niger to investigate a U.S. intelligence claim that Saddam Hussein had attempted to purchase yellowcake uranium for use in manufacturing nuclear weapons. Wilson refuted the claim, which had been included as proven fact in President Bush's January 28, 2003, State of the Union address. Wilson asserted that the "outing" of his wife was administration retaliation for his article, and the subsequent federal prosecution of vice presidential aid I. Lewis "Scooter" Libby bore this out.

Presidents have always sought to prevail over critics, and most have taken an active role in shaping public perception, but the Bush administration carried these presidential functions to an extraordinary level by cherry-picking, interpreting, even distorting putatively objective military intelligence to justify a desired course of action, then acting ruthlessly to suppress those who dissented from the administration's line.

Failure and a Faith in History

Although the Iraq War became increasingly unpopular—especially since no WMDs were ever discovered—President Bush nevertheless won reelection in 2004, running against the lackluster Massachusetts senator John Kerry.

It was during his second term that President Bush's approval rating declined most dramatically. In August 2005, Hurricane Katrina tore across Florida, then slammed into the Gulf Coast with devastating winds and even more destructive floodwaters. Hardest hit by the floods was New Orleans, much of which was submerged under some 20 feet of water after the city's levees and flood walls failed.

Katrina did not strike without warning; indeed, it had been national news for several days before it made landfall on the Gulf shore. As Katrina approached the United States, President Bush enjoyed the latest in a series of long vacations at his ranch in Crawford, Texas, a five-week getaway that was his forty-ninth trip to the ranch since he had taken office. He left management of the impending hurricane to the Federal Emergency Management Agency (FEMA), the funding of which had been drastically cut on his watch and the direction of which had been put in the hands of Michael Brown, who had no significant experience in disaster management, his prior employment having been as commissioner of the International Arabian Horse Association.

 Tally

President Bush enjoyed long and numerous vacations. By August 2005, the president had spent, cumulatively, nearly a year at his ranch, about 20 percent of his presidency.

The federal response to Katrina was, in a word, feckless. The American people saw daily TV images of desperate survivors clinging to the rooftops of their submerged houses, waving signs pleading for help; saw bodies floating down flooded streets; and saw refugees packed into the makeshift shelter of the city's Superdome and convention center, could do little more than gasp in disbelief: "I can't believe this is America."

For many, Katrina was the final straw for the Bush administration as a credible presidency. George W. Bush himself deflected criticism of the failed federal response to Katrina in much the same way as he had deflected criticism of the Iraq War, with an appeal to history, a claim that his presidency be accurately judged only after the passage of time.

The Campaign and Election of 2008

In the midst of the 2008 presidential campaign, which pitted Republican John McCain and running mate Sarah Palin against the first African American nominated by a major party as its presidential candidate, Democrat Barack Obama, and his running mate, Joe Biden, Americans suddenly realized that they did not have time to wait for the judgment of history.

As home real estate prices, vastly inflated for years, tanked, millions of Americans defaulted on unaffordable mortgages obtained during the years the Bush administration had rolled back federal regulation of financial institutions. With the mortgage meltdown, securities markets derived from mortgages likewise collapsed. Mortgage lenders, as well as major banks and investment houses, failed. The three major U.S. automobile manufacturers careened toward bankruptcy, as did tens of thousands of smaller businesses of all kinds. As Christmas approached, consumers, having lost their jobs or fearful of losing them, having seen their savings and investments wither along with the value of their homes, tightened their belts, giving retailers one of their worst seasons on record.

Tally

Barack Obama became the first African American U.S. president, winning 66,882,230 votes (53 percent) and defeating Republican John McCain, who polled 58,343,671 (46 percent). Obama took 365 electoral votes to McCain's 173.

Unfolding during the worst economic collapse since the Great Depression, the campaign took on an urgency that had been missing from the elections of 2000 and 2004. Both candidates, Democrat and Republican, campaigned against George W. Bush as much as they did against one another, but in the end, John McCain could not disassociate himself from the incumbent, and Barack Obama prevailed.

Looking Ahead

Barack Obama is a gifted speaker. Already, as this chapter is being written, little more than a month after he was sworn in, it is clear that the rhetorical presidency has returned. The eager, even desperate, expectation of the American people, those who voted for him and surely many who did not, is that they will be inspired by their president again. But that is hardly all that they want.

Doubtless, some wish to see a less powerful presidency, a restoration of proportion among the three branches of government, but most are willing to give the new executive whatever authority—within constitutional limits—he may claim. For these people, the failure of the Bush presidency was not in its having claimed much authority, but in having claimed it in the absence of the judgment and competence to use it wisely and effectively. The hope of the American people is that the new president will bring these qualities to bear on the exercise of power to help the nation recover from war and economic catastrophe, in the process providing a new model for all the presidents who will succeed him.

The Least You Need to Know

◆ The flawed election of 2000 raised disturbing issues about the state of the American democracy, from the mechanics and ethics of elections to the lack of interest among voters in the candidates.

◆ George W. Bush built a conservative presidency that combined moderate, centrist elements with a Reagan-style ideological conservatism, a commitment to the Christian Right, and the foreign affairs outlook of neoconservative Republican thinkers.

◆ The combination of the "permanent campaign" approach to governing and the urgent demands of the "War on Terror" allowed the Bush administration to consolidate a great deal of power in the White House, creating a strong "unitary executive" that often accepted little input from Congress or the judiciary.

◆ The cost, frustrations, and length of the Iraq War, the inept federal response to the Hurricane Katrina disaster in 2005, and catastrophic economic collapse of the economy in 2008 combined to persuade many Americans that the Bush presidency had been a failure.

◆ In 2008, voters elected the nation's first African American president, Democrat Barack Obama, in the hope that he would revitalize and remodel the presidency.

Appendix A

The Presidents and Vice Presidents

For each administration, the president is listed first, followed by the vice president(s) on the next line.

1 George Washington (April 30, 1789–March 4, 1797) No party
John Adams

2 John Adams (March 4, 1797–March 4, 1801) Federalist
Thomas Jefferson   Democratic-Republican

3 Thomas Jefferson (March 4, 1801–March 4, 1809) Democratic-Republican
Aaron Burr; George Clinton

4 James Madison (March 4, 1809–March 4, 1817) Democratic-Republican
George Clinton (died April 12, 1812); **Elbridge Gerry** (died November 23, 1814)

5 James Monroe (March 4, 1817–March 4, 1825) Democratic-Republican
Daniel D. Tompkins

6 John Quincy Adams (March 4, 1825–March 4, 1829) Democratic-Republican/National Republican
John C. Calhoun Democratic-Republican/Democratic

7 **Andrew Jackson** (March 4, 1829–March 4, 1837) Democratic
John C. Calhoun (resigned December 28, 1832); **Martin Van Buren**

8 **Martin Van Buren** (March 4, 1837–March 4, 1841) Democratic
Richard Mentor Johnson

9 **William Henry Harrison** (March 4, 1841–died April 4, 1841) Whig
John Tyler

10 **John Tyler** (April 6, 1841–March 4, 1845) Whig (but expelled from the party
in 1841)
No vice president

11 **James K. Polk** (March 4, 1845–March 4, 1849) Democratic
George M. Dallas

12 **Zachary Taylor** (March 4, 1849–died July 9, 1850) Whig
Millard Fillmore

13 **Millard Fillmore** (July 10, 1850–March 4, 1853) Whig
No vice president

14 **Franklin Pierce** (March 4, 1853–March 4, 1857) Democratic
William R. King (died April 18, 1853)

15 **James Buchanan** (March 4, 1857–March 4, 1861) Democratic
John C. Breckinridge

16 **Abraham Lincoln** (March 4, 1861–died April 15, 1865) Republican
Hannibal Hamlin; Andrew Johnson Democratic (when he ran with Lincoln
in 1864, the two men identified themselves as "National Unionists")

17 **Andrew Johnson** (April 15, 1865–March 4, 1869) Democratic/National Union
No vice president

18 **Ulysses S. Grant** (March 4, 1869–March 4, 1877) Republican
Schuyler Colfax; Henry Wilson (died November 22, 1875)

19 **Rutherford B. Hayes** (March 4, 1877–March 4, 1881) Republican
William A. Wheeler

20 **James A. Garfield** (March 4, 1881–died September 19, 1881) Republican
Chester A. Arthur

21 **Chester A. Arthur** (September 20, 1881–March 4, 1885) Republican
No vice president

22 **Grover Cleveland** (March 4, 1885–March 4, 1889) Democratic
Thomas A. Hendricks (died November 25, 1885)

23 **Benjamin Harrison** (March 4, 1889–March 4, 1893) Republican
Levi P. Morton

24 **Grover Cleveland** (March 4, 1893–March 4, 1897) Democratic
Adlai E. Stevenson I

25 **William McKinley** (March 4, 1897–died September 14, 1901) Republican
Garret Hobart (died November 21, 1899); **Theodore Roosevelt**

26 **Theodore Roosevelt** (September 14, 1901–March 4, 1909) Republican
No vice president (September 14, 1901–March 4, 1905); **Charles W. Fairbanks**

27 **William Howard Taft** (March 4, 1909–March 4, 1913) Republican
James S. Sherman (died October 30, 1912)

28 **Woodrow Wilson** (March 4, 1913–March 4, 1921) Democratic
Thomas R. Marshall

29 **Warren G. Harding** (March 4, 1921–died August 2, 1923) Republican
Calvin Coolidge

30 **Calvin Coolidge** (August 3, 1923–March 4, 1929) Republican
No vice president (August 3, 1923–March 4, 1925); **Charles G. Dawes**

31 **Herbert Hoover** (March 4, 1929–March 4, 1933) Republican
Charles Curtis

32 **Franklin D. Roosevelt** (March 4, 1933–died April 12, 1945) Democratic
John Nance Garner (terms 1 and 2); **Henry A. Wallace** (term 3); **Harry S. Truman** (term 4)

33 **Harry S. Truman** (April 12, 1945–January 20, 1953) Democratic
No vice president (April 12, 1945–January 20, 1949); **Alben W. Barkley**

34 **Dwight D. Eisenhower** (January 20, 1953–January 20, 1961) Republican
Richard Nixon

35 **John F. Kennedy** (January 20, 1961–died November 22, 1963) Democratic
Lyndon B. Johnson

36 **Lyndon B. Johnson** (November 22, 1963–January 20, 1969) Democratic
No vice president (November 22, 1963–January 20, 1964); **Hubert Humphrey**

37 Richard Nixon (January 20, 1969–resigned August 9, 1974) Republican
Spiro T. Agnew (resigned October 10, 1973); **Gerald R. Ford** (appointed December 6, 1973)

38 Gerald R. Ford (August 9, 1974–January 20, 1977) Republican
Nelson Rockefeller (appointed December 19, 1974)

39 Jimmy Carter (January 20, 1977–January 20, 1981) Democratic
Walter Mondale

40 Ronald Reagan (January 20, 1981–January 20, 1989) Republican
George H. W. Bush

41 George H. W. Bush (January 20, 1989–January 20, 1993) Republican
Dan Quayle

42 Bill Clinton (January 20, 1993–January 20, 2001) Democratic
Al Gore

43 George W. Bush (January 20, 2001–January 20, 2009) Republican
Dick Cheney

44 Barack Obama (January 20, 2009–) Democratic
Joe Biden

Appendix B

The Elections

The winner is listed first, with electoral and popular vote totals. Other major contenders follow. Prior to ratification of the Twelfth Amendment (1804), the electoral runner-up became vice president; the 1804 election was the first in which electors voted separately for president and vice president. No popular vote totals are given for elections before 1824 because reliable and meaningful data is unavailable. Reliable popular vote data is not available for all minor-party candidates.

1st 1789

George Washington (no party) 69

John Adams (no party) 34

John Jay (no party) 9

Robert H. Harrison (no party) 6

John Rutledge (no party) 6

Under the pre–Twelfth Amendment Constitution, each elector voted for two candidates, one of whom had to be from a state different than the elector's. All 69 electors cast one of their votes for Washington. Electors from 10 states voted; North Carolina and Rhode Island had yet to ratify the Constitution, and New York could not decide in time which electors to send.

2nd 1792

George Washington (no party) 132

John Adams (Federalist) 77

George Clinton (Democratic-Republican) 50

Again, all electors cast one of their votes for Washington; 15 states were represented.

3rd 1796

John Adams (Federalist) 71

Thomas Jefferson (Democratic-Republican) 68

Thomas Pinckney (Federalist) 59

Aaron Burr (Democratic-Republican) 30

Samuel Adams (Democratic-Republican) 15

Oliver Ellsworth (Federalist) 11

George Clinton (Democratic-Republican) 7

4th 1800

Thomas Jefferson (Democratic-Republican) 73

Aaron Burr (Democratic-Republican) 73 (tie broken by House)

John Adams (Federalist) 65

Charles Cotesworth Pinckney (Federalist) 64

5th 1804

Thomas Jefferson (Democratic-Republican) 162

Charles Cotesworth Pinckney (Federalist) 14

6th 1808

James Madison (Democratic-Republican) 122

Charles Cotesworth Pinckney (Federalist) 47

George Clinton (Democratic-Republican) 6

James Monroe (Democratic-Republican) 0

7th 1812

James Madison (Democratic-Republican) 128

DeWitt Clinton (Federalist) 89

8th 1816

James Monroe (Democratic-Republican) 183

Rufus King (Federalist) 34

9th 1820

James Monroe (Democratic-Republican) 231

John Quincy Adams (Democratic-Republican) 1

Monroe ran unopposed; however, one elector, Governor William Plumer of New Hampshire, cast a ballot for Adams. Some believe this was a symbolic gesture intended to preserve Washington's record as the only president elected unanimously; others hold that Plumer personally despised Monroe and cast his vote against him in earnest.

10th 1824

John Quincy Adams (Democratic-Republican) 84 115,696 (32%)

Andrew Jackson (Democratic-Republican) 99 152,933 (42%)

Henry Clay (Democratic-Republican) 37 47,136 (13%)

William H. Crawford (Democratic-Republican) 41 46,979 (13%)

Each candidate represented a faction of the splintered Democratic-Republican Party; because no candidate won an electoral majority, the election was decided in the House.

11th 1828

Andrew Jackson (Democratic) 178 642,553 (56.0%)

John Quincy Adams (National Republican) 83 500,897 (43.6%)

12th 1832

Andrew Jackson (Democratic) 219 701,780 (54.2%)

Henry Clay (National Republican) 49 484,205 (37.4%)

John Floyd (Nullifier) 11

William Wirt (Anti-Masonic) 7

13th 1836

Martin Van Buren (Democratic) 170 762,678 (51%)

William Henry Harrison (Whig) 73 548,007 (36%)

Hugh Lawson White (Whig) 26 145,396 (10%)

Daniel Webster (Whig) 14 42,247 (3%)

Willie Person Mangum (Whig, undeclared candidate) 11

14th 1840

William Henry Harrison (Whig) 234 1,275,390 (52.9%)

Martin Van Buren (Democratic) 60 1,128,854 (46.8%)

15th 1844

James K. Polk (Democratic) 170 1,339,494 (49.5%)

Henry Clay (Whig) 105 1,300,004 (48.1%)

James G. Birney (Liberty) 0 62,300 (2%)

16th 1848

Zachary Taylor (Whig) 163 1,363,393 (47%)

Lewis Cass (Democratic) 127 1,223,460 (43%)

Martin Van Buren (Free Soil) 0 291,263 (10%)

17th 1852

Franklin Pierce (Democratic) 254 1,607,510 (50.8%)

Winfield Scott (Whig) 42 1,386,942 (43.9%)

John P. Hale (Free Soil) 0

18th 1856

James Buchanan (Democratic) 174 1,838,169 (45%)

John C. Frémont (Republican) 114 1,335,264 (33%)

Millard Fillmore (American Party/Whig) 8 874.534 (22%)

19th 1860

Abraham Lincoln (Republican) 180 1,865,908 (39.8%)

John C. Breckinridge (Southern Democratic) 72 854,763 (18%)

John Bell (Constitutional Union) 39 589,581 (13%)

Stephen A. Douglas (Northern Democratic) 12 1,375,157 (29.5%)

20th 1864

Abraham Lincoln (Republican/National Union) 212 2,218,388 (55%)

George B. McClellan (Democratic) 11 1,812,807 (45%)

21st 1868

Ulysses S. Grant (Republican) 214 3,013,650 (52.7%)

Horatio Seymour (Democratic) 80 2,708,744 (47.3%)

22nd 1872

Ulysses S. Grant (Republican) 286 3,598,235 (55.6%)

Horace Greeley (Democratic/Liberal Republican) 0 2,834,761 (43%)

Thomas A. Hendricks (Democratic) 42

B. Gratz Brown (Democratic/Liberal Republican) 18

Charles J. Jenkins (Democratic) 2

23rd 1876

Rutherford B. Hayes (Republican) 185 4,033,950 (48%)

Samuel J. Tilden (Democratic) 184 4,284,757 (51%)

24th 1880

James A. Garfield (Republican) 214 4,454,416 (48.3%)

Winfield Scott Hancock (Democratic) 155 4,444,952 (48.2%)

James Weaver (Greenback) 0

25th 1884

Grover Cleveland (Democratic) 219 4,911,017 (49%)

James G. Blaine (Republican) 182 4,848,334 (48%)

John St. John (Prohibition) 0

Benjamin Butler (Greenback) 0

26th 1888
Benjamin Harrison (Republican) 233 5,439,853 (48%)
Grover Cleveland (Democratic) 168 5,540,329 (49%)
Clinton B. Fisk (Prohibition) 0
Alson Streeter (Union Labor) 0

27th 1892
Grover Cleveland (Democratic) 277 5,556,918 (46%)
Benjamin Harrison (Republican) 145 5,176,108 (43%)
James Weaver (Populist) 22 1,041,028 (9%)
John Bidwell (Prohibition) 0

28th 1896
William McKinley (Republican) 271 7,035,638 (51%)
William Jennings Bryan (Democratic/Populist) 176 6,467,946 (47%)

29th 1900
William McKinley (Republican) 292 7,219,530 (29%)
William Jennings Bryan (Democratic) 155 6,358,071 (46%)
John Woolley (Prohibition) 0

30th 1904
Theodore Roosevelt (Republican) 336 7,628,834 (56%)
Alton B. Parker (Democratic) 140 5,084,401 (38%)
Eugene V. Debs (Socialist) 0 402,714 (3%)
Silas Swallow (Prohibition) 0

31st 1908
William Howard Taft (Republican) 321 7,679,006 (52%)
William Jennings Bryan (Democratic) 162 6,409,106 (43%)
Eugene V. Debs (Socialist) 0 420,858 (3%)
Eugene Chafin (Prohibition) 0

32nd 1912
Woodrow Wilson (Democratic) 435 6,286,820 (42%)
Theodore Roosevelt (Progressive ["Bull Moose"]) 88 4,126,020 (27%)
William Howard Taft (Republican) 8 3,483,922 (23%)
Eugene V. Debs (Socialist) 0 901,255 (6%)
Eugene Chafin (Prohibition) 0

33rd 1916

Woodrow Wilson (Democratic) 277 9,129,606 (49%)
Charles Evans Hughes (Republican) 254 8,538,221 (46%)
Allan L. Benson (Socialist) 0
James Hanly (Prohibition) 0

34th 1920

Warren G. Harding (Republican) 404 16,152,200 (61%)
James M. Cox (Democratic) 127 9,147,252 (35%)
Eugene V. Debs (Socialist) 0 915,490 (3%)
This was the first election in which women were enfranchised.

35th 1924

Calvin Coolidge (Republican) 382 15,725,016 (54%)
John W. Davis (Democratic) 136 8,385,586 (29%)
Robert M. La Follette, Sr. (Progressive) 13 4,822,856 (17%)

36th 1928

Herbert Hoover (Republican) 444 21,392,190 (58%)
Al Smith (Democratic) 87 15,016,443 (41%)

37th 1932

Franklin D. Roosevelt (Democratic) 472 22,821,857 (57%)
Herbert Hoover (Republican) 59 15,761,841 (40%)
Norman Thomas (Socialist) 0

38th 1936

Franklin D. Roosevelt (Democratic) 523 27,751,597 (61%)
Alf Landon (Republican) 8 16,679,583 (37%)
William Lemke (Union) 0

39th 1940

Franklin D. Roosevelt (Democratic) 449 27,243,466 (55%)
Wendell Willkie (Republican) 82 22,304,755 (45%)

40th 1944

Franklin D. Roosevelt (Democratic) 432 25,602,505 (53%)
Thomas E. Dewey (Republican) 99 22,006,278 (46%)

41st 1948

Harry S. Truman (Democratic) 303 24,105,812 (49%)
Thomas E. Dewey (Republican) 189 21,970,065 (45%)
Strom Thurmond (States' Rights [Dixiecrat]) 39 1,169,063 (2%)
Henry A. Wallace (Progressive/Labor) 0 1,157,172 (2%)

42nd 1952
Dwight D. Eisenhower (Republican) 442 33,936,234 (55%)
Adlai Stevenson (Democratic) 89 27,314,992 (44%)

43rd 1956
Dwight D. Eisenhower (Republican) 457 35,590,472 (57%)
Adlai Stevenson (Democratic) 73 26,031,322 (42%)

44th 1960
John F. Kennedy (Democratic) 303 34,227,096 (49.7%)
Richard Nixon (Republican) 219 34,108,546 (49.5%)
Harry F. Byrd (Democratic, but not a party candidate) 15

45th 1964
Lyndon B. Johnson (Democratic) 486 43,126,506 (61%)
Barry Goldwater (Republican) 52 27,176,799 (39%)

46th 1968
Richard Nixon (Republican) 301 31,785,480 (43.4%)
Hubert Humphrey (Democratic) 191 31,275,166 (42.7%)
George Wallace (American Independent) 46 9,906,473 (13.5%)

47th 1972
Richard Nixon (Republican) 520 47,165,234 (61%)
George McGovern (Democratic) 17 29,168,110 (38%)
John G. Schmitz (American) 0

48th 1976
Jimmy Carter (Democratic) 297 40,825,839 (50%)
Gerald Ford (Republican) 240 39,147,770 (48%)

49th 1980
Ronald Reagan (Republican) 489 43,899,248 (51%)
Jimmy Carter (Democratic) 49 35,481,435 (41%)
John B. Anderson (Independent) 0 5,719,437 (7%)
Ed Clark (Libertarian) 0

50th 1984
Ronald Reagan (Republican) 525 54,281,858 (59%)
Walter Mondale (Democratic) 13 37,457,215 (41%)

51st 1988
George H. W. Bush (Republican) 426 47,946,422 (54%)
Michael Dukakis (Democratic) 111 41,016,429 (46%)

52nd 1992
Bill Clinton (Democratic) 370 44,908,233 (43%)
George H. W. Bush (Republican) 168 39,102,282 (37%)
Ross Perot (Independent) 0 19,741,048 (19%)

53rd 1996
Bill Clinton (Democratic) 379 47,402,357 (49.2%)
Bob Dole (Republican) 159 39,198,755 (40.7%)
Ross Perot (Reform) 0 8,085,402 (8.4%)

54th 2000
George W. Bush (Republican) 271 50,456,167 (48%)
Al Gore (Democratic) 266 50,996,064 (48.5%)
Ralph Nader (Green) 0 2,864,810 (2.7%)
Pat Buchanan (Reform) 0 448,750 (0.4%)
Harry Browne (Libertarian) 0 386,024 (0.4%)

55th 2004
George W. Bush (Republican) 286 62,028,285 (51%)
John Kerry (Democratic) 251 59,028,109 (48%)
Ralph Nader (Independent) 0 406.924 (1%)

56th 2008
Barack Obama (Democratic) 365 66,882,230 (53%)
John McCain (Republican) 173 58,343,671 (46%)
Ralph Nader (no party) 0 736,773 (0.56%)
Bob Barr (Libertarian) 0 524,237 (0.4%)
Chuck Baldwin (Constitution) 0 194,869 (0.15%)
Cynthia McKinney (Green) 0 161,134 (0.12%)

Appendix C

Further Reading

General Books

Brinkley, Alan, and Davis Dyer. *The American Presidency*. Boston: Mariner Books, 2004.

DeGregorio, William A. *The Complete Book of U.S. Presidents*. 6th ed. Fort Lee, NJ: Barricade, 2005.

Milkis, Sidney M., and Michael Nelson. *The American Presidency: Origins and Development, 1776–2007*. 5th ed. Washington, D.C.: CQ Press, 2008.

Neustadt, Richard E. *Presidential Power and the Modern Presidents*. New York: Free Press, 1991.

Ornstein, Norman J., and Thomas E. Mann. *The Permanent Campaign*. Washington, D.C.: American Enterprise Institute Press, 2000.

Skowronek, Stephen. *The Politics Presidents Make: Leadership from John Adams to Bill Clinton*. Cambridge, MA: Oxford University Press, 1997.

Truman, Margaret, ed. *Where the Buck Stops: The Personal and Private Writings of Harry S. Truman*. New York: Warner Books, 1989.

Individual Presidents

George Washington

Flexner, James Thomas. *George Washington*. 4 vols. Boston: Houghton Mifflin, 1965–1972.

Schwartz, Barry. *George Washington: The Making of an American Symbol*. Ithaca, NY: Cornell University Press, 1990.

John Adams

McCullough, David. *John Adams*. New York: Simon and Schuster, 2001.

Thomas Jefferson

Horn, James, Jan Lewis, and Peter Onuf, eds. *The Election of 1800*. Charlottesville, VA: University of Virginia Press, 2002.

Malone, Dumas. *Jefferson and His Times*. 6 vols. Boston: Houghton Mifflin, 1948–1991.

Peterson, Merrill D. *Thomas Jefferson and the New Nation: A Biography*. London and New York: Oxford University Press, 1986.

James Madison

Ketcham, Ralph. *James Madison: A Biography*. New York: Macmillan, 1971.

Rutland, Robert A. *The Presidency of James Madison*. Lawrence, KS: University of Kansas Press, 1990.

James Monroe

Cunningham, Noble E., Jr. *The Presidency of James Monroe*. Lawrence, KS: University of Kansas Press, 1996.

John Quincy Adams

Parsons, Lynn Hudson. *John Quincy Adams*. Madison, WI: University of Wisconsin Press, 1998.

Andrew Jackson

Cole, Donald B. *The Presidency of Andrew Jackson.* Lawrence, KS: University of Kansas Press, 1993.

Remini, Robert V. *Andrew Jackson.* Newtown, CT: American Political Biography Press, 2003.

Watson, Harry L. *Liberty and Power: The Politics of Jacksonian America.* New York: Hill and Wang, 1990.

Martin Van Buren

Wilson, Major J. *The Presidency of Martin Van Buren.* Lawrence, KS: University of Kansas Press, 1984.

William Henry Harrison and John Tyler

McCormick, Richard P. *The Presidential Game: The Origins of American Presidential Politics.* New York: Oxford University Press, 1982.

Peterson, Norma Lois. *The Presidencies of William Henry Harrison and John Tyler.* Lawrence, KS: University of Kansas Press, 1989.

James K. Polk

Bergeron, Paul H. *The Presidency of James K. Polk.* Lawrence, KS: University of Kansas Press, 1987.

Sellers, Charles. *James K. Polk.* 2 vols. Princeton, NJ: Princeton University Press, 1957–1966.

Zachary Taylor and Millard Fillmore

Rayback, Robert J. *Millard Fillmore: Biography of a President.* Buffalo: Buffalo Historical Society, 1959.

Smith, Elbert B. *The Presidencies of Zachary Taylor and Millard Fillmore.* Lawrence, KS: University of Kansas Press, 1988.

Franklin Pierce

Gara, Larry. *The Presidency of Franklin Pierce*. Lawrence, KS: University of Kansas Press, 1991.

James Buchanan

Klein, Philip S. *President James Buchanan*. University Park, PA: Pennsylvania State University Press, 1962.

Smith, Elbert B. *The Presidency of James Buchanan*. Lawrence, KS: University of Kansas Press, 1975.

Abraham Lincoln

Goodwin, Doris Kerns. *Team of Rivals: The Political Genius of Abraham Lincoln*. New York: Simon and Schuster, 2006.

Lincoln, Abraham. *Speeches and Writings*. New York: Library of America, 1992.

Paludan, Philip Shaw. *The Presidency of Abraham Lincoln*. Lawrence, KS: University of Kansas Press, 1994.

Randall, James. *Lincoln the President*. 4 vols. New York: Dodd, Mead, 1945–1955.

Andrew Johnson

Trefousse, Hans L. *Andrew Johnson: A Biography*. New York: Norton, 1989.

Ulysses S. Grant

McFeely, William S. *Grant: A Biography*. New York: Norton, 1982.

Perret, Geoffrey. *Ulysses S. Grant: Soldier and President*. New York: Random House, 1997.

Rutherford B. Hayes

Hoogenboom, Ari. *Rutherford B. Hayes: Warrior and President*. Lawrence, KS: University of Kansas Press, 1995.

James A. Garfield and Chester A. Arthur

Doenecke, Justus D. *The Presidencies of James A. Garfield and Chester A. Arthur.* Lawrence, KS: University of Kansas Press, 1981.

Peskin, Allan. *Garfield: A Biography.* Kent, OH: Kent State University Press, 1999.

Grover Cleveland

Welch, Richard. *The Presidencies of Grover Cleveland.* Lawrence, KS: University of Kansas Press, 1988.

Benjamin Harrison

Socolofsky, Homer E., and Allen B. Spetter. *The Presidency of Benjamin Harrison.* Lawrence, KS: University of Kansas Press, 1987.

William McKinley

Gould, Lewis L. *The Presidency of William McKinley.* Lawrence, KS: University of Kansas Press, 1980.

Leech, Margaret. *In the Days of McKinley.* New York: Harper, 1959.

Theodore Roosevelt

Blum, John Morton. *The Republican Roosevelt.* Cambridge, MA: Harvard University Press, 1977.

Hunt, John Gabriel, ed. *The Essential Theodore Roosevelt.* New York: Gramercy Books, 1994.

Morris, Edmund. *Theodore Rex.* New York: Random House, 2001.

Roosevelt, Theodore. *An Autobiography.* New York: Da Capo, 1985.

William Howard Taft

Anderson, Donald F. *William Howard Taft: A Conservative's Conception of the Presidency.* Ithaca, NY: Cornell University Press, 1973.

Coletta, Paolo E. *The Presidency of William Howard Taft.* Lawrence, KS: University of Kansas Press, 1973.

Woodrow Wilson

Link, Arthur S. *Woodrow Wilson*. 5 vols. Princeton, NJ: Princeton University Press, 1947–1966.

Thompson, John A. *Woodrow Wilson*. London and New York: Oxford University Press, 2002.

Warren G. Harding

Murray, Robert K. *The Harding Era: Warren G. Harding and His Administration*. Minneapolis: University of Minnesota Press, 1969.

Calvin Coolidge

McCoy, Donald R. *Calvin Coolidge: The Quiet President*. New York: Macmillan, 1967.

Herbert Hoover

Fausold, Martin L. *The Presidency of Herbert C. Hoover*. Lawrence, KS: University of Kansas Press, 1988.

Franklin D. Roosevelt

Davis, Kenneth Sydney. *FDR*. 5 vols. New York: Random House, 1971–2000.

Freidel, Frank. *Franklin D. Roosevelt: A Rendezvous with Destiny*. Boston: Little, Brown, 1990.

McJimsey, George. *The Presidency of Franklin Delano Roosevelt*. Lawrence, KS: University of Kansas Press, 2000.

Harry S. Truman

McCullough, David. *Truman*. New York: Simon and Schuster, 1992.

Truman, Harry S. *Memoirs*. 2 vols. Garden City, NY: Doubleday, 1955–1956.

Dwight D. Eisenhower

Ambrose, Stephen E. *Eisenhower*. 2 vols. New York: Simon and Schuster, 1983–1984.

Pach, Chester J., Jr., and Elmo Richardson. *The Presidency of Dwight D. Eisenhower.* Lawrence, KS: University of Kansas Press, 1991.

John F. Kennedy

Dallek, Robert. *An Unfinished Life: John F. Kennedy, 1917–1963.* Boston: Little, Brown, 2003.

Giglio, James N. *The Presidency of John F. Kennedy.* Lawrence, KS: University of Kansas Press, 2006.

Lyndon B. Johnson

Bornet, Vaughn. *The Presidency of Lyndon Johnson.* Lawrence, KS: University of Kansas Press, 1983.

Dallek, Robert. *Flawed Giant: Lyndon Johnson and His Times, 1961–1973.* Boston: Little, Borwn, 1998.

Richard Nixon

Ambrose, Stephen E. *Nixon.* 3 vols. New York: Simon and Schuster, 1988–1991.

Nixon, Richard. *RN: The Memoirs of Richard Nixon.* New York: Simon and Schuster, 1978.

Small, Melvin. *The Presidency of Richard Nixon.* Lawrence, KS: University of Kansas Press, 1999.

Gerald Ford

Greene, John Robert. *The Presidency of Gerald R. Ford.* Lawrence, KS: University of Kansas Press, 1995.

Jimmy Carter

Carter, Jimmy. *Keeping Faith: Memoirs of a President.* New York: Bantam, 1982.

Kaufman, Burton. *The Presidency of James Earl Carter.* Lawrence, KS: University of Kansas Press, 1993.

Ronald Reagan

Morris, Edmund. *Dutch: A Memoir of Ronald Reagan*. New York: Simon and Schuster, 1999.

Reagan, Ronald, et al. *In His Own Hand: The Writings of Ronald Reagan That Reveal His Revolutionary Vision for America*. New York: Free Press, 2001.

Bill Clinton

Drew, Elizabeth. *On the Edge: The Clinton Presidency*. New York: Touchstone, 1995.

———. *Showdown: The Struggle Between the Gingrich Congress and the Clinton White House*. New York: Simon and Schuster, 1996.

Klein, Joe. *The Natural: The Misunderstood Presidency of Bill Clinton*. New York: Doubleday, 2002.

George W. Bush

Draper, Robert. *Dead Certain: The Presidency of George W. Bush*. New York: Free Press, 2008.

Hayes, Stephen F. *Cheney: The Untold Story of America's Most Powerful and Controversial Vice President*. New York: HarperCollins, 2007.

McClellan, Scott. *What Happened: Inside the Bush White House and Washington's Culture of Deception*. New York: Public Affairs, 2008.

Weisberg, Jacob. *The Bush Tragedy*. New York: Random House, 2008.

Barack Obama

Obama, Barack. *The Audacity of Hope: Thoughts on Reclaiming the American Dream*. New York: Crown, 2006.

Index

O

Let history be your guide!